Carolina Flare

Outer Banks Boatbuilding
& Sportfishing Heritage

[NEAL, JOHN & JIM CONOLEY]

[CAROLINA FLARE]

www.carolinaflare.com

Published by Carolina Flare, LLC
525 Old Zebulon Road • Wendell, N.C. 27591

Edited by Larry Earley • Designed by Linda Noble

First Edition • Library of Congress
ISBN 978-0-9791177-0-1

Printed by Hickory Printing Company
Hickory, North Carolina

We dedicate this book to our families for their unwavering support and encouragement...
and to the legacies of boatbuilders and charter fishermen, past and present,
along North Carolina's famed Outer Banks.

Best wishes,
Neal
John

[ACKNOWLEDGEMENTS]

This book would not have been possible without the assistance and support of many, many people. First, we sincerely thank all of the boatbuilders and fishermen who provided valuable information and insight into the rich history of the Outer Banks. We also thank all those who participated in interviews and provided photographs for this project.

On the northern Outer Banks, we especially recognize and acknowledge the support of Captain Sunny Briggs and Captain Omie Tillett for sharing their wealth of knowledge and experience about boatbuilding and sportfishing. They guided us through the people, places and events that were important to our study.

Among many others who helped, the staff at the Outer Banks History Center graciously provided access to photographs and historical information that was critical in this effort. In addition, Stuart Bell provided many family photographs; Captain Bobby Scarborough added his sportfishing knowledge and experience; Brian Edwards supplied historic information and family photographs; and, Captain Moon Tillett and Billy Carl Tillett added to the storied history of charter fishing.

John Wilson, Faye Austin, Earl Willis, Wilson Snowden, Captain Ernie Foster and Lynne Foster, Mrs. Kathleen Styron, Allen Burrus, Marlene Matthews, Captain Sam Stokes, Captain Tony Tillett, the Herbert Perry family, Mike Midgett, Gerald Craddock, Melvin Twiddy, Melody Leckie, Steve Hutchins and Captain Billy Brown were all instrumental in providing both important information and photographs.

On the southern Outer Banks, we especially acknowledge the support and assistance of Pam Morris, Karen and Jimmy Amspacher, Reggie Lewis, Captain George Bedsworth and Heber Guthrie. They provided guidance and direction as we traced the boatbuilding and sportfishing legacies of Carteret County.

In addition, Bob Simpson, John Tunnell and Tony Seamon Jr. graciously provided many photographs that were very important in documenting sportfishing and boatbuilding on the southern Outer Banks. Others who provided information and support include James Allen Rose, Captain Terrell Gould, Ann Rose, Becky Paul, Joanne Brooks, Bob Dance, Mrs. Rilla Gould, Julia G. Charles, Jack Dudley, Phyllis O. Gentry, Lina B. Willis, Sunny Williamson, Ed Pond, Bernie Davis, Kenneth Ball and Wes Seegars.

The Core Sound Waterfowl Museum and the Carteret County History Center opened their collections and they were most helpful in allowing us to use documents and photographs. The Wilson Library at the University of North Carolina, Chapel Hill; the Museum of the Albemarle; the North Carolina Division of Archives and History; the North Carolina Division of Marine Fisheries; North Carolina Sea Grant and, the North Carolina Maritime Museum also provided many photographs.

One of the most important ways to document history is through photographs. We respectfully acknowledge the legacies of Aycock Brown, Reginald Lewis, Jerry Schumacher, Dan Wade and Bob Simpson in documenting the sportfishing history of the Outer Banks. These excellent photographers took many of the historical photographs used in this book.

Of special significance is the invaluable support and assistance provided by Ray Matthews and Scott Taylor. These two outstanding photographers provided most of the contemporary images of sportfishing boats and offshore sportfishing used in this book. We admire their skills and talents and greatly appreciate their advice, guidance and generosity. We also thank Melton International Tackle, Black Bart Lures, Applied Concepts Unleashed, and Sea Striker for providing graphic images.

We are very grateful to Linda Noble for wholeheartedly jumping into this complex project and for applying her tremendous skills and expertise in designing this book. She worked magic while overcoming our tedious suggestions. We also thank Larry Earley for his much-needed editorial support and advice.

Our intent with this book is to present an overview and survey of the boatbuilding and sportfishing heritage along the Outer Banks. Any historical documentation will inevitably be incomplete and we apologize to anyone that we inadvertently left out or whom we failed to acknowledge.

The North Carolina Outer Banks is a unique place. For centuries this narrow strip of sand has greeted explorers, pirates, sailors and fishermen. Sometimes the welcome is warm and cordial, framed by Carolina-blue skies, emerald green waters and gentle rolling waves. Other encounters are harsh and foreboding with hurricane-force winds, fierce waves, storm-tossed shoals and treacherous inlets. No matter what Mother Nature offers, mariners can always count on the hospitality, generosity and integrity of the "Bankers." This book is a tribute to these wonderful people and their boatbuilding and sportfishing heritage.

During our research, we found that many of the boatbuilding pioneers and sportfishing legends continue to be active and involved in their craft. In addition, we were overwhelmed by the enthusiasm and support offered by everyone who participated in this effort. Boatbuilders stopped building, fishermen stopped fishing and families put dinner on hold to talk about their coastal heritage. We are most appreciative for this kindness, and we can report that the famed Outer Banks reputation for hospitality is alive and well!

Boaters and fishermen from around the world associate Manteo, Wanchese, Harkers Island, Marshallberg and Morehead City with Carolina-style custom offshore fishing boats. Likewise, Oregon Inlet, Wimble Shoals, Cape Hatteras and Cape Lookout are synonymous with great offshore fishing. Legendary boatbuilders, ageless charter captains and knowledgeable historians along the Outer Banks eagerly tell of their exploits and we have attempted to capture their spirit and enthusiasm.

Boatbuilding and sportfishing continue to be vital parts of the culture of the Outer Banks. To document this heritage, we focused primarily on the history of custom sportfishing boats and sportfishing, and to tell this story, we incorporated many historical and contemporary photographs as well as personal interviews. Our research led us from backyard boat sheds to state-of-the-art boatbuilding facilities. We walked the docks with boat captains and sat on front porches with old-timers as they reminisced about "their good old fishing days." We made many new friends and we thoroughly enjoyed our journey.

We started this effort as a family project to survey and document the Outer Banks custom boatbuilding and sportfishing heritage. It was to be a book about boats and fishing, but what we learned is that it's really about people— extraordinary people. We hope our effort is a tribute to them.

Neal Conoley
John Conoley
Jim Conoley

[TABLE OF CONTENTS]

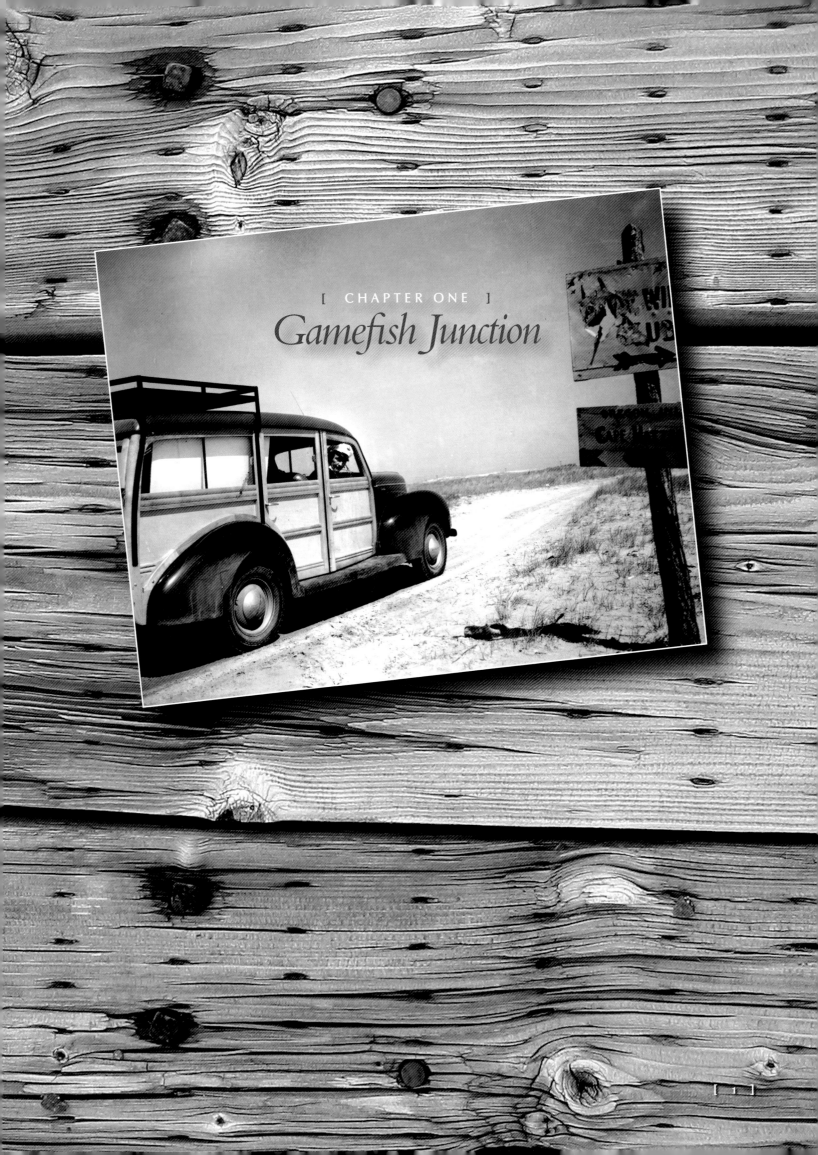

[CHAPTER ONE]

Gamefish Junction

Gamefish Junction

Late June, off Cape Hatteras. The emerald green waters are alive with sparkling schools of twisting baitfish trying to elude the watchful eyes patrolling nearby. On occasion, a dark shape disrupts this idyllic setting with a quick flash through the school. When this happens, both predator and prey gets airborne in a hurry and the fight for survival begins. After a few moments, the ocean calms and the scene returns to normal, just as it has millions of times before. Through all the commotion, the Diamond Shoals Lightship is a silent witness to the ebb and flow of nature, beckoning a growing legion of charter boat captains and their queasy anglers out for a day of fun and sun. Life is good.

Not exactly so for Ernal Foster. He is on a mission and his focus is intense. Over the past few years he has tangled unsuccessfully with numerous blue marlin. Maybe it was fate, bad luck or any of a hundred different explanations, but the simple fact remains, he has landed no marlin.

On charter trips during the past few days, Ernal has seen some huge blue ones roaming the edges of the Gulf Stream, taunting him to take another shot. Now, he is frustrated and ready for his bad luck to end. Bring 'em on—and this time, no excuses.

According to Ernal's son, Captain Ernie Foster, his bad luck ended on June 25, 1951. This is how it happened.

The *Albatross II* eased through Hatteras Inlet on a beautifully calm day and headed for the tried and true fishing grounds in the Graveyard of the Atlantic. Captain Ernal Foster was at the helm of his prized new vessel and the mate was younger brother Gaston. Their fishing party consisted of four older gentlemen who were on an outing simply to catch a few fish and enjoy a relaxing day on the water.

When the *Albatross II* reached the tip of the shoals and the bottom fell away, Ernal motioned for Gaston to put out the baits. Four lines were set, two connected to the trademark red-and-white-striped bamboo outriggers and two rested in the gunwale-mounted rod holders. Only farmers and duck hunters could complain about this kind of weather, but it really was too calm. Ernal knew it would be a difficult day trolling and he was right. After a few hours, the party had managed only a couple of dolphin and one small wahoo.

All morning Ernal had been quietly "working to the east'erd," and now the opaque green inshore swells had given way to the clear blue water of the Gulf Stream. It was lunchtime and the fishermen were relaxing in the shade of the cabin. Even though the party didn't want to catch a marlin, Captain Foster decided to try the large Spanish mackerel that was rigged and ready. He instructed Gaston to set the bait on his best

He is on a mission and his focus is intense. Over the past few years he has tangled unsuccessfully with numerous blue marlin. Maybe it was fate, bad luck or any of a hundred different explanations but the simple fact remains, he has landed no marlin.

rod and reel, a 9/0 Penn Senator mounted on a Jersey Coast rod. In no time, a familiar silhouette crashed the mackerel and the Senator reacted with a scream. Figuring the ferocious strike to be that of a shark or a marlin, either of which were way too big and sinister to mess with, no one in the fishing party moved an inch. One man even hollered at Captain Foster, "You hooked it, you catch it!" Having seen the big marlin inhale the mackerel, Ernal concluded that this might be the opportunity he had long been waiting for.

Above • 1:

Captain Ernal Foster with the first documented blue marlin caught in North Carolina waters after WW II. Hatteras, June 25, 1951.

In an instant, Ernal and Gaston swapped places. Ernal wrestled the rod from its holder as Gaston grabbed the wheel. The fight was on. The big blue headed deep and Gaston threw the boat into reverse hoping to make up some line. Ernal struggled but he managed to get in the sturdy fighting chair and stab the butt of the rod into the gimbal. The braided line was disappearing fast and the marlin was in complete control. This fight, however, was unlike the others—this time Captain Foster was in the chair.

The tug of war continued for an hour, then two. Each time Ernal got a little line back, the marlin responded. When the marlin made a run, Ernal countered. Back and forth it went. For this fish, going deep was an exit strategy. No magnificent jumps or tail-walking aerial displays, just straight down, head-shaking, back-breaking runs. Almost three hours into the fight, Ernal was exhausted. Something had to give and this time, for the first time, it was the giant.

The big blue was still deep but it no longer stirred and Ernal could sense a definite change in the fight. He braced himself against the gunwales to put more pressure the rod. The response from below was now muted. With no more deep dives or long runs to endure, Ernal started gaining line and he felt his own strength revive. He was still cautious because he had witnessed the power of these fish before and he was taking no chances with this one. He kept the pressure steady as he brought the marlin along side his boat. After a quick jab of the gaff, all six men strained just to pull the fallen warrior over the gunwales and onto the wooden deck.

His battles were over—both of them: the battle with the marlin and the one with those who had claimed he was foolish for trying to build a future in sportfishing. Now he was on his way back through Hatteras Inlet with a 475-pound blue marlin onboard, the first one landed on the Outer Banks since World War II. We can only imagine the smile on his face and the feeling in his heart that he had accomplished something special— Ernal Foster had just realized his dream.

Overview

The easternmost edges of Cape Hatteras stretch far into the Atlantic Ocean as if reaching out for the Gulf Stream. This is a special place where lazy tropical waters from the south skirt the coastline, only to be met in a massive collision with the cold currents swirling in from the north. It's a special place where seemingly endless lines of sargassum, rafted up by the wind and tide, make their timeless journey northward. This special place is called the Outer Banks, and it is home to some of the world's best boatbuilders and offshore sportfishing.

The Outer Banks is a unique environment that includes inlets, shoals, wind and waves. None is more foreboding or more widely recognized by mariners than Diamond Shoals. Here the shallow, wave-tossed waters are both fierce and fickle. It's a place that has earned the Outer Banks a well-deserved moniker: "Graveyard of the Atlantic."

Left • 2: *Map of coastal North Carolina by Captain John White. 1585.*

On the other hand, this same spot, with its close proximity to the Gulf Stream, is teeming with schools of baitfish and alive with predators eager for a passing bite. Marlin, tuna, wahoo and dolphin congregate along the edges of this vast underwater river, and fishermen know this place as "Gamefish Junction."

Outer Bankers are no less diverse than the environment they inhabit. For generations, residents have adapted to life on this narrow strip of sand and their tenacity and resilience are legendary. These are people who have enjoyed the best and endured the worst that nature has to offer. The Outer Banks is indeed a unique environment.

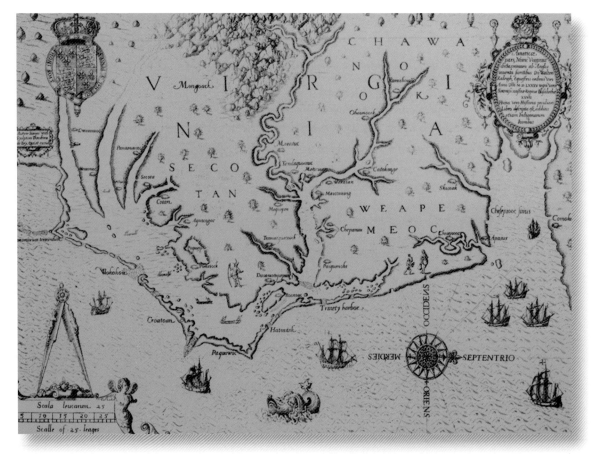

Right • 3:

Map of coastal North

Carolina. 1590.

A chain of barrier islands stretches approximately 300 miles along the entire length of the North Carolina coast. These geologic formations might best be described as "offshore sandbars" resulting from centuries of accumulating sand deposits. Along the northern part of the coast, the barrier islands are long, narrow "ribbons of sand" that are often separated from the mainland by miles of large, shallow sounds. Along the southern part of the coast, the barrier islands are relatively small and close to the mainland.

Barrier islands share common features. Ocean surf zones, where the tide ebbs and flows, are the high-energy areas where storms can make significant changes to the island in just a matter of hours. Barrier islands also include a sand beach zone that stretches from the reach of high tides all the way to the primary dunes. The dune line is a zone where the first vegetation grows, usually sea oats and other salt-tolerant, low-growing grasses. Just beyond the dunes, shrubs and smaller trees begin to emerge in a zone where wax myrtle and yaupon are found. Farther from the effects of the salt spray and blowing sand is the maritime forest where cedars, pines, live oaks and a variety of shrubs flourish.

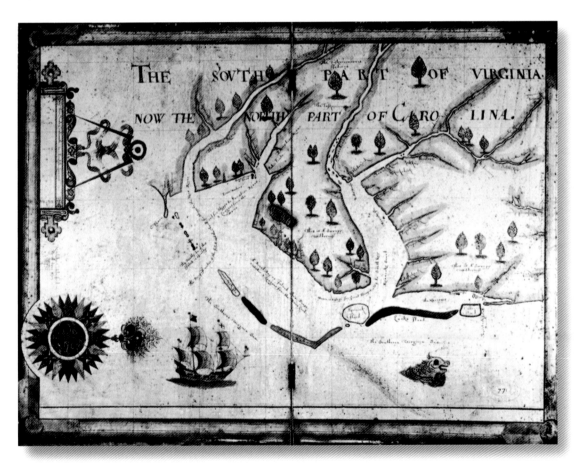

Maritime forests often contain freshwater ponds or interconnected marshes. On the backside of the island, the maritime forest flattens to meet the salt marsh grasses and the open waters of the sound. Unlike contemporary coastal developments, early settlers on the Outer Banks lived primarily in the protected, heavily vegetated maritime forest.

The North Carolina Outer Banks are separated by a series of inlets linking the ocean and the sound. These inlets are often formed by an ocean storm surge that breaches the dune line and washes a channel through the barrier island to the sound. Inlets can also be created when the pressure of water from the sound erodes a channel through the dunes to the ocean. These natural processes result in a mixing of salt and fresh waters that creates a habitat conducive to a rich and diverse population of aquatic life. This biodiversity is the foundation for a dynamic fishery resource.

Left • 4:

Map of coastal North Carolina. 1657.

Once an inlet has formed, it functions more like an "outlet" because it allows huge volumes of water from the rivers and sounds to flow into the ocean. Depending on the position of a storm, the inland pressure from rainwater and wind-driven tides can be much greater than the push of water from the ocean. This complex interaction of currents, tides and winds in an inlet creates a constantly changing environment.

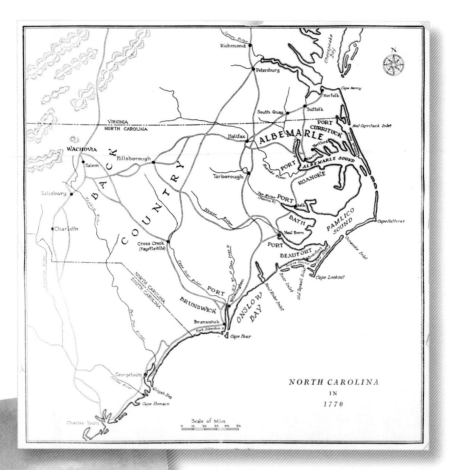

Boaters are well aware of the navigational challenges presented by the inlets along the North Carolina coast. These features also create an environment where baitfish and sportfish converge and where some of the best fishing in the world can be found.

Our review of boatbuilding and sportfishing focuses on the 175-mile portion of the Outer Banks from the North Carolina border with Virginia to Beaufort Inlet. The northern Outer Banks extends from the border with Virginia to Ocracoke Inlet, and the Southern Outer Banks stretches from the north end of Portsmouth Island to Beaufort Inlet.

The Northern Outer Banks

The northern Outer Banks begins at the border with Virginia in the vicinity of the Old Currituck Inlet. This shallow opening in the barrier island existed prior to 1657, when it was documented on an early chart of the region. Colonial records indicate that the inlet closed during the 1730s. The land from this inlet to just north of the village of Duck is known as the "Currituck Outer Banks," and it is a part of Currituck County.

Waterfowlers are familiar with Currituck County for its rich hunting and decoy-making heritage. A large part of this history can be attributed to the ecology of Currituck Sound and the habitat created for wintering waterfowl. With the closing of the Old Currituck Inlet in the 1730s and the subsequent closings of the New Currituck Inlet and Caffee's Inlet in the early 1800s, Currituck Sound became a large, freshwater sound. Only during strong winds and tides does Currituck Sound become slightly brackish. Along with this transition to fresh water came the succulent grasses and marsh

Top • 5: *Map of the Outer Banks. 1770.*

Bottom • 6: *Currituck Beach Lighthouse and keeper's quarters. Corolla, 1905.*

habitats that attracted waterfowl by the millions. Wildlife surveys from the early 1900s
suggest that more than 10 percent of the waterfowl along the entire Atlantic Flyway
wintered in Currituck Sound.

     The tremendous flocks of waterfowl in Currituck Sound attracted hunters from
around the country. Local residents established businesses that offered guide services,
lodging, decoys and skiffs to the incoming sportsmen. Gunning clubs sprang up along
the Outer Banks, and many of them were impressive facilities. The Whalehead Club
in Corolla, with its magnificent copper roof, is a prime example of the golden era of
waterfowl hunting. Thanks to the vision and commitment of leaders in Currituck
County, the Whalehead Club and, next door, the N.C. Wildlife Resources Commission's
Outer Banks Center for Wildlife Education are preserving the rich waterfowling heritage
of the region.

Left • 7:

Fishermen

display their

catch on

the Manteo

waterfront.

1905.

     The Dare County portion of the barrier islands begins just north of Duck and
continues to Hatteras Inlet. This section of the northern Outer Banks offers some of the
most famous beaches on the entire Atlantic seaboard. The communities of Kitty Hawk,
Kill Devil Hills and Nags Head are steeped in legend and history.

     The name Kitty Hawk might have originated from the Indian term "killy hawk,"
loosely meaning "goose hunting." Or it could have come from shortening the term
"mosquito hawk," or dragonfly, to "skeeter hawk" and then to "kitty hawk." Dragonflies
feed on mosquitoes that abound in low-lying areas of the region. Regardless of its origin,

The Tranquil House

All the Name Implies

MANTEO - N. C.

Right on the island. Just a stone's throw from the wharf.

Caters to Fishing Parties

Homelike Atmosphere

Large Rooms   Good Table

Box Luncheons
for
Early Morning Parties

MRS. N. E. GOULD
Proprietress

MANTEO
NORTH CAROLINA
Truly the Fisherman's Paradise

Game Fish and their Season in this Locality

HORACE DOUGH
Fishing Guide
P. O. Box 77   -   -   MANTEO, North Carolina

CHANNEL BASS

BULL dogs of the sea. May be caught casting or trolling. Frequently in schools from April 15 to June 15. A real test for your ability and tackle. Doubting Thomases take home real remembrances of thrill and skill.

Last season one party caught 90 in one day. These fish weigh from 12 to 60 pounds each. Some Channel Bass remain in these waters throughout the entire summer season. Artificial bait spoons best for trolling.

STRIPED BASS or ROCK

THE striped bass season is probably the most extensive of all fishing periods, lasting from May 1 to December 1. The big season, however, is from September 1 to November 15, when they may be caught in large schools, trolling with artificial bait (spoons).

These fish run from 2 to 20 pounds, excepting in May and June, when smaller rock are caught, averaging from 1½ to 3 pounds each. A party of two caught 200 pounds of Rockfish in this vicinity in one day, last season.

Left • 8: Fisherman with a channel bass caught at Oregon Inlet. 1928.

Right • 9: Brochure advertising Horace Dough's fishing guide service. Manteo, 1928.

Kitty Hawk played an important role in the history of the Outer Banks as the site where the Wright brothers telegraphed their news about the first successful airplane flight.

Kill Devil Hills shares an equally muddled name derivation. One theory proposes that the name originated with a report by William Byrd, a colonial surveyor, when he suggested that local residents made an alcoholic brew so distasteful that it would "kill the devil." According to a similar story, locals salvaged kegs of "kill devil rum" from shipwrecked cargo vessels and the myth grew with each successive drunken party. The first documented use of the name was in 1808 on a map of the Outer Banks. The huge sand dunes in Kill Devil Hills are where the Wright brothers made their historic flight on December 17, 1903, and where the Wright Brothers National Memorial commemorates this feat today.

The folklore surrounding the name Nags Head may be the most colorful of all Outer Banks communities. The first documentation of this name was in 1738 and stories have abounded since. One theory suggests that the early colonists brought the name from England where at least

one community was called Nags Head. A more popular version describes the natives as "pirates" who ventured out at night with a devious plan for passing ships. They reportedly tied a lantern around the neck of a horse and walked the "old nag" up and down the sand dunes. Passing vessels were deceived into thinking that the light was a ship rocking gently in safe harbor. When they approached, their vessels ran aground on the beach and looters quickly overtook the ship and make off with the bounty.

Just west of Nags Head is historic Roanoke Island. Surrounded by the Roanoke and Croatan Sounds, Roanoke Island dates to 1584 and is considered to be the home of the first English settlement in America. The communities of Manteo and Wanchese, both named for Indian leaders, are famous for their "lost colony" history and they are also widely recognized as the focal point for boatbuilding and offshore sportfishing on the northern Outer Banks.

Just to the east of Roanoke Island is Whalebone Junction and Bodie Island. At this point the "ribbon of sand" begins to stretch from the mainland farther into the waters of the Atlantic. Before 1810, Bodie Island was separated from Nags Head by Roanoke Inlet. With the closing of this inlet, however, Bodie Island became a part of the contiguous barrier island chain from the border with Virginia to Oregon Inlet.

The southern tip of Bodie Island is marked by Oregon Inlet, one of the most famous, or infamous, inlets along the Atlantic seaboard. Oregon Inlet was opened by a fierce hurricane on September 7, 1846. Accounts from residents indicate that a hard west wind pushed 2 to 3 feet of water from the sound onto the west side of Bodie Island. This pressure started

Top • 10:

Fisherman lands a channel bass from a shad boat. Oregon Inlet, 1928.

Bottom • 11:

Boatbuilder and charter fisherman Jerry Turner at his home in Wanchese. The stern of the boat protrudes from the other side of his house. 1955.

Top • 12: *Vehicle on the sand road to Oregon Inlet. 1949.*

Bottom • 13: *Bodie Island Lighthouse stands guard over Oregon Inlet. 1900.*

eroding a narrow channel into the backside of the dunes until it suddenly pushed through to the ocean. Over the next couple of months, the prevailing southwesterly winds kept the waters churning through this small opening until an inlet more than 100 yards wide was formed. In October 1846, a strong gale sent waters rushing through the channel with such force that the inlet widened further and the bottom was scoured deep enough to allow passage of large ships. Oregon Inlet is named for the side-wheeler *Oregon*, the first vessel to successfully navigate its treacherous shoals and shifting channel.

From the mid-1920s through the early 1950s, Captain Toby Tillett of Wanchese offered a ferry service across Oregon Inlet. Access from Nags Head to the ferry landing was either down the oceanfront on the hard beach or on a narrow sand path. To summon the ferry, a customer simply hoisted a flag at the landing as a signal for Captain Tillett to come pick them up.

Depending on the tides and wind, the ferry often could not reach the shore and vehicles had to negotiate more than 100 yards of shallow water before reaching dry land.

Once on Hatteras Island, visitors could travel down the oceanfront on the beach or take the inland route on a sand path. Reportedly, one cantankerous "drummer," or salesman, asked Toby about the best way to get from Oregon Inlet to Cape Hatteras. Without hesitation Captain Tillett replied: "Just take Highway 108." The motorist asked for directions to the highway only to be told: "Mister, there are 108 tire tracks to Hatteras, just pick one and stay in it."

In 1951, the sand road from Nags Head to Oregon Inlet was paved and named N.C. Highway 12. The highway was connected to Hatteras Island with the opening of the Bonner Bridge in 1962.

Top • 14: *Captain Toby Tillett's ferry,* Barcelona, *prepares to take cars and passengers across Oregon Inlet. 1938.*

Bottom • 15: *Charter fishing party with a nice catch of channel bass at Oregon Inlet. Circa 1915.*

Constantly changing winds, currents, tides and shoals make Oregon Inlet one of the most dynamic spots along the Outer Banks. As if this was not enough, the inlet is migrating southward and the channel is ever-shifting. This inlet, no matter how fickle, is vitally important to the Outer Banks. It provides the only boating access to the ocean from the Virginia border to Hatteras Inlet, and it is the lifeline for a thriving commercial and sportfishing industry.

Across Oregon Inlet is Hatteras Island. This part of Dare County stretches southward approximately 60 miles to Hatteras Inlet. Many small inlets have divided this vulnerable stretch of island over the last 400 years. The northern part, once called Chicamacomico Banks, is now known as Pea Island. This section was separated by

Text continued on page 15

Top • 16: *Captain Will*
Etheridge, Jr., right, with a
fishing party and their catch.
Oregon Inlet, 1955.
Middle • 17: *Cape Hatteras*
Lighthouse. 1893.

Bottom • 18:
Captain Charles Midgett on
the Lois C *at the Oregon Inlet*
Fishing Center. 1957.

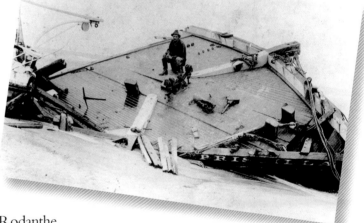

Oregon Inlet to the north and by New Inlet to the south, but when New Inlet closed in the 1930s, Pea Island became a contiguous part of Hatteras Island. Even though engineers have tried to stabilize the dunes several times at the New Inlet site, strong storms continue to break through and threaten once again to divide Hatteras Island. The remnants of an old wooden bridge across New Inlet still stand as a reminder of the fragility of these barrier islands.

South of Pea Island is a region once called Kinnakeet Banks. This stretch of the island runs from New Inlet all the way to Hatteras Inlet. The communities of Rodanthe, Waves, Salvo, Avon, Buxton, Frisco and Hatteras dot the narrow strip of sand that extends into the Atlantic some 20 miles across Pamlico Sound from the mainland. This beach provides excellent surf fishing and boasts of the world record channel bass, 94 pounds, caught at Rodanthe in 1984.

Cape Hatteras is one of the most prominent geographical features on the East Coast. Located at Buxton, Cape Point is the easternmost tip of North Carolina, and is famous as a surf-fishing destination for anglers eager to catch large bluefish, channel bass and striped bass. Cape Hatteras is also where the barrier islands deviate from their north–south orientation and make a turn to the southwest towards Ocracoke Island and Cape Lookout.

Text continued on page 18

Top • 19:

Creed's Hill Lifesaving Station

is located just south of Buxton

near Diamond Shoals. 1895.

Bottom • 20: *Wreck of the*

Priscilla at Cape Hatteras.

1899.

Top • 21: *A soundside windmill at Buxton was used for grinding corn and was one of over 30 windmills along the Outer Banks. Circa 1900.*

Bottom Left • 22: *Captain Hallas Foster on the charter boat KoKo is navigating Hatteras Inlet. 1948.*

Bottom Right • 23: *H.H. Brimley, first Director of the North Carolina Museum of Natural Sciences, caught a nice channel bass on a collecting trip to Cape Hatteras. 1905.*

Top Left • 24: *Hugo Rutherford, left, and Captain Lloyd Styron, right, pose with a 439-pound blue marlin, the first recorded in North Carolina. Hatteras, July, 1938.* Top Right • 25: *Captain Ernal Foster with a sailfish caught on the Albatross. Hatteras, 1939.* Bottom Left • 26: *Fishing with Captain Ernal Foster on the charter boat Albatross off Cape Hatteras. 1948.*

Bottom Right • 27: *The first time two marlin were boated in one day, on the same boat. Mrs. Lucy Stowe, Twins II. Hatteras, 1953.*

Top • 28: *The U.S. Weather Station at Cape Hatteras was among the first in the nation. 1893.*

Bottom • 29:

Lightship Diamond Shoals *washed ashore at Cape Hatteras in the San Ciriaco Hurricane. 1899.*

Cape Hatteras has become synonymous with shipwrecks and violent storms. It is also widely known by fishermen as the closest port to the Gulf Stream along the mid–Atlantic coast. The present day Hatteras Inlet opened in the same storm that carved Oregon Inlet on September 7, 1846. With the shoals and the Gulf Stream so close to shore, early sailing vessels had to select either the treacherous inside route near Cape Point or go outside east of the shoals near the Gulf Stream. The inside journey was plagued by shifting channels and shallow water and the outside route exposed vessels to wicked currents and storms that rode the warm waters of the Gulf Stream.

With so many shipwrecks, Hatteras Island was a logical choice as a location for several U.S. Lifesaving Stations, one of the first U.S. Weather Stations and the Cape Hatteras Lighthouse. Local residents tell of one particularly bad stretch of weather in the late 1800s that lasted 26 straight days and prevented more than 100 sailing vessels from rounding Cape Point. The sight of all these large sailing ships anchored in the lee of the Cape was such an awesome experience that descriptions have been passed down through generations and are still told by Hatteras Island residents.

During World War II, Cape Hatteras and Diamond Shoals were known as "Torpedo Alley." German submarines patrolled the shipping lanes around the Cape and sank over 100 vessels in this area. Local residents report that explosions were common with some so violent that dishes shook in the kitchen cupboard. Curfews were in effect and a lights-out policy was implemented to prevent the island from becoming a military target. Islanders routinely saw ships burning in the distance, and there are reports that German soldiers were even spotted among the sand dunes just north of Cape Point.

Across Hatteras Inlet is Ocracoke Island, one of the most remote locations along the coast. Early traders found the shipping channels ominously close to shore and if they successfully made it through the weather and the shoals, they had another menace to worry about—pirates. Ocracoke was home to many noted pirates including the infamous Captain Edward Teach, "Blackbeard." Other pirates that terrorized the area included Stede Bonnet, "Bluebeard," and "Calico" Jack Rackham. These pirates used fast, shallow-draft sailboats, and they learned how to navigate the shoals and inlets. In 1718, "Blackbeard" was captured and beheaded off Ocracoke Island and other pirates were driven out of the area in an effort to rid the coast of this danger.

Left • 30: *Captain Thurston Gaskill poses with a catch beside his charter boat* Southwind. *Ocracoke, 1949.* Right • 31: *Ocracoke Lighthouse and keeper. Ocracoke, 1890.*

FISHING PARTIES

EX. C. G. BOAT
"HATTERAS"

LEAVE		RETURN
7 a.m.	to	10 a.m.
12 p.m.	to	3 p.m.
3 p.m.	to	6 p.m.

FROM WAHAB PIER
OCRACOKE, N. C.

6 PERSONS	2.00	EACH TRIP
5 "	2.00	"
4 "	2.50	"
3 "	3.50	"
2 "	5.00	"
1 "	10.00	"

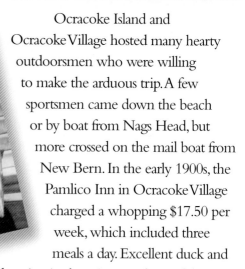

Top Left • 32: Poster advertising sportfishing at Ocracoke. Circa 1947.

Top Right • 33: Angler on the Fear-Mac lands a channel bass. Bottom • 34: Six nice channel bass caught in Ocracoke Inlet by Captain Thurston Gaskill. 1952.

Ocracoke Island and Ocracoke Village hosted many hearty outdoorsmen who were willing to make the arduous trip. A few sportsmen came down the beach or by boat from Nags Head, but more crossed on the mail boat from New Bern. In the early 1900s, the Pamlico Inn in Ocracoke Village charged a whopping $17.50 per week, which included three meals a day. Excellent duck and goose hunting in the winter and sportfishing in the spring, summer and fall rewarded the sportsmen that got here. Hunting guides took parties to the shoals behind Ocracoke in search of pintails, redheads, brant and geese, and fishermen trolled near the Ocracoke Inlet for channel bass, bluefish and Spanish mackerel. In the 1920s, Captain Thurston Gaskill, one of the most widely acclaimed local guides, proved that a loon bone skirted with chicken feathers was an exceptional lure for channel bass.

Ocracoke Inlet was also significant for maritime trade in North Carolina. This inlet was more stable than most others along the northern Outer Banks, and it provided ocean access to and from markets in the central part of the state.

The Southern Outer Banks

The tip of Portsmouth Island, or North Core Banks, lies just across Ocracoke Inlet. This long, thin barrier island stretches 56 miles around Cape Lookout to Beaufort Inlet. In 1976, the entire island was named the Cape Lookout National Seashore to protect its natural and cultural history.

In 1753, Portsmouth Village was founded as an important seaport where cargo from large ships entering Ocracoke Inlet could be "lightered," or off-loaded, for shipment to inland cities. Portsmouth was a thriving village with over 700 annual residents until a succession of strong storms and severe shoaling in the inlet occurred during the late 1800s. From 1900 through the 1940s, Portsmouth Village began a slow decline. By the 1950s, almost everyone had left except for a few families that stayed on simply because of their intense love for the island and the lifestyle it afforded. In 1971, even the hardiest permanent residents gave up and Portsmouth Island became uninhabited. Several houses still remain in the village along with the Portsmouth Lifesaving Station, a post office and the general store. The National Park Service is working to restore the village and to interpret the lifestyle on the barrier islands.

Left • 35: *Aerial view of Cape Lookout and Barden's Inlet. 1963.*

Top • 36: *The Cape Lookout*

Shoals Lightship. *1897.*

Bottom • 37: *A Morehead*

City charter boat

fishes near

the Lightship

Relief. *These*

ships provided

"relief" while the

regular lightship

was ashore making

repairs and getting

supplies. 1947.

South of Portsmouth Village is the Atlantic Lifesaving Station, Old Drum Inlet and New Drum Inlet. These two inlets frequently open and close with storms and are generally too shallow for navigation. Portsmouth Island is a long uninhabited portion of the southern Outer Banks with only a few hunting and fishing camps dotting its landscape. Surf fishermen find this stretch appealing for its excellent channel bass and bluefish runs.

Southern Portsmouth Island, or South Core Banks, was the location of Diamond City and Cape Lookout Village. From the late 1800s through the early 1900s, both villages were thriving fishing and whaling communities. Several violent hurricanes, especially the San Ciriaco Hurricane of August 17, 1899, caused the residents of Cape Lookout Village, Diamond City and Shackleford to leave the islands and resettle on the mainland. With winds reportedly in excess of 140 miles per hour for two full days, the beaches and interior islands were devastated. The hearty residents, known as "Ca'e Bankers," began to leave the islands for more protected areas in Marshallberg, Harkers Island and Morehead City. These strong, independent and resourceful islanders are the forefathers of many of the famous boatbuilders in Carteret County.

The barrier islands along the North Carolina coast have three major capes, each with their own distinctive features. Cape Hatteras, on the northern Outer Banks, and Cape Lookout, on the southern Outer Banks, frame the "Graveyard of the Atlantic." Cape Fear, in the southern part of the state, actually has the most extensive shoals but there are more pathways around this dangerous area.

The famous Cape Lookout Lighthouse warns mariners about the shifting shoals along the central coast. This lighthouse is 165 feet tall and was commissioned in 1859. The black and white diamonds, originally called checkers, were added in 1873.

Harkers Island is only a short distance from the Cape Lookout Lighthouse. Originally called Craney Island, Harkers Island was founded in the early 1700s as a fishing community, but its main legacy is boatbuilding. Some local residents believe that "boatbuilding genes" have been passed down through generations of islanders. One legend even tells of a youngster who was taken from the island when he was 2 years old and upon his return, 20 years later, he built a beautiful skiff with no plans or assistance.

Top • 38: *Anglers on the charter boat* Ocean Spray *show off a nice sailfish. Harkers Island, 1958.* Bottom • 39: *Cape Lookout Lighthouse and keeper's quarters. 1895.*

Whether this is true or not, some of North Carolina's most renowned boatbuilders are from Harkers Island.

Other Down East communities such as Marshallberg, Gloucester, Davis, Otway, Atlantic, Stacy and Cedar Island claim boatbuilders who have contributed to our rich fishing heritage. This entire area became a center for building sportfishing boats with the Willises, Guthries, Roses, Gillikins and many other local families leading the way.

Top • 40: Captain Claude Brown caught this sailfish onboard his Marshallberg charter boat, Miss Belle. 1955.

Bottom • 41: Captain Jimmy Harker, on the charter boat Gale Ann, shows off a couple of nice bluefish. 1967.

Even though many of the sportfishing boats were built Down East, there were also some outstanding builders in Morehead City and the South River sections of Carteret County.

On the mainland just north of Beaufort Inlet is the town of Beaufort, the county seat of Carteret County and the third-oldest community in the state. The history of Beaufort dates to the late 1600s when the town was settled as a seaport and fishing community. The earliest settlers were whalers who hunted the offshore waters near Beaufort Inlet for several species of whales that migrated up and down the coast. These hearty fishermen brought their catch to villages located on Core Banks and Shackleford Banks where they cleaned the whales and turned their harvest into oil and food.

Beaufort is located at a strategic point on the trade route between the northern

Top • 42:

The Morehead

City charter

boat, Helen.

Circa 1938.

Bottom • 43:

Captain Tony

Seamon with a

sailfish landed on

the Monnie M.

Morehead City, 1938.

markets on the Atlantic coast and the West Indies. Ships making these treks would often stop at Beaufort for supplies and rest. Many sailing vessels anchored at Cape Lookout Bight where they were protected from the north winds off the ocean. Much like its northern neighbor Ocracoke, Beaufort was a favorite haunt of pirates. In August 1747, privateers actually raided Beaufort and took control of the town. Local militia responded and the pirates were driven out after only a few days.

Beaufort also played an important role in the Civil War, World War I and World War II. The inlet was considered a strategic vantage point for entrance to inland North Carolina. Fort Macon, a major fortification, was built on the southern tip of the Inlet between 1826 and 1834. In 1862, Union forces captured the fort along with Roanoke Island, Hatteras and Ocracoke. With control of the Outer Banks, the northern forces had access to the inland towns and soon captured Elizabeth City, Washington and New Bern. With the inlets secured, the Outer Banks became a staging area for Union forces and their naval war efforts.

After the Civil War, Beaufort commercial fishermen resumed whaling for a time but soon turned to mullet and menhaden as the primary fishery. The maritime shipping trade also became more important with increasing demand for forest and agricultural products. In the 1920s, a small fleet of four or five boats took sportfishing parties from the waterfront, but this was a secondary business to commercial fishing and shipping.

Morehead City is a thriving town that dates to the 1840s. The Governor of North Carolina, John Motley Morehead, dreamed of having a

Top • 44: *John Tunnell at the Morehead City Yacht Basin with his first marlin. 1958.*

Bottom • 45: *Captain Ottis Purifoy posing with a catch on one of his Lucky 7 Fishing Fleet boats. Morehead City, 1949.*

major seaport at Shepard's Point where the Newport River and Beaufort Inlet converge. This idea evolved into a planned city where sections of the land at Shepard's Point were laid out in square blocks consisting of 16 houses each. This development style was called the "Philadelphia plan" after a similar planned community on the outskirts of Philadelphia, Pennsylvania.

After the Civil War, Morehead City began to develop as a maritime trade center. With its close proximity to beautiful ocean beaches and with the construction of the Atlantic Hotel in the 1880s, Morehead City became a tourist destination. The name "Summer Capital by the Sea" was used to promote the area in an attempt to increase tourist traffic. Unfortunately, the grand Atlantic Hotel was destroyed by fire in 1933 and coupled with the Depression, tourism faltered for a few years.

During the 1880s and 1890s, many fishing families were displaced from Core Banks and Shackleford Banks by hurricanes. These "Bankers" began to settle in Morehead City in an area between 10th Street and 15th Street. This community was called the "Promise Land," so named because of the promise for a better life among those who had endured the worst of Outer Banks weather.

Top • 46: *Lucky angler with a sailfish caught on the charter boat* Blue Water. *Morehead City, 1950.* Bottom • 47: *Two sailfish caught by Kinston physicians Dr. T. Leslie Lee, left, and Dr. Branch Moore, right, on the* Moonglow. *This is the first documented catch of two sailfish on one boat in one day. Morehead City, 1949.*

Morehead City became the center for sportfishing on the southern Outer Banks. In the early 1930s, fishing parties departed from the waterfront docks in search of inshore fish such as channel bass, bluefish and trout along with Spanish and King mackerel. Bottom fishing in the channels and near wrecks also produced nice catches of croakers, spots and other inshore fish. Occasionally, a boat would venture a few miles offshore where sailfish roamed the waters.

Many of the Morehead City charter boats were concentrated between the Sanitary Fish Market and Captain Bill's Restaurant on the waterfront. This was a perfect place to entice tourists into booking a fishing trip. One of the first entrepreneurs to recognize the potential for sportfishing was Captain Tony Seamon. He began charter fishing in 1935 and was soon a key promoter of the Morehead City charter fleet.

Top • 48: *Party boat* Danco *prepares to depart for a day of fishing. Morehead City, 1953.*

Bottom • 49: *Photographer and artist, Reginald Lewis, paints one of his famous mermaids on the Lucky 7 booking headquarters. Morehead City, 1952.*

Seamon expanded his offerings when he and partner Ted Garner opened the Sanitary Fish Market in 1938.

Captain Ottis Purifoy was another a pioneer of the charter fishing industry on the Southern Outer Banks. He founded the Lucky 7 Fleet that catered to sportfishing customers from around the world. The Lucky 7 Fleet docked at the Morehead City waterfront while a few sportfishing charter boats and private boats docked at the Morehead City Yacht Basin.

[CHAPTER TWO]
Backyard Boatbuilders

Backyard Boatbuilders

The setting is Harkers Island and the year is 1946. James Allen Rose is only 11 years old but he has already acquired considerable experience working on the water. He can hardly wait until Saturday when his father's first sportfishing party of the year arrives. James Allen spent more than six hours on his chores, removing the trawl nets from the boat and hanging canvas curtains in the riggings to provide shade for the ladies. He loaded all of their modest fishing tackle onboard in anticipation of a fun day at Cape Lookout. James Allen is thrilled and ready to go.

When the party arrives, all the way from Tarboro, James Allen helps unload trays of ham biscuits and coolers of drinks. Soon the dock lines are cast off and the adventure begins. Their old boat, the *Rose Brothers I*, putt-putts down the channel toward "the Drain," a local name for Bardens Inlet. As soon as they enter the ocean waters, James Allen casts two hand-lines over the stern for bluefish or Spanish mackerel. Attached to the end of the line is the only lure they have ever used—a short, white "tube bait" fashioned from a loon bone fitted over a small hook. Somehow, the twisting, spinning loon bone does the job and a nice Spanish is boated. Twenty more are caught over the next two hours until the party tires of trolling.

Captain Rose decides to anchor near an inshore shipwreck for sea bass and trout. The fishing is good, and the distraction provides just the opportunity James needs to dive into his favorite "up-state" treat, those country ham biscuits. After he devours five or six of them, James Allen is ready for a break and fortunately the party is, too. As they head back to shore, with stomachs and fish boxes full, it is apparent to everyone why Harkers Island is called "Fisherman's Paradise."

With plenty of daylight left, the fishing party offers to hire the precocious young James as their guide for a driving tour of the island. This is the perfect ending to a great day because James Allen knows almost everyone and everything about this close-knit community. As they motor down the dirt lanes, it seems as if a boat is under construction in every backyard and all along the waterfront. James notes that there are 40 boatbuilders on the island. While this is astonishing to the group, it is a part of everyday life for James Allen. He easily recounts stories of the Willises, Guthries, Gillikins, Roses, Lewises and other legendary boatbuilding families, and he relates his own family's boatbuilding prowess.

By the end of the tour, this family from Tarboro knows a lot more about the astonishing Harkers Island boatbuilding heritage, but, more important, they have stimulated a young man to better appreciate his own island heritage. These events would

As they head back to shore,

with stomachs and

fish boxes

full, it is apparent to everyone

why Harkers Island is called

"Fisherman's Paradise."

Top • 50: *Rose Brothers I,*

with canvas in the riggings,

is ready for fishing at Cape

Lookout. Harkers Island, 1949.

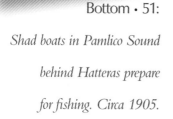

Bottom • 51:

Shad boats in Pamlico Sound

behind Hatteras prepare

for fishing. Circa 1905.

lead James to spend his lifetime preserving this legacy. In 2000, at the age of 65, James Allen Rose received the prestigious North Carolina Folklife Award in recognition of his model boatbuilding and maritime heritage achievements.

Outer Banks families like the Roses are proud of their coastal heritage and their rich boatbuilding history. Often without formal training, with simple tools and native materials, these backyard boatbuilders were a significant part of commercial and sportfishing history. They had a great sense of the water and they knew what it took to make a boat that fit both the environment and the job. These traditions were passed down through generations with every new builder adding his own touch. Driven by the need for a fast, comfortable, safe boat for ocean fishing, the magnificent custom sportfishing boats of today evolved from the designs of these early builders.

A survey of these backyard boatbuilders and their craft provides a foundation for understanding the history of custom sportfishing boats built on the North Carolina Outer Banks.

Overview

For half a century, from the 1880s through the 1930s, backyard boatbuilders on the North Carolina Outer Banks made many important advances in the evolution of sportfishing boats. Among the most significant was the development of the shad boat on Roanoke Island by George Washington Creef.

Top • 52: *The sharpie,* Three Friends, *sails near Beaufort. 1900.*

Bottom • 53: *Ray Davis used the Core Sounder,* Sallie D, *for sport and commercial fishing. Marshallberg, 1947.*

Otis, Lee, Horace and Worden Dough improved on this design and built hundreds of these adaptable boats. When Ben Daniels of Wanchese added the first gasoline engine to a shad boat, the revolution from sail to motorized vessels was underway.

The sharpie and Core Sounder evolved on the southern Outer Banks. Brady Lewis, a master boatbuilder from Harkers Island, designed the first North Carolina boat with a flared bow. The Core Sounder became the standard craft for commercial fishermen and charter boat captains along the North Carolina coast.

The origins of sportfishing also emerged during this period. Some commercial fishermen began to adapt their boats to carry sportfishing parties, while others, like Ernal Foster, an enterprising fisherman from Hatteras, commissioned boats specifically for sportfishing. Mildon Willis of Marshallberg built the famous charter boat *Albatross* for Captain Foster.

Backyard boatbuilders provided the foundation for today's sportfishing boats. Their stylish boats were simple, functional and well-made, classic traits still observed by contemporary boatbuilders on the Outer Banks.

The Shad Boat: Born on the Northern Outer Banks

One of the most significant developments in North Carolina boatbuilding history occurred on the north end of Roanoke Island around 1880 when George Washington Creef designed and built a unique craft called the "shad boat." This vessel was used for fishing pound nets during the spring runs of American and Hickory shad. In the late 1800s and early 1900s, shad was one of the most important commercial fisheries on the northern Outer Banks.

Most early shad boats were 20 to 30 feet long. The 20- to 25-foot vessels were called "net boats" because they were used to maneuver around the pound nets when shad were being harvested. Larger boats, from 25 to 30 feet, were known as "stake boats." They were used to transport the long, heavy gum trees out to the fishing grounds. These trees were driven into the bottom and became the stakes that supported the nets.

According to Earl W. Willis Jr., who documented much of the historical information about shad boats, fishermen used these adaptable boats much like farmers use pick-up trucks. Shad boats were modified for sportfishing in the 1920s and 1930s when commercial fishermen began to take parties to the shoals behind Oregon Inlet in search of channel bass, bluefish, trout and other inshore species.

Top • 54: *Portrait of George Washington Creef. Roanoke Island, 1895.*

Bottom • 55: *Shad boat fishing a pound net near Manns Harbor. Circa 1925.*

Dugout canoes, fashioned from three large cypress or juniper logs, were predecessors of the shad boat. These vessels were called "kunners," local slang for canoes, and they were slow, heavy and sat low in the water. One Manteo boatbuilder recalls his grandfather describing kunners "as a boat that sailed as well under the water as it did on top of it."

"Wash" Creef started building kunners in the mid-1800s but they required large trees, backbreaking labor and months to construct. There had to be a better design. On a trading voyage to the Caribbean, Creef stumbled across a small boat called the "Bahamas dinghy." This craft resembled the kunner but it had more sweeping lines and it was built using a new construction technique called "plank-on-frame." Creef immediately recognized this design as the model he had been seeking.

Top • 56: *George Washington Creef works on shad boats at his boat shed on the north end of Roanoke Island. Circa 1890.*

Bottom • 57: *Shad boats were versatile and used for many applications like this water taxi that ran from Manteo to Nags Head. 1920.*

Text continued on page 38

Top • 58: *Otis Dough, Lee Dough and Worden Dough add the "shutter plank," or the last board that "shuts up" the hull. Roanoke Island, circa 1915.* Middle Left • 59: *The 55-foot shad boat Hattie Creef ferried the Wright brothers and their flying machine from Elizabeth City to Nags Head. 1902.*

Middle Right • 60: *Otis Dough works on a small "runabout." Roanoke Island. Circa 1915.*

Bottom • 61: *Letterhead for W.O. (Otis) Dough and Sons, builders of shad boats. Circa 1920.*

Top • 62: *Lee Dough working on a shad boat with the classic, champagne glass-shaped stern. Roanoke Island, 1936.*

Bottom Left • 63: *The typical sharp bow of a shad boat is displayed as Lee Dough prepares to plank the deck. Roanoke Island, 1936.*

Middle Right • 64: *Lee Dough resting beside a shad boat. Roanoke Island, circa 1930.*

Bottom Right • 65: *The shad boat, Madge, built by the Dough family. Circa 1935.*

Left • 66: Captain Clarence Holmes, right, works alongside his mate on the charter boat Secotan *at Manns Harbor. 1947.* Right • 67: *Oregon Inlet fisherman catches a bluefish as guide Horace Dough watches. 1928.*

Upon his return to Roanoke Island, Wash Creef and his partner, Mann H. Basnight, started working on a plank-on-frame boat that was a hybrid between the kunner and the Bahama dinghy. This new craft had sweeping lines, juniper plank sides, a wide mid-section, rounded bottom, straight bow stem and a champagne glass-shaped stern. Even with these innovations, Creef still had not completely overcome the challenges in the design and construction of the shad boat. To get the transition from the sides to the bottom, Creef continued to use the spreading roots or limbs from juniper trees for the frames and keel. This approach required an ever-expanding search of the swamps for the just right tree and it required skilled workers, both hard to find.

Around 1910, the construction of shad boats evolved from the round bottomed skiff into a Vee-bottom, or deadrise skiff. This design solved many of the problems with materials and labor since both the frames and keel could now be made from boards instead of roots and limbs. These craft are known as "round-chine, deadrise shad boats."

Even though shad boats were relatively small, they often required two people to sail properly. Depending on the load, one person steered the boat and worked the sail while the other person, standing in the bow, moved ballast bags to compensate for the conditions. These canvas ballast bags were filled with gravel and weighed up to 50 pounds each. When properly balanced, shad boats were fast, capable of carrying large loads and steady in the waves.

One of the most famous shad boats built by Wash Creef was named for his daughter, Hattie. The *Hattie Creef* was a large vessel, 55 feet long, and was originally used for oyster dredging. She was later adapted as a ferry and she carried passengers, supplies and mail to many ports around northeastern North Carolina. The *Hattie Creef* was the vessel that transported the Wright brothers and their new flying machine from Elizabeth City to the Outer Banks.

With demand for shad boats spreading, other local boatbuilders started constructing these popular vessels. Otis Dough and his sons Horace, Lee and Worden became known throughout the eastern seaboard for their construction of quality shad boats. In addition to their reputation as premier boatbuilders, the Dough family was also involved in commercial fishing and sportfishing. Horace Dough was among the first to realize the potential for sportfishing when in the late 1920s he started a guide service and began advertising for charter fishing trips from the Manteo waterfront.

In the 1920s and 1930s, Belove Tillett from Manns Harbor began building charter boats based on the shad boat design. These boats were round-chine, deadrise boats that had a sweeping sheer, straight stem and round stern, but they also had a cabin, removable chairs, and other amenities not found on early workboats. Captain Clarence Holmes, *Secotan*; Captains Les and "Grizz" Evans, *Ranger*, and Jerry Turner, *Jerry Jr.*, are charter captains that represent the early transition from commercial to charter fishing.

Another excellent boatbuilder in the Manteo area, Ken Mann, lived on the Dare County mainland between Manns Harbor and Mashoes and built shad boats from the early 1900s through the 1920s. He is considered one of the best boatbuilders of that time.

Thirty miles down the Pamlico Sound shore from Manns Harbor, is the village of Engelhard and the home of Captain Rynald "Nal" Midyette, also an accomplished shad boat builder. According to Earl Willis, Captain Nal built a stylish and functional boat that was well suited to the open waters of Pamlico Sound.

In 1906, Ben Daniels from Wanchese contributed an important innovation to boatbuilding on the Outer Banks by adding a small, three-and-a-half horsepower Lathrop

Text continued on page 41

Top • 68:

Captain Moon Tillett, left, and his son Billy Carl Tillett, holding bill, display a marlin caught on the Ranger. *Wanchese, 1957.*

Bottom • 69: *Shad boat heading for the nets. Manns Harbor, circa 1925.*

Top • 70: *Captain Omie Tillett holds a nice wahoo caught on the round-stern charter boat, Jerry Jr. Oregon Inlet, 1953.* Bottom Left • 71: *Shad boats line the canal at Manns Harbor. 1946.* Middle Right • 72: *Horace Dough takes a ride on one of his beautifully balanced shad boats. Manns Harbor, circa 1935.* Bottom Right • 73: *Shad boat made by Ken Mann, right, prepares for a Sunday afternoon boat ride. Manns Harbor, circa 1920.*

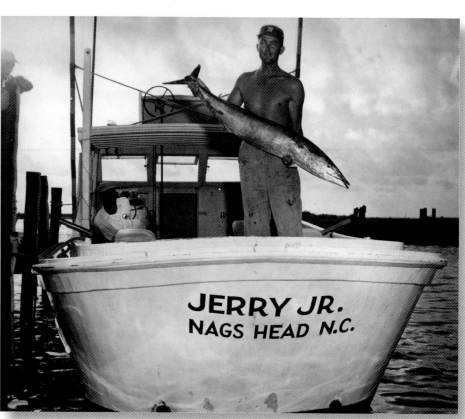

engine to a shad boat. Even though his boat was slow, it was still more versatile than the sail-powered model it replaced, and the improvement signaled the end of the sail craft era. With more and more fishermen eager to use gas engines and with their expanding availability, the transition to gasoline engines proved to be rapid. By the 1930s, almost all shad boats were gas powered. Daniels is credited with making an already efficient vessel into a boat that eventually would be the foundation for a growing commercial and sportfishing industry on the northern Outer Banks.

Thanks to the efforts of Earl Willis, the North Carolina General Assembly named the shad boat the Official State Boat in 1987. This extraordinary vessel embodies the ingenuity and craftsmanship of the early backyard boatbuilders on the northern Outer Banks. The shad boat started the modern era of boatbuilding and is an important ancestor in the lineage of custom sportfishing boats.

Sharpies and Core Sounders on the Southern Outer Banks

One of the early, and important, workboats used in North Carolina waters is the sharpie. This sail craft was originally designed and built in New Haven, Connecticut, during the mid-1840s. These flat-bottomed boats were long and narrow, generally measuring between 27 to 35 feet in length. They were shallow draft and included a retractable centerboard so they were ideal for inshore commercial use. Sharpies also had a straight stem, low bulging sides and a round stern. They could carry large loads and still be operated by a two-man crew. Sharpies were not designed for work or travel in the ocean.

Above • 74: *The sharpie,*

Bessie B, sails near

Morehead City. Circa 1900.

In the mid-1870s, George Ives, a Connecticut businessman, brought two sharpies, the *Lucia* and the *Ella,* from New England to Beaufort hoping to convince local oystermen to use this new craft. When local fishermen stubbornly refused to change from their flat-bottomed sail skiffs, Ives arranged a boat race to demonstrate the virtues of his new craft. The *Lucia* was pitted against the *Sunny Side,* a 28-foot open sail skiff owned by Daniel Bell. The race was from Harkers Island to Beaufort Inlet and the New England sharpie easily won. Bell and other local boatbuilders decided to construct the Core Sound version of a sharpie based on the design of the *Lucia*. A year later, Bell challenged Ives to another race pitting his newly completed *Julia Bell* against the *Lucia*. This race took place in New Bern on the Neuse River and this time the winner was the *Julia Bell*. Word spread about this new style vessel and boatbuilders soon began construction of the Core

Above • 75: *The sharpie,*

Iowa, *heading for the oyster*

beds in Pamlico Sound.

Circa 1900.

Sound sharpie. This craft was shaped like the New England version except the Core Sound model used a different sail configuration.

For a half-century, from the 1870s through the 1920s, sharpies became the standard craft for inshore commercial use along the southern Outer Banks. Goods and supplies were shipped by large ocean-going vessels through Hatteras Inlet and Beaufort Inlet. Since these deep draft vessels could not navigate in the shallow sounds, their cargo was "lightered," or off-loaded, onto a fleet of waiting sharpies for distribution to inland destinations such as New Bern, Washington, Edenton and Elizabeth City. Farm and forest products along with many other goods were shipped back on the sharpies for export to other parts of the east coast and the Caribbean.

According to Mike Alford, retired curator at the North Carolina Maritime Museum, many of the attributes of today's commercial and sportfishing boats can be traced to the sharpie. If not in looks, the lineage can be followed through construction techniques. The Core Sound sink-net boat is an example of the sharpie's evolution into a dominant fishing vessel adapted for use in the shallow waters of Core Sound.

Following the same timeline and transition of the shad boat, the sailing sharpie was adapted for gasoline engines during the 1920s and 1930s. By the end of the 1930s, almost all of the sharpies still in use were powered by gas engines. In order to accommodate bigger nets and larger crews, the old sharpie evolved into a new boat called a Core Sound sink-netter, or simply, the Core Sounder. A functional and cost-efficient vessel, the Core Sounder soon became the mainstay for commercial fishermen along the southern Outer Banks.

The Core Sounder's lines are similar to those of the sharpies they replaced. Although Core Sounders are deadrise boats, they typically have a straight bow stem, low flaring sides, a sweeping sheer and a round stern. Originally, Core Sounders were built using the relatively narrow 4 to 1 length-to-beam ratio. Since most Core Sounders were 36 to 40 feet long, the beam measured 9 to 10 feet. As engines became more powerful and fishermen wanted to carry heavier loads, the length-to-beam ratio decreased to 3 to 1 and a 36- to 40-foot Core Sounder evolved into a boat with a wider 12- to 13-foot beam.

All of these attributes contributed to a perfectly suited vessel for the region. Sink nets and trawls could easily be handled over the round stern without snags or tangles, and fishermen could work crab pots or oyster tongs over the low sides. Unlike the shad boat or the sharpie, Core Sounders were well suited for inshore ocean waters. With more length, deadrise and beam, a Core Sounder could easily handle a load of fish in rough seas. The relative speed, ride and sea-handling capabilities of the Core Sounder also afforded a better experience for sportfishermen. As a result, this vessel became the most widely used craft for charter fishing on the Outer Banks.

Core Sound sink-net boats were built throughout the southern region of the Outer Banks, particularly at Harkers Island, Marshallberg and in many other Down East communities of Carteret County. Most of the legendary boatbuilders in this area started by building Core Sounders and their influence on the sportfishing boats of today is apparent.

One of the area's best boatbuilders was Brady Lewis. Like so many others along the Outer Banks, Lewis started building boats in his backyard on the Harkers Island shoreline. His first effort was a 26-foot skiff called the *Dogfly*. Completed in 1938, this boat set into motion a long and important career that made a significant impact on the boatbuilding history of North Carolina.

Born in 1904, Brady Lewis had an innate sense of the relationship between the lines and curves of a boat and her sea-keeping abilities. He also was a master at translating these characteristics into the design and construction process. Without any formal training or apprenticeship, Brady Lewis learned to build boats using his own intuition. He became so adept and successful that other boatbuilders came to him for guidance, earning him the unofficial title, "father of Harkers Island boatbuilders." Clem Willis, also a very skilled boatbuilder who apprenticed with Lewis, once commented that Brady was so talented he surely must have been born with a hammer in his hand.

Top • 76: *"Backyard boatbuilder" Burgess Lewis works on a boat in Brady Lewis' boat yard on the Harkers Island waterfront. 1947.* Bottom • 77: *The* Jean Dale, *a famous Core Sound sink-net boat, rests at harbor. Harkers Island, 1968.*

Brady Lewis constructed boats using a technique called the "rack of the eye" or "rock of the eye," the spelling depending on where you live on the Outer Banks. This approach simply means that there are no construction plans or guides. Each vessel is built using the proportions, lines, curves and shapes that look right in the "eye" of the builder. Boatbuilders using the rack-of-the-eye method constantly step back to assess the look of their boat. If the lines don't appear "right," they make adjustments. This process is repeated over and over until the boat is finished. If the builder has a good "rack of the eye," the boat turns out to be beautifully proportioned and well shaped. This method has proven to be a very effective way to build boats. Since most early boatbuilders either had no plans or could not read plans, the "rack-of-the-eye" approach was widely practiced. When asked if he had ever used plans to build a boat, Brady Lewis's quick response was: "No, I don't need plans. I know what a boat looks like."

Top • 78: *Brady Lewis, father of the "Carolina flare," in front of his last skiff. Harkers Island, 1967.*

Bottom • 79: *The flared bow of* Jean Dale *is widely recognized as the predecessor to the "Carolina flare" of contemporary sportfishing boats. Harkers Island, 1968.*

Brady Lewis's most important innovation in boatbuilding was the flared bow. Built in 1941, his 40-foot Core Sounder, the *Jean Dale*, is widely considered to be the first North Carolina boat built with a distinctive "flare." The *Jean Dale* was built for Harry M. Lewis and named for his two children. She was used for sink-net and long-haul fishing, two widely practiced commercial fishing techniques for catching mullets, croakers, spots, trout and other inshore species.

Clem Willis said that Brady Lewis selected the frames for the *Jean Dale* from red cedar trees that grew on Core Banks. Cedar trees are common along the Outer Banks where they are sculpted by constant winds and salt spray into unusual, gnarly shapes.

Brady handpicked limbs that had a peculiar "elbow" as they emerged from the trunk of the tree. Using only his hatchet, he fashioned each limb into the exact shape and size for the frame he needed. With the frames in place, Brady Lewis attached juniper strip planking with copper nails into the familiar bow "flar" (local pronunciation of flare). He used heart pine for the keel, stem and cabin framing. At a cost of $750, the *Jean Dale* was the most expensive boat built on Harkers Island at that time.

The *Jean Dale* also had another feature common to early Core Sounders—the "doghouse." This is a small, windowed compartment into which the boat captain sticks his head so he can see how to navigate the vessel. One style of doghouse is the "cabin doghouse" where the compartment is a fixed part of the cabin. The other type is the "sliding doghouse" that is built on runners and capable of being pushed forward or backwards over a hole in the roof of the cabin.

Above • 80: *The sliding doghouse on the* Jean Dale *allows the captain to operate the vessel in any weather. 1968.*

The sliding doghouse affords the option of moving the doghouse out of the way so the captain can enjoy the breezes on calm days. On rough days, he can slide the doghouse forward and be protected from the rain and salt spray. The doghouse design exemplifies the oft-quoted description of Harkers Island boats: "practical design and quality construction equals great results."

Over the past 65 years, the *Jean Dale* has been a warrior, surviving a fire and two sinkings while doing what she was designed to do—carry heavy loads of fish in unforgiving seas. Through each adversity the *Jean Dale* was dried out, cleaned up and returned to duty. Thanks to the efforts of the Core Sound Waterfowl Museum, the *Jean Dale* is being restored today. She will be on public display at the museum as a tribute to Brady Lewis and all of the Harkers Island boatbuilders. No one vessel epitomizes the heritage of commercial fishing and the origins of sportfishing boats on the Outer Banks better than the *Jean Dale*, a classic Core Sound sink-netter.

On Harkers Island, Captain Stacy Guthrie built many Core Sound sink-net boats for commercial fishermen and even a few that were used in the area's growing charter business. Guthrie was born in 1882 on Shackleford Banks and moved to Harkers Island at the age of 17, when fierce hurricanes in 1898 and 1899 forced all of the Bankers to the mainland. Captain Guthrie was one of the last islanders who could give a first-hand account of the whaling industry on the southern Outer Banks. In the mid-1890s, he was involved in the harvest of three whales off Cape Lookout at a time when the entire community depended on this resource for subsistence.

Captain Guthrie was an excellent boatbuilder. He started constructing boats with his father Devine Guthrie in 1892 and he continued for 80 years until 1972 when he retired. His largest vessel was a 54-foot party boat, but he built "hundreds" of boats between 30 and 40 feet. He is particularly noted for a small lapstrake skiff that was sharp on both ends. These sail craft were built in the 1920s and 1930s and were used to fish pound nets. Local fishermen called them "clinker boats." When Captain Guthrie retired, he said: "I have built enough boats that when set side by side would stretch from Harkers Island all the way to the Banks." No one doubted his claim.

Clem Willis was also a noted boatbuilder and contributed to the transition from commercial vessels to charter boats. Willis moved from Salter Path to Harkers Island in the early 1900s where he began his boatbuilding career with his father, Brady Willis. They first built sail skiffs for family transportation and for hauling supplies to their fish camp at Cape Lookout. Clem continued to build small boats and commercial fish until the late 1930s when he went to work with Brady Lewis. Clem describes the boats that he and Lewis built as "classics" that everybody else wanted to copy. Willis also described Brady Lewis as one of the smartest and most mild-mannered of all the local boatbuilders.

Most of the boats built by Clem Willis were commercial vessels, but he did build several square-stern boats for sportfishing. In the late 1940s, Clem Willis and James Gilliken teamed up to build party boats and sportfishing boats for the charter fleets. In the 1950s, Willis worked for Earl Wade in the boat repair shop at the Morehead City Yacht Basin.

Bernie Gillikin was a noted boatbuilder who worked in an area between Marshallberg and Smyrna called "Tusk." This community was so small that local residents teased the few people who lived in Tusk by saying there was no such place. They

Top • 81: *Devine Guthrie constructing a boat used for whaling at Cape Lookout. Circa, 1895.* Bottom • 82: *Stacy Guthrie is a well-known boatbuilder on Harkers Island. 1950.*

declared that Tusk was either lower Smyrna or upper Marshallberg depending on how cruel they wanted to be. Bernie Gillikin built many Core Sound sink-net boats that were used for commercial and sportfishing. Gillikin was born in 1890 and died in 1979.

Some of the most talented boatbuilders along the entire Outer Banks are from the Down East community of Marshallberg. Mildon W. Willis is one of the earliest and most well known of this famous boatbuilding community. Born in 1886, Willis began his career in the early 1920s building sharpies and sail skiffs from his "backyard" on the harbor in Marshallberg. Like others in the area, Willis built mostly Core Sound sink-netters under the name Willis Boatworks. In 1936, Willis was commissioned by Captain Ernal Foster to build a boat that could be used for commercial fishing in the winter and for charter fishing in the summer. With the launching of *Albatross* in April 1937, at a cost of $805, the beginning of sportfishing on the Outer Banks was underway. Mildon Willis went on to build the *Albatross II* in 1948 and the *Albatross III* in 1952 to complete Captain Foster's famous Albatross Fleet.

Mildon Willis built about 50 commercial and sportfishing boats between 1945 and 1960. During this time, Mildon's two sons, Grayer and Kenneth, joined the business and the name was changed to M.W. Willis and Sons Boatworks. Keith Willis, grandson of Mildon Willis and also a noted boatbuilder, worked with M.W. Willis and Sons, as did Ray LeMay. Collectively these fine craftsmen and boatbuilders constructed more than 30 sport cruisers and sportfishing boats known as Willis Craft. In the late 1960s, M.W. Willis and Sons Boatworks stopped building boats and began a reconstruction and repair service at their Marshallberg boat house. Mildon died in 1969 at the age of 83. In addition to the Albatross Fleet, Mildon Willis and the Willis family are known throughout the Atlantic seaboard for their classic Carolina-style cruisers and sportfishing boats. The M.W. Willis family made a significant contribution to the boatbuilding history and the early years of sportfishing along the southern Outer Banks.

Text continued on page 50

Top • 83: *Bernie Gillikin built the charter boat,* Rose Brothers I. *Harkers Island, circa 1940.* Bottom • 84: *Mildon Willis, right, and his son Grayer Willis, take a break from boatbuilding at their Marshallberg boat shed. 1940.*

Top • 85: *Interior of M.W. Willis Boatworks in Marshallberg. 1956.*

Bottom Left • 86: *Exterior of M.W. Willis boat shed with two trawlers under construction. 1956.*

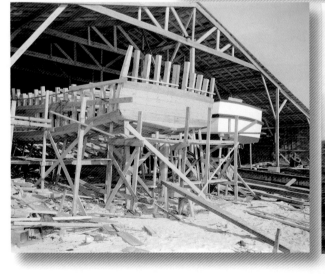

Bottom Right • 87: *Albatross II trolling off Cape Hatteras. 1949.*

Top Left • 88: *Profile of the* Albatross, *built by Mildon Willis for Captain Ernal Foster. Hatteras, 1955.* Top Right • 89: *Captain Bill Foster, left, and Oliver O'Neal, right, with a blue marlin caught on the* Albatross II. *1962.*

Bottom Left • 90: *Boat framed up in M.W. Willis boat shed. Marshallberg, 1956.* Bottom Right • 91: Albatross II *with Ernie Foster sitting in front. She was hauled for repainting. 1953.*

Top • 92: *Cagie*

Adams, center, is

ready for charter on the

Phyllis. *Morehead City,*

1950. Bottom • 93:

Cagie Adams at the helm

of the Phyllis. *1950.*

One of the earliest and most notable backyard boatbuilders from Morehead City was Captain Macajah "Cagie" Adams. Born in 1877 on the western end of Bogue Banks, Captain Adams began his boatbuilding career at the age of 19 from his backyard in Salter Path. From the late 1890s through the 1920s, Cagie built mostly small skiffs used by local fishermen to harvest oysters and scallops from the teeming eelgrass flats behind Bogue Banks. His reputation as a boatbuilder and craftsman became widespread.

Captain Adams was also well known for his involvement and active participation in religious and political affairs. According to his granddaughter, Phyllis O. Gentry, Cagie had the somber responsibility as "keeper of the cooling board." This contrivance was simply two wooden planks, glued side by side, each measuring 8 feet long, 18 inches wide and 2 inches thick. When a death occurred in the community, Adams was summoned to bring the cooling board to the home of the deceased. The body was placed on the board and measured using notches that had been carved into the edges of the plank. The departed was covered with a white linen sheet to "cool" while friends and relatives paid their respects. These ceremonies usually lasted a couple of days allowing time for Cagie to build and deliver a custom-fitted casket.

After a brief ceremony at home, the casket was placed in a wooden skiff, often one used by the deceased. A line of boats filled with family and friends followed in a funeral procession from Salter Path, across Bogue Sound, to the Gales Creek Cemetery on the Carteret County mainland. Local stories still exist about the eerie sounds and unforgettable wailing that echoed across the water as mourners cried out for their loved ones.

Text continued on page 52

Top • 94: *Cagie Adams built his own charter boat and named her* Phyllis *for his granddaughter. Morehead City, 1948.*

Middle Left • 95: *The* Sea Fox, *built by Cagie Adams, is ready for launch. The flag was added to alert patrolling dirigibles during and after WW II that the vessel was American. 1945.*

Middle Right • 96: *Cagie*

Adams boat yard with a boat under construction. Circa 1930. Bottom Left • 97: *Portrait of Macajah "Cagie" Adams. Salter Path, 1910.* Bottom Right • 98: *Cagie Adams in front of a boat under construction at his South 14th Street yard in the "Promise Land." Morehead City, 1946.*

Top • 99: *The* Mattie G., *a classic Core Sound sink-netter, was the charter boat used by noted fisherman Captain Leroy Gould. Morehead City, 1950.*

Bottom • 100: *Captain Cagie Adams, left, inspects the charter boat* Harriet L. *with Captain Dave Gould, center, and Captain Leroy Gould, right. Adams is building the* Harriet L. *on the waterfront at the end of 14th Street on the Bogue Sound waterfront in Morehead City. 1938.*

In 1918, Macajah Adams moved from Salter Path to Shackleford Street in Morehead City and quickly set up his boatbuilding shop at the end of 14th Street in the "Promise Land." Captain Adams, like most other local boatbuilders, did not use blueprints or "formal" plans; rather he sketched his

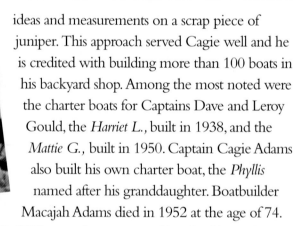

ideas and measurements on a scrap piece of juniper. This approach served Cagie well and he is credited with building more than 100 boats in his backyard shop. Among the most noted were the charter boats for Captains Dave and Leroy Gould, the *Harriet L.*, built in 1938, and the *Mattie G.*, built in 1950. Captain Cagie Adams also built his own charter boat, the *Phyllis* named after his granddaughter. Boatbuilder Macajah Adams died in 1952 at the age of 74.

Captain William R. Willis was also a respected boatbuilder and contemporary of Cagie Adams. Willis operated his shop on 10th Street in the "Promise Land" where he began building boats in the 1920s. In 1933, Captain Willis christened the 36-foot *Sylvia II,* a classic Core Sounder, reportedly by smashing a bottle of clam juice over her bow. With Prohibition laws in effect this seemed like the proper thing to do. Willis reportedly said: "Why waste my limited supply of spirits just to launch a boat?"

Bob Simpson, one of North Carolina's most celebrated and respected outdoor journalists and owner of the *Sylvia II,* confirms that Captain Willis was indeed a special character who was known by the descriptive nicknames "Double Dip" or "Just Right" Willis. In both cases, the names are synonymous with his insistence on using the best materials, like double-dip galvanized fasteners, as well as the latest construction techniques.

The *Sylvia II* was used as a commercial fishing vessel, mail boat and for harbor patrol in World War II. After the War, Captain Theodore Lewis returned the *Sylvia II* to active duty as a charter boat where she became one of the most popular vessels in the Morehead City charter fleet. The *Sylvia II* sank at the dock in the Great Groundhog Day Storm of 1976 and was rescued and refurbished under the watchful care of Bob Simpson. The *Sylvia II* now stands ready to continue her service as a training vessel for groups interested in learning about our maritime heritage.

Asa B. Buck was another noted Morehead City boatbuilder during the time of transition from commercial to sportfishing. Born in 1890, Buck was a contemporary of Cagie Adams and the two worked together on several boats before Asa set up his own shop on Calico Creek in Morehead City. Established in 1927 and known as A.B. Buck Boatworks, the Calico Creek shop is where some of the best-known early sportfishing boats were constructed. Included in this long list are the charter boats *Harriet L. II* and the *Mattie G. II* made for Captains Dave and Leroy Gould.

According to Mrs. Lina Buck Willis, Asa's daughter, Buck prepared half-models before beginning most of his boats. He also made drawings on butcher paper using a scale of 1 inch for 1 foot. Once the drawings were complete, the butcher paper was laid on the floor of his boat shop and the plans were transferred from the 1-foot scale to the floor where they were marked at full scale. The wooden beam for the keel, usually heart pine, was laid on the floor and guide marks were transferred from the floor to "boat stations" along the keel. Large timbers were cut for ribs and fitted to the keel at each station.

Left • 101: Captain Theodore Lewis displays a small sailfish as he sits on the Sylvia II. *1949.* Right • 102: *The* Little Sister, *built by Asa Buck, was a part of the Lucky 7 Charter Fleet in Morehead City. 1949.*

Text continued on page 55

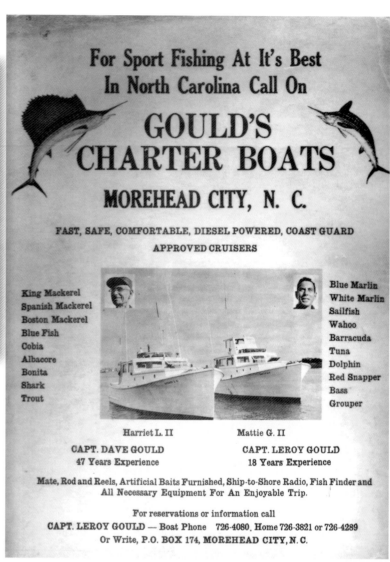

Top Left • 103: *Asa Buck standing on the* Flying Fish *at his Calico Creek boat dock. Morehead City, 1948.*

Top Right • 104: *A poster advertises charter fishing with Captain Dave Gould,* Harriet L. II, *and Captain Leroy Gould,* Mattie G. II. *Morehead City, 1961.* Bottom • 105: *Asa Buck built the* Harriet L. II *for Captain Dave Gould. Morehead City, 1958.*

Once the boat had its shape and the stations were in place, Buck started the process of attaching the battens and planking to the hull. This construction method was common among early boatbuilders on the southern Outer Banks. Even with his sophisticated use of models and scale drawings, Buck still used the "rack of the eye" to tell if everything was level, square and in the right proportions. His boats display a timeless quality that comes only from the hands of a skilled designer and craftsman. Asa Buck was both.

During the Depression, Asa Buck not only built boats but he offered a repair service and a railway for hauling boats out of the water. In those days the price for hauling was $2 with an additional $1 per day for storage. All of the repair work was billed separately and usually amounted to no more than $4 per day. It was common for Buck to be paid with scallops and oysters. Mrs. Willis said that one of the many black commercial

Top • 106: Mattie G. *backs into her slip on the Morehead City waterfront. 1957.* Bottom • 107: *The charter boat Mattie G. II was built by Asa Buck for Captain Leroy Gould. Morehead City, 1960.*

fishermen in the community needed to have some repair work done and he inquired about the fee to have his boat hauled. When Asa replied that it was $2, the fisherman dejectedly said he only had 50 cents. Buck thought for a moment and said, "Well, that's more than I've got. Go get your boat."

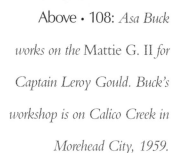

Above • 108: *Asa Buck works on the* Mattie G. II *for Captain Leroy Gould. Buck's workshop is on Calico Creek in Morehead City, 1959.*

During World War II, Asa Buck was employed at the Bell Wallace Shipyard on Fisher Street in Morehead City and later he worked at the shipyard in New Bern. After the War, Buck returned to his boatbuilding business with a renewed desire and a broader perspective. Even though he experimented with several plans and modifications, he never lost his passion for the Core Sounder. In the 1950s, Asa Buck had five boats in the Lucky 7 Fishing Fleet and all were Core Sounders. With the help of Clyde Guthrie, Asa Buck continued building boats at Calico Creek until his death in 1969.

These backyard boatbuilders, with their shad boats, sharpies and Core Sound sink-netters, opened the door to the growing world of sportfishing. They provided the foundation for many innovative design and construction techniques, and they humbly passed along their knowledge and skills to the next generation of boatbuilders. They deserve much credit in the evolution of today's Carolina-style sportfishing boat.

[CHAPTER THREE]

Origins of Charter Fishing on the Northern Outer Banks

Origins of Charter Fishing on the Northern Outer Banks

It's well before daylight and the air is heavy with that familiar salty smell of the ocean. The Oregon Inlet Fishing Center is buzzing with activity as charter captains, mates and fishermen scurry about attending to last-minute details. Harrowing little questions keep popping up. Where's the coffee? Did you remember the sunscreen? Is the cooler on the boat? Who has the car keys? Oh yeah, where is the camera? And on and on. Amid this confusion, the charter captains calmly go about checking the vital signs of their boats: fuel, oil, bait, batteries, ice. They feel secure knowing that their preparation for today was done before quitting yesterday. Plus, they have seen it all before and there's not much that can cause concern.

On this day in August 1964, Captain Omie Tillett boards the *Sportsman*, a 42-foot charter boat he built with Warren O'Neal. His mate is Sunny Briggs, a future charter captain and exceptional boatbuilder. Omie works tirelessly. He is just as excited about this trip as he was when he took his first charter back in 1945. Omie knows the waters around Oregon Inlet better than anyone and he fishes with a passion that few possess. Even though his reputation has spread throughout the sportfishing community, today he is only focused on providing a great experience for the people paying to fish with him on the *Sportsman*.

Although still a teenager, Sunny is an experienced mate and he knows exactly what to do. The connection between captain and mate is a fundamental part of charter fishing and this one is especially rare. Sunny anticipates what the captain wants just by watching Omie move about the bridge. No words are exchanged. Both men are professionals and they have a bond strengthened by many days together on the water.

Finally, preparations are complete and the party is situated onboard. They've forgotten only a few things, but it's okay because the adrenalin is flowing. Just as the fleet leaves the harbor, the sun peeps over the horizon and the sky is aglow with orange shafts of light against a deep blue background. This is the best part of the day for Omie. He says a quiet prayer giving thanks for his good fortune and for the safety of the fleet. Little does he know that in years to come he will establish a tradition for blessing the Oregon Inlet fleet, a tradition that has spread to other charter fleets and tournaments around the world.

Twenty-three sportfishing boats fall in line and snake their way through a narrow channel towards the inlet. Once clear of the shoals and into the ocean, the fleet fans out

Twenty-three sportfishing boats fall in line and snake their way through a narrow channel towards the inlet. Once clear of the shoals and into the ocean, the fleet fans out and each captain heads for his favorite spot about 40 miles away in the Gulf Stream.

Above • 109: *Captain Omie Tillett and mate Sunny Briggs with a 325-pound marlin caught on the* Sportsman. Oregon Inlet *Fishing Center, June 21, 1964.*

and each captain heads for his favorite spot about 40 miles away in the Gulf Stream. Some go north, some south and a few head due east with plans to fish south. Captain Tillett has a "feeling" that today is the day to go south. Sunny has already begun arranging colorful artificial baits and soaking ballyhoo. The hooks are sharp and the tackle is in perfect condition. Everything is ready.

At about 8 a.m., the lines go overboard. The ocean is flat, the air is cool and the water is blue. The big diesel engine on the *Sportsman* drones into the depths calling out for any tuna, wahoo or marlin looking for an easy meal. Omie and Sunny exchange glances and they know the ocean is about to explode with fish. *Get ready!*

A 10 a.m., the lines are still overboard. No fish. Not one single strike. Omie wonders about his decision to go south and he gets on the radio to check out the fleet. One by one the reports come in—no fish, no fish, no fish. It seems as though everyone hesitated to call for fear that they had made the wrong decision. Disappointed but relieved, Omie tries a spot farther out in the Gulf Stream. Three more hours and still no fish. Now it's approaching 2 p.m. and almost time to pick up for the trip home. One by one the fleet calls it quits but Omie desperately wants his party to catch a few fish. In his typical understated manner, Omie quietly leans over the rail and whispers to Sunny, "Change the baits, I'm going to try one more sally to the east'erd." The *Sportsman* makes a big arc and, right on cue, Captain Tillett spots a dense weed line filled with dolphin. As the baits pass within striking distance, the drags begin to sing. In short order, all the boxes are packed and Omie and Sunny are elated.

The trip back is going to be much better now. Sunny quickly cleans up, puts away and he is set for home. With the ocean so calm, Captain Tillett calls on Sunny to put out a couple of lines for a chance at a wahoo on the run in. Great idea, and Sunny is eager to see if it will work.

The party settles in for a relaxing ride back to shore. About an hour into the trip, with the diesel humming and the ocean slick, everyone is fast asleep, including Sunny. Omie had warned him about staying out too late at night but Sunny is a teenager and he obviously knows better than the captain.

On days when the lines are out, it's customary for Omie to make a slight speed adjustment and the resulting variation in engine pitch is a signal for Sunny to bring in the baits. On this day, however, Omie notices Sunny curled up in the corner and he decides to teach him a lesson. The *Sportsman* charges through the inlet, up the channel and almost into the basin at the Fishing Center. When Omie finally slows, Sunny jumps up only to realize that it is too late. The lines he was supposed to be tending have fallen limp and the baits are sitting on the bottom. With the fleet rocking from *Sportsman's* wake, all the captains and mates stop their chores to see what's happening. In front of everyone, Sunny has to reel in the lines and suffer the ultimate embarrassment for a mate. Omie docks the boat and quietly climbs down from the bridge as if nothing had happened. Sunny unloads the dolphin and goes to work cleaning the boat, also without speaking a word.

This is what a great captain does and, as Sunny puts it, "lesson learned and never forgotten." Sunny continues to have the greatest respect and admiration for Omie and their lifelong friendship is stronger now than ever.

Overview

Charter fishing on the northern Outer Banks can be traced to the early 1900s when visiting waterfowl hunters heard about the tremendous schools of channel bass and bluefish that migrated through the inlets each spring and fall. Returning after the duck and goose season ended, these sportsmen hired local guides for fishing and they had great success. Soon, other visitors to the Outer Banks learned of the exceptional fishing. Local commercial fishermen responded by modifying their workboats to carry fishing parties. In the 1920s, Horace Dough was among the first to promote fishing on the Outer Banks when he began an advertising program to recruit customers.

The Oregon Inlet charter fleet had its modest beginnings in a roadside canal between Manteo and Nags Head called Dykstra's ditch. In the early 1950s, the fleet moved to Oregon Inlet and expanded to become one of the premier fishing destinations on the east coast. On July 26, 1974, Jack Herrington landed a 1,142-pound blue marlin,

Top · 110:

Captain Horace Dough was among the first to promote sportfishing as a business on the Outer Banks. Manteo, 1927. Bottom · 111: *Captain Dough gets the gaff as an angler brings another channel bass to the boat. Oregon Inlet, 1930.*

then a world record, on the *Jo-Boy* with Captain Harry Baum at the helm. Charter captains at Oregon Inlet quickly became some of the most recognized offshore fishermen in the country. Names like Tillett, Midgett, Baum, Etheridge, Perry, O'Neal, Basnight, Scarborough, Dough, Cannady, Briggs, Davis and many others established a legacy that continues in the Oregon Inlet Fleet.

At Hatteras, Ernal Foster led the way with the construction of the Albatross Fleet and sportfishing was off and running. Known as the "Billfish Capital of the World," Hatteras became a world-class destination for offshore angling. The charter boats that assembled at Oden's Dock and the private boats fishing out of the Hatteras Marlin Club included some of the best fishermen anywhere. Since Hatteras is ideally situated near Diamond Shoals with close proximity to the Gulf Stream, it remains a time-honored location for offshore fishermen.

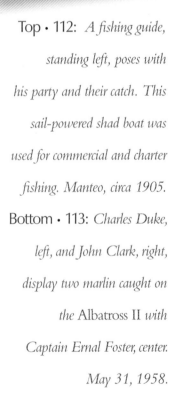

Top • 112: *A fishing guide, standing left, poses with his party and their catch. This sail-powered shad boat was used for commercial and charter fishing. Manteo, circa 1905.*

Bottom • 113: *Charles Duke, left, and John Clark, right, display two marlin caught on the* Albatross II *with Captain Ernal Foster, center. May 31, 1958.*

Early Charter Fishing

Captain Horace Dough was one of the pioneers of charter fishing on the northern Outer Banks. Born in 1892 into the famous Dough boatbuilding family, he grew up on Roanoke Island where he acquired first-hand experience in boatbuilding and fishing. He also served as caretaker of the Wright Brothers National Memorial from 1933 through 1941 and as superintendent until his retirement in 1962. Dough was in a unique position to understand both the growing tourist industry and the possibilities for charter fishing.

Horace Dough began charter fishing in the mid-1920s from the Manteo waterfront. He used a shad boat powered by a small gasoline engine and he carried fishermen to the shoals behind Oregon Inlet for channel bass, striped bass, bluefish, trout and other inshore species. His reputation and success as a charter captain spread along the entire Atlantic seaboard and he became recognized as the spokesman for sportfishing on the Outer Banks. As early as the mid-1930s, Horace developed brochures, conducted radio interviews and sent photographs of fish catches to newspapers in Washington and Baltimore. Dough was among the first to actively promote sportfishing on the northern Outer Banks. His most widely publicized catch occurred on April 7, 1928 when his party landed over 2,000 pounds of channel bass in one day. Forty-two of the fish they caught averaged more than 50 pounds each.

Captain Dough suspended his sportfishing business with the outbreak of World War II but he picked it up with an even more aggressive campaign afterwards. The results he achieved in attracting more and more fishermen to the area caught the attention of other local fishermen who began to focus on their charter businesses. Dough also persuaded local government leaders to establish funds for promoting charter fishing on the Outer Banks. Today these efforts have been expanded and sportfishing has become an important part of tourism development along the Outer Banks.

In addition to Horace Dough, Clyde Hassel took charter parties from the Manteo waterfront in the 1930s and 1940s. His boat, the *Clyde,* was built on

Above • 114: *Part of a brochure for Horace Dough's guide service. Manteo, 1928.*

Left • 115: *Fisherman displays a sailfish caught with Captain J.F. "Jerry" Turner. Wanchese, circa 1947.* Right • 116: *The Caredwyn with Captain Jesse Etheridge, right front, and a catch of striped bass caught at the Manns Harbor Bridge in Croatan Sound. 1958.*

Harkers Island and was a Core Sound sink-netter. Several other charter fishermen docked in Manteo including Captain Lee Dough, *Libby-D*; Captain Ken Ward, *Cherokee*; and Captain Lannis Midgett on a big shad boat named *Lucy*.

During the 1930s and 1940s, several charter fisherman took parties from the docks at Wanchese. These included Captain Wayland Baum, *Alethia;* Captain Jesse Etheridge, *Caredwyn;* Captain Will Etheridge, Jr., *Carrie;* Captain Will Etheridge, Sr., *Boys;* and Captain Gilbert "Moon" Tillett, *Bumbaloo*. These captains fished around Oregon Inlet and into the nearshore waters of the ocean, mostly trolling for channel bass and bluefish. If the ocean was calm and the weather forecast good, they might venture out to the sea buoy and troll until they reached the first grass line. Here they readily caught great numbers of dolphin and returned with happy parties.

Moon Tillett succinctly describes a typical offshore trip from Wanchese during the 1940s: "At best, our old round-stern boats only made about 8 knots. We left Wanchese at 6 a.m. and it took an hour to reach the sea buoy. We put the lines overboard and trolled for four hours straight out, and then we turned around and trolled for four hours straight back. If all went well, we came back to that same sea buoy around 3 p.m. and then back to the dock by 4 o'clock. This gave us time to unload and get ready for the next day."

Captain Will Etheridge, Jr., also described his charters as "close to home fishing" since they had no instruments or electronics to guide them offshore. They used the lighthouses and sand dunes as navigational aids. Other charter captains that fished from Wanchese include Chester Tillett, Dewey Tillett, Kermit Godsey and Billy Tillett.

Top • 117: *Captain Will Etheridge, Jr., kneeling, with a day's catch of dolphin and wahoo. Captain Etheridge is legendary for his fishing ability. One charter captain even accused him of having to shake the scales out of his underwear every night because he was convinced that "Captain Will" was part fish. Oregon Inlet Fishing Center, 1957.*

Bottom • 118: *Captain Moon Tillett, seated, Billy Carl Tillett, left, and mate Fred Parker, right, with a white marlin caught on the* Bumbaloo. *Oregon Inlet, 1959.*

The Oregon Inlet Charter Fleet

After World War II, better roads and new bridges began connecting the "ribbon of sand" to population centers in the northeast. Improved transportation led to a rapidly growing summer tourist population, and the charter captains realized they needed to increase their public visibility. In 1946, a small group of captains informally decided to combine efforts by concentrating their boats in a high traffic area and by consolidating the booking process. The perfect place to implement this plan was the stretch along Highway 64 that connected Manteo to Nags Head. One spot, a narrow roadside canal named for George Dykstra and locally known as Dykstra's ditch, had it all. This canal started at the base of the Roanoke Sound Bridge and ran westward about a half-mile almost to the intersection between Manteo and Wanchese. Dykstra's ditch was deep enough to maneuver the boats, it lay beside a major road, it afforded deep-water access all the way to Oregon Inlet, and it had a store, Dykstra's or Dykes, to handle bookings and promote the fleet. Today the east end of Dykstra's canal is a public boat

Top • 119: *Stuart Rogers'*
store on the roadside canal
between Manteo and Nags
Head. This store pre-dates
George Dykstra's and was
a popular spot where parties
booked charter fishing trips
and bought supplies. 1939.

Bottom • 120: *Dykstra's*
canal and store as viewed
from Roanoke Sound toward
Manteo. Captain Ken Ward is
sitting on the Cherokee *at the*
near end of the canal. 1949.

ramp, and the entrance to Pirates
Cove Marina is the approximate site
of Dykes store.

As bookings increased, other
charter boats that had been docking
in Manteo and Wanchese moved to
Dykstra's. By the late 1940s, more
than 20 boats called Dykstra's home
and a charter fleet was born.

The captains and boats using
Dykstra's read like a Sportfishermen's
Hall of Fame. Included in this list
are Chick Craddock, *Mary Jane*;
Lee Dough, *Libby-D*; Kenneth
Ward, *Cherokee*; Dan and Rhondall Lewark, *Rita*; Sam Tillett, *Spur*; Will Etheridge, Jr.,
Carrie; Omie Tillett, *Jerry Jr.*; Fred Basnight, *Slow An Easy*; Joe Berry, *Phyllis Mae*; Clarence
Holmes, *Secotan*; Les and Griz Evans, *Ranger*; Herbert Perry, *Mildred I*; Charlie Perry,
Maggie; Lawrence Perry, *Spotty Boy*; Jesse Etheridge, *Caredwyn*; Warren O'Neal, *Pearl*; and
Balfour Baum, *Butch*. These legendary characters and classic vessels set a high standard for
the generations of charter fishermen to follow.

Stories abound describing the practical jokes of Ken Ward, the meticulous
organization of Lee Dough, the fishing prowess of Will Etheridge, Jr., the leadership of
Sam Tillett and the intensity of Fred Basnight. But perhaps the most endearing stories
involve Captain Joe Berry, the only black captain in the fleet. Berry is recognized by his

peers not only for his abilities as a captain and fisherman but also for his compassion and willingness to risk his own safety to assist fellow fishermen. On several occasions, Berry was the first one to aid a charter boat that wandered too close to the shoals, got caught in a storm or even ravaged by fire. Joe Berry was a well-liked and respected member of the charter fleet.

Encouraged by their great success at Dykstra's, several charter captains began to look for ways to expand their businesses. One of the fleet leaders, Sam "Sambo" Tillett, had a perfect solution. Ten years earlier, in 1936, Sambo contracted with John Ferebee to relocate a small house from Wanchese to his property at Whalebone Junction in Nags Head. Ferebee moved the house by barge to its current site and Tillett named it Sambo's. Opening on June 5, 1937, Sambo's became a popular spot for commercial fishermen to get an early breakfast, or dinner and refreshments after a long day on the water. Tillett decided that Sambo's would be an ideal location to promote the charter fleet. In 1947, when his oldest son Omie joined the business, Sambo changed the name of the restaurant to Sam & Omie's and he started a booking service for the charter boats at Dykstra's. The Tilletts managed the restaurant, booked parties and operated charter boats until 1951 when they sold the restaurant to Tom McKinmey. Although the charter fleet moved from Dykstra's to Oregon Inlet in the early 1950s, many boats continued booking charters from Sam & Omie's through the early 1960s.

Text continued on page 70

Top • 121: *Herbert Perry brings the* Mildred I *to the docks on a postcard advertising Dykstra's canal and sportfishing on the northern Outer Banks. Circa 1948.*

Bottom • 122: *The* Spur, *Captain Sam Tillett's charter boat, docked at Dykstra's canal. 1947.*

Top Left • 123: *Captain Joe Berry with mate Billy Brown hold a marlin while their catch of dolphin is displayed in back. Dykstra's canal, 1950.* Top Right • 124: *Captain Ken Ward, left, and a happy fisherman with a marlin caught on the* Cherokee. *Captain Ward was noted among the charter captains as a prankster. Circa 1955.* Bottom Left • 125: *Captain Dan Lewark, left, and Rhondall Lewark with a sailfish caught on their charter boat,* Rita. *Dykstra's canal, 1948.* Bottom Right • 126: *Captain Charlie Perry, back row center, and brother Lawrence Perry, back row right, return to Dykstra's canal with a nice catch of dolphin on the* Maggie. *1947.*

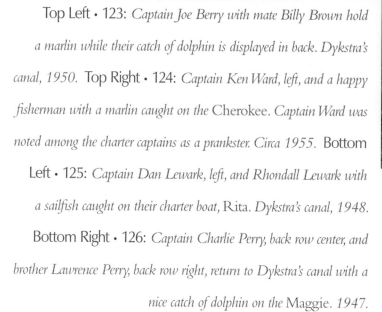

Top Left • 127: *Captain Joe Berry, the only black captain in the fleet, with a fisherman and nice channel bass caught on the Phyllis Mae. Captain Berry was one of the most respected and popular charter boat captains. Dykstra's canal, 1949.* Top Right • 128: *Aerial view of Dykstra's canal. Circa 1954.* Bottom Left • 129: *Captain Herbert Perry and an unidentified boy prepare for a fishing trip on the Mildred I. This charter boat docked at Dykstra's canal and was a popular inshore sportfishing vessel. Circa 1946.* Bottom Right • 130: *The charter boat Secotan with Captain Clarence Holmes at the helm arrives at the Dykstra's canal dock after a day of fishing. 1947.*

According to McKimmey, Sam & Omie's started serving breakfast and a favorite local beverage, Pabst Blue Ribbons, at 3 a.m. The restaurant stayed open for dinner and more PBRs until 11 p.m. The charter captains were regularly the first ones to arrive and the last ones to leave. In fact, on many nights, Tom figures some never left at all.

McKimmey typically picked up his cook and wait staff every morning on his way to the restaurant.

Top • 131: *Captain Sam Tillett, kneeling right, with a fishing party beside his restaurant, Sam and Omie's. Nags Head, 1950.* Bottom • 132: *In addition to its restaurant business, Sam and Omie's was the early booking headquarters for the Oregon Inlet fishing fleet. Nags Head, 1953.*

By the time he got there, a few of the early-rising charter captains had already opened up, made coffee, taken orders and cooked breakfast. This "helping hand" earned Sam & Omie's an infamous reputation: "customers can order anything they want but

what they're going to get is salty scrambled eggs, hard bacon, burnt toast and strong coffee."

As the central booking headquarters for the fleet at Oregon Inlet, Sam & Omie's played an important role in the development of charter fishing on the Outer Banks. The window where parties registered remains in the kitchen wall and photographs of fishermen and their catch are displayed throughout the restaurant as reminders of our sportfishing heritage. Jakie and Judy Waits purchased the restaurant in 1971 and operated

it until 1987 when it was purchased by its current owners Teresa Merritt and Carol Sikes. Sam & Omie's still operates on the same site and it remains a popular place to relax, enjoy a meal and talk about fishing.

In the late 1940s, Charlie and Lawrence Perry moved their boats from Dykstra's to a small creek on the south end of Bodie Island near Oregon Inlet. This tidal creek was both wide and deep enough to hold a few boats, and it was a much closer location to the fishing grounds around the inlet. The Perry brothers, who lived in Kitty Hawk, reportedly made getting to the dock an adventure. They met their parties at 4 a.m. in a designated spot, drove their old station wagon down the paved road to Whalebone Junction, then traversed the last eight miles of their journey on a deep sand path where the party might have to get out and help push the car just to keep it going.

In 1951, the state remedied this situation with a paved road from Whalebone Junction to Oregon Inlet. The door was opened for development of the charter fishing fleet, but the area was still isolated so fuel and supplies had to be trucked in daily.

Authorized in 1937, it was January 12, 1953 before the National Park Service established and opened the Cape Hatteras National Seashore. All of the property on the south end of Bodie Island, including the creek where the Perry brothers kept their boats, became part of the National Seashore. In early 1954, a lease to manage the concession for recreational fishing was awarded by the Park Service to Toby Tillett, who had previously operated the Oregon Inlet ferry from this site. Tillett immediately had the creek dredged and a bulkhead added to form a basin. A small marina and bait shop was erected on the east side of the canal and longer docks were constructed. Tillett also had gasoline tanks installed and offered a booking service for the fleet. With these additions, the charter fleet was quick to move from Dykstra's to this new site called the Oregon Inlet Fishing Center.

Above • 133: *Aerial view of Oregon Inlet Fishing Center. The basin had not been dredged and charter boats pulled bow first into slips beside long finger piers because the water was too shallow to back in.* *1952.*

Text continued on page 74

Top Left • 134: *The charter boat* Sam and Omie *with a big catch of striped bass. Captain Omie Tillett, left rear, and his uncle Chester Tillett, right rear, provided a good fishing experience. Manns Harbor, circa 1965.*

Top Right • 135: *Tony Tillett with two marlin caught on the* Carolinian. *Oregon Inlet Fishing Center, 1960.*

Bottom Left • 136: *Captain Tony Tillett, standing right, and mate Sunny Briggs, kneeling right, with a blue marlin caught on the* Carolinian. *Oregon Inlet Fishing Center, July 25, 1968.* Bottom Right • 137: *Captain Omie Tillett, kneeling right with mate Buddy Davis beside him, display a day's catch of dolphin onboard the* Sportsman. *Oregon Inlet Fishing Center, 1966.*

Top • 138: *The first meeting of the Oregon Inlet Guides Association took place in 1955 at the Shrine Club in Nags Head. Captain Will Etheridge, Jr., front left, was elected President. Members and their boats on the front row, left to right, are: Will Etheridge, Jr.,*

Chee Chee; Billy Baum, Kay; Harry Baum, Jo-Boy; Marvin Daniels, Mar-Pete; Moon Tillett, Bumbaloo; Fred Basnight, Slow An Easy; Charles Midgett, Lois C; Lee Dough, Libby-D; Warren O'Neal, Pearl; Melvin Perry, Golden Dawn; Wayland Baum, Alethia. Back row, left to right, are: Tony Tillett, Carolinian; Omie Tillett, Sportsman; Buddy Cannady, Mel-O-Dee; H. T. Gaskins, Erma Queen; Carson Stallings, Carrov; Warren Gallop, Margie C; Kenneth Ward, Cherokee; Jesse Etheridge, Caredwyn; Lee Perry, Jinny B. 1955. Bottom Left • 139: *Captain Will Etheridge, Jr., kneeling left, and mate Bobby Scarborough, kneeling right, with a day's catch on the* Chee Chee. *Captain Etheridge and Bobby Scarborough were among the best fishermen on the Outer Banks. Oregon Inlet, 1956.* Bottom Right • 140: *Postcard advertising the big channel bass caught at Oregon Inlet. Circa 1930.*

Left • 141: *Dover Hinton holds a nice channel bass caught with Captain Will Etheridge, Jr., on the Chee Chee. Oregon Inlet, 1952.* Right • 142: *The charter boat Kay, captained by noted fisherman and boatbuilder Billy Baum, enters the basin at the Oregon Inlet Fishing Center. Circa 1957.*

In 1956, Tillett added additional parking and moved the expanded tackle shop to the north end of the creek. The Oregon Inlet Fishing Center had grown to a fleet of 32 boats and the demand for charter fishing was increasing every year. In 1957, Toby Tillett transferred the concession to George and H.A. Creef who managed the site until 1965 when it was leased to Dick O'Neal from nearby Hyde County.

A significant event that affected the development of the Oregon Inlet Fishing Center was the organization of the charter captains and the formation of the Oregon Inlet Guides Association in 1955. This association provided input from the charter captains to the management, structure and development of the Fishing Center.

Another major event occurred on March 7, 1962, when the Ash Wednesday Storm struck the Outer Banks. This powerful northeaster ripped along the coast and inflicted more damage than most hurricanes. Captain Will Etheridge, Jr., reported that water washed over the entire Fishing Center, destroying the tackle shop and all of the docks. When the storm subsided and the captains returned to assess the damage, they were equally awed by the widespread destruction and by the survival of Balfour Baum's little charter boat *Butch*. Untouched, she bobbed quietly amid the devastation.

When Dick O'Neal retired in 1968, the Oregon Inlet Guides Association leased the management rights from the Park Service and has continuously operated the Fishing Center since that time. The fleet has now grown to more than 50 boats and is recognized around the world as a premier destination for offshore sportfishing.

In the formative years of the Oregon Inlet Fishing Center, several factors converged to make the charter fleet successful: experienced captains, efficient boats and lots of fish. In the 1940s and 1950s, the captains were primarily local watermen who commercially fished in the area. They had an intimate knowledge of when, where and how to catch fish, and they were very familiar with the idiosyncrasies of the wind, tide and currents around Oregon Inlet. In addition, all of the captains could handle a boat and they were proficient at reading the water and putting their parties on fish. These men were dedicated and hard working, often at the docks by 4:30 a.m. and not returning to their homes before 6:30 p.m. At $12 per person per day, including fuel, ice, bait and tackle, their compensation was modest. The mate was paid a small hourly wage by the captain and worked for tips from the party. Even though charter captains didn't make much money, they were respected in the community for their work ethic and their knowledge and skills on the water.

At the heart of the Oregon Inlet fleet were the captains who moved from Dykstra's. Sam and Omie Tillett, Will Etheridge, Jr., Fred Basnight, Moon Tillett, Wayland Baum, Warren O'Neal, Balfour Baum, Lee Dough, Joe Berry, Carson Stallings, Delton Dowdy, Matt Spivey and Kenneth Ward were among this list of early Oregon Inlet charter captains. From the 1950s through the 1970s, other notable fishermen joined the Oregon Inlet fleet including Harry and Billy Baum, Tony Tillett, Marvin Daniels, Lee Perry, Charles Midgett, Melvin Perry, Buddy Cannady, H. T. Gaskins, Buddy Davis, Sunny Briggs, Sam Stokes, Charles Scarborough and Bobby Sullivan. All of the captains who have served in the Oregon Inlet charter fleet contributed to a well-deserved international reputation for excellence.

Top • 143: *The charter boat* Libby-D *returns to the Oregon Inlet Fishing Center with Captain Lee Dough at the helm. 1955.* Bottom • 144: *Captain Delton Dowdy on his charter boat* Connie Dionne *with two marlin. Oregon Inlet Fishing Center, 1960.*

An efficient boat is another component of a successful charter business, and the captains at the Oregon Inlet Fishing Center started with some of the best. Most of the early vessels were either shad boats or Core Sounders, but as sportfishing

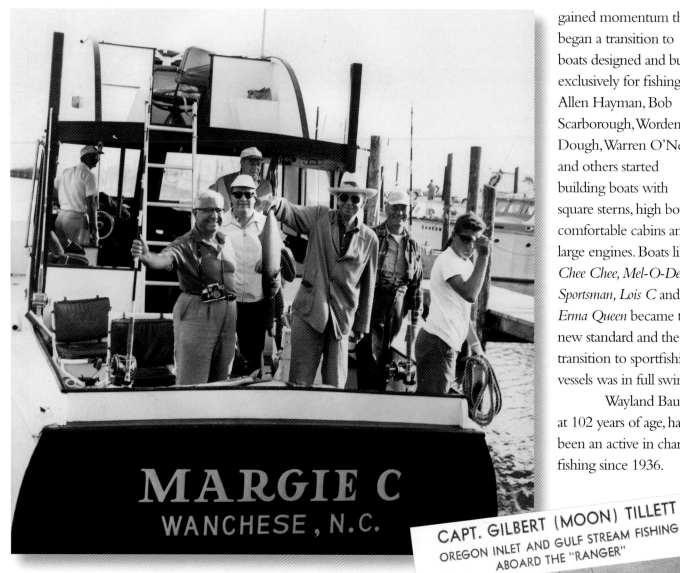

gained momentum they began a transition to boats designed and built exclusively for fishing. Allen Hayman, Bob Scarborough, Worden Dough, Warren O'Neal and others started building boats with square sterns, high bows, comfortable cabins and large engines. Boats like *Chee Chee, Mel-O-Dee, Sportsman, Lois C* and *Erma Queen* became the new standard and the transition to sportfishing vessels was in full swing.

Wayland Baum, at 102 years of age, has been an active in charter fishing since 1936.

CAPT. GILBERT (MOON) TILLETT
OREGON INLET AND GULF STREAM FISHING
ABOARD THE "RANGER"

DIESEL POWERED — RADIO-TELEPHONE
THE BEST IN ACCOMMODATIONS   WANCHESE, N. C.
PHONE 165-J1

Left • 145: *Captain Warren Gallop backs the charter boat Margie C into her dock at the Oregon Inlet Fishing Center. 1955.* Right • 146: *Business card advertising offshore fishing with Captain Moon Tillett on the* Ranger. *Oregon Inlet Fishing Center, circa 1955.*

Captain Baum described fishing on a big shad boat built by Worden Dough and his struggles with early gasoline engines. Dough helped Captain Baum equip the *Alethia* with a Chrysler engine and, as Wayland aptly put it, "The engine made more noise than it provided power. Everyone could hear me coming down the sound but I couldn't catch anyone."

Another boat Worden Dough built for charter fishing was the *Connie Dionne*. Captained by Delton Dowdy and Dan Lewark, this vessel was the first boat at Oregon Inlet to be outfitted with a diesel engine and a giant step was taken in the transition to today's sportfishing boats.

A third ingredient for a successful charter fishing business is having lots of fish to catch, and the offshore waters out of Oregon Inlet are among the best. In the late 1940s and early 1950s, the fleet began trolling at the sea buoy to catch dolphin, wahoo and occasionally a sailfish. The captains began to offer more trips to the Gulf Stream as their boats acquired more range and better electronics.

Top • 147: *Captain Delton Dowdy, left, with a bull dolphin caught on the* Connie Dionne. *Oregon Inlet, 1955.* Bottom • 148: *Fishermen pose with Captain Buddy Cannady, left, and mate Billy Holton, beside Cannady, onboard the* Mel-O-Dee. *Oregon Inlet Fishing Center, 1963.*

At first, dolphin were caught in great numbers and occasionally a marlin was hooked. Most captains reported that marlin were a nuisance because they took a long time to fight and they always escaped. In 1953, Captain Will Etheridge, Jr., on the *Chee Chee* landed a 192-pound blue marlin, the first at Oregon Inlet. The next day Captain Etheridge boated another small marlin while a much larger 476-pound blue marlin was boated by Les Evans on the *Ranger*. Word spread quickly about the huge fish being caught at the Oregon Inlet Fishing Center. When stronger tackle became available and the mates started rigging baits for marlin, they began to have much more success. Charter parties started booking trips just for a chance to catch a marlin or sailfish along with yellowfin, bluefin, big-eye tuna, wahoo and dolphin.

Text continued on page 84

Top Right • 149: *Fishermen on the* Phyllis Mae *pose with Captain Joe Berry, right, and mate Billy Brown, next to Captain Berry, at the Oregon Inlet Fishing Center. 1956.*

Below • 150: *Captain Matt Spivey brings the charter boat* Jean Ann *into the Oregon Inlet Fishing Center. 1958.*

Above • 151: *Charter boat Lois C, with Captain Charles Midgett, approaches the Oregon Inlet Fishing Center. 1956.*

Bottom Right • 152: *Legendary Captain Warren O'Neal, center, with a marlin caught on the* Pearl II. *Oregon Inlet Fishing Center, August 14, 1966.*

Top Left • 153: *Captain Fred Basnight, standing right, and Johnny Booth, kneeling right, pose with a fisherman and a nice tuna caught on the Slow An Easy. Oregon Inlet Fishing Center, circa 1960.*

Top Right • 154: *Fishermen pose with Captain Fred Basnight, front row second from left, and their catch on the Slow An Easy. Oregon Inlet Fishing Center, 1966.*

Bottom Left • 155: *Captain Charles Midgett, right, with a marlin caught on the Skipper. Oregon Inlet Fishing Center, 1960.*

Bottom Right • 156: *Party with catch of inshore bottom fish caught on the Lollypop with Captain Chick Craddock, in boat on left, and mate Gerald Craddock, in boat on right. Oregon Inlet Fishing Center, circa 1964.*

Top Right • 157: *Captain Sunny Briggs, center, and mate Buddy Davis, right, with bull dolphin caught on the* Jerry, Jr. *Sunny Briggs and Buddy Davis are both renowned boatbuilders. Oregon Inlet Fishing Center, 1967.*

Below • 158: *Charter boat* Sea Fever, *with Captain Sunny Briggs, returns to the Oregon Inlet Fishing Center after a day of trolling. 1971.*

Above • 159: *Captain Chick Craddock, kneeling left, and mate Gerald Craddock, kneeling right, with a party and catch on the* Lollypop. *Oregon Inlet Fishing Center, July 25, 1963.*

Bottom Right • 160: *Buddy Davis, captain of the charter boat* Sportfisher, *backs into his slip at the Oregon Inlet Fishing Center. Circa 1970.*

Top Left • 161: *Captain Buddy Davis, kneeling right, and mate Irving Forbes, kneeling left, with a catch on the* Sportfisher. *Oregon Inlet Fishing Center, July 7, 1970.* **Top Right • 162:** *Captain Joe Berry, right, and mate Billy Baum, left, pose with a nice catch on the charter boat* Phyllis Mae. *Oregon Inlet Fishing Center, 1956.*

Bottom Left • 163: *Captain Charles Scarborough, right, with a sailfish caught on his charter boat* Andrea. *Fellow captains nicknamed him "No fish Charlie" because he seemed to catch less than the other boats. Oregon Inlet Fishing Center, 1962.* **Bottom Right • 164:** *The* Fight-N-Lady *and Captain Sam Stokes return to the Oregon Inlet Fishing Center with 12 white marlin release flags flying. 1978.*

Top Left • 165: *Captain Bobby Sullivan, right, with a marlin caught on his charter boat Wahoo. Oregon Inlet Fishing Center, August 15, 1970.* Top Right • 166: *Captain Sam Stokes, second from right in rear, and mate Mike Bennett, back left, pose with a party on the Fight-N-Lady. Oregon Inlet Fishing Center, 1972.* Middle Right • 167: *Captain Harry Baum, holding a King mackerel, with a fishing party on the Jo-Boy. Oregon Inlet, 1968.* Bottom Right • 168: *Captain Delton Dowdy with a nice sailfish caught on his charter boat the Connie Dionne. Oregon Inlet Fishing Center, 1957.*

Top Left • 169: *Jack Herrington caught the world record blue marlin on the Jo-Boy with Captain Harry Baum. The huge fish is hoisted to the scales at the Oregon Inlet Fishing Center and moments later, the support pole snapped and the marlin fell to the ground. The marlin was*

loaded onto a truck and driven to the Hatteras Marlin Club, about 40 miles away, where another set of large scales were located. Oregon Inlet, July 26, 1974. Top Right • 170: *Angler Jack Herrington, right, and Captain Harry Baum, left, pose with the 1,142-pound marlin. The fish was so long that a hole had to be dug for the bill in order for the marlin to be completely suspended on the scales. Hatteras, July 26, 1974.* Bottom Left • 171: *World record blue marlin is brought back to the Oregon Inlet Fishing Center after being weighed at the Hatteras Marlin Club. Oregon Inlet Fishing Center, July 27, 1974.* Bottom Right • 172: *Six blue marlin caught on July 31, 1970 at the Oregon Inlet Fishing Center. Standing, left to right, are Captains Sam Stokes,* Fight-N-Lady, *Lee Perry,* Deepwater, *Arvin Midgett,* Miss Boo, *Bobby Sullivan,* Wahoo, *and Buddy Davis,* Sportfisher. *Missing from photo is Captain Chick Craddock,* Lollypop. *Oregon Inlet, July 31, 1970.*

Captain Harry Baum, fishing with a party on his boat the *Jo-Boy,* landed a huge blue marlin on July 26, 1974. When the giant fish was weighed at the Fishing Center, the marlin was so heavy that the support pole snapped. Captain Baum and a crew of onlookers loaded the marlin onto a truck and drove it 40 miles to the Hatteras Marlin Club where the closest large scales were located. The marlin weighed 1,142 pounds and was certified as a world record. One local captain estimated that the marlin might have lost more than 100 pounds in its travels. This record stood for several years as a testament to big game fishing at the Oregon Inlet Fishing Center.

Top • 173: *Charter captains, left to right, are H. T. Gaskins, Warren Gallop, Jack Hoffler, Charles Midgett, Tony Tillett, Delton Dowdy, and Matt Spivey. Oregon Inlet Fishing Center, circa 1956.*

Bottom • 174: *Captains Mike Merritt, left, and Sam Stokes, right, shake hands in front of four giant marlin caught in a three day period from August 20-22, 1987. Oregon Inlet Fishing Center, August 22, 1987.*

Over the past 70 years, thousands of charter parties have passed through the narrow channel at Oregon Inlet on their way to the Gulf Stream. While captains, boats and fishing techniques have changed, the fundamentals remain the same. The crews are still professional and they work hard to insure a memorable trip for their party.

The Albatross Fleet

Captain Ernal Foster was a central figure in the early years of Outer Banks sportfishing. Born in 1910 at Hatteras village, Captain Foster began his career on the water as a commercial fisherman. He trawled for shrimp and fished nets in Pamlico Sound. He even operated a small ferry from Hatteras Island to Ocracoke.

Ernal joined the Lifesaving Service in 1928 and was stationed on the east end of Long Island. During the Depression, Captain Foster decided to return to Hatteras where he knew he could make a living on the water.

In the mid-1930s, Ernal bucked traditional wisdom when he decided to start a charter business from the docks in Hatteras harbor. His first task was to acquire a fishing vessel and he visualized exactly what he wanted. The Core Sound sink-netters were the preferred boats of that era so Captain Foster made a trip to Harkers Island and Marshallberg to select a builder. He approached several before Mildon Willis in Marshallberg agreed to build the boat exactly as Captain Foster described. In 1937, the 41-foot *Albatross*, a classic Core Sound sink-net boat with a straight stem and round stern, was completed. Her sweeping lines and broad beam were

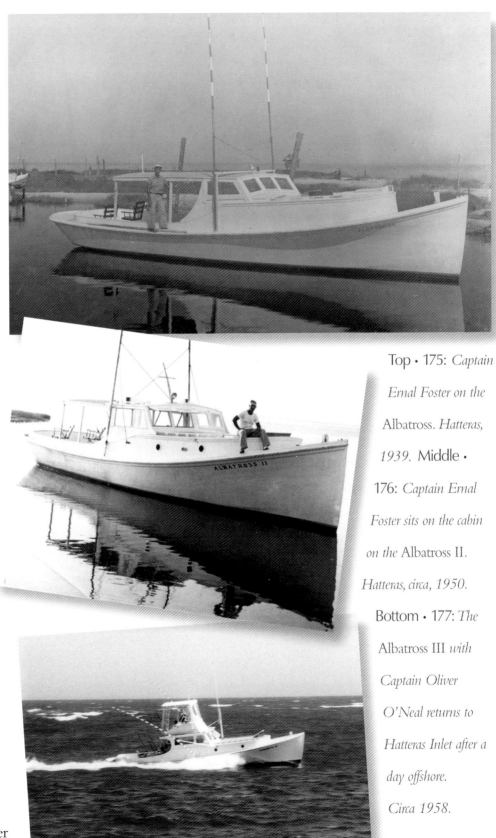

Top • 175: *Captain Ernal Foster on the* Albatross. *Hatteras, 1939.* Middle • 176: *Captain Ernal Foster sits on the cabin on the* Albatross II. *Hatteras, circa, 1950.*

Bottom • 177: *The* Albatross III *with Captain Oliver O'Neal returns to Hatteras Inlet after a day offshore. Circa 1958.*

Top Left • 178: *The Albatross Fleet resting at Foster's Quay. Hatteras, circa 1967.* Bottom Left • 179: *The* Albatross *at Hatteras with a sportfishing catch. A top deck was added to the* Albatross *a few years later. 1939.* Right • 180: *Ernal Foster with a blue marlin caught by Mrs. Ross Walker. Hatteras, 1951.*

ideal for the kind of sportfishing Captain Foster envisioned. The *Albatross* was equipped with everything, including a sliding doghouse, but at a cost of $805 she was expensive. Ernal knew he was taking a big risk so he hedged his bet by operating the *Albatross* as a commercial vessel in the winter and taking sportfishing parties in the spring, summer and fall. According to family records, the price for a Gulf Stream trip in the late 1930s was $25 and an inshore trip was $15.

Captain Foster and the *Albatross* quickly earned a reputation for sportfishing prowess. While vacationing in Hatteras, an outdoor writer from Boston chartered with Ernal and was treated not only to excellent fishing but also to traditional Outer Banks hospitality. He wrote several newspaper articles about Captain Foster and his bookings began to grow.

Hugo Rutherford, an avid sportfisherman from New Jersey, read about the excellent offshore fishing and he journeyed to Hatteras on his boat *Mako* in search of marlin. During the summer of 1938, while fishing with local guide Captain Lloyd Styron, Rutherford landed the first two recorded blue marlin caught in North Carolina waters.

Left • 181: *The first blue marlin caught in North Carolina by a woman angler, Mrs. Betsy Walker, on the* Albatross. *Captain Ernal Foster, holding the marlin's bill, and mate Milton Stowe, with the gaff, pose with Mr. Ross Walker and Betsy. Hatteras, July 13, 1951.*

Right • 182: *Dr. J.C. Overby poses with two marlin caught with Captain Ernal Foster at Foster's Quay. Hatteras, circa 1958.*

Rutherford befriended Captain Foster and taught him the secrets of rigging baits and tackle for marlin. Rutherford also gave Ernal his first set of outriggers and the hunt for marlin at Hatteras began.

Captain Foster hooked several marlin that year but his tackle could not stand up to the giant fish. Ernal finally landed a sailfish on the *Albatross* in 1939, marking the first of many billfish caught onboard this legendary vessel.

During World War II, Captain Foster served in the Coast Guard and was stationed in Baltimore, Morehead City and Norfolk. The *Albatross* was commandeered for duty as a patrol boat and sent to Morehead City. In 1945, Ernal returned to his beloved Hatteras and his sportfishing business. Picking up right where he left off, Ernal's charter bookings boomed. In 1947, Captain Foster contacted Mildon Willis to build a second charter boat, the 44-foot *Albatross II,* so he could better accommodate his growing clientele. Ernal convinced his brother Bill to operate the *Albatross II* and a perfect union was formed.

In 1952, M. W. Willis Boatworks built the 45-foot *Albatross III* and Captain Foster got his cousin, Milton Meekins, to skipper the new vessel. The Albatross Fleet, with its three Core Sounders, was now complete. With the death of Milton in 1953, Captain Foster hired family friend and local guide Oliver O'Neal to take Meekins' place. Bill Foster ran the *Albatross,* Ernal captained the *Albatross II,* Oliver O'Neal became skipper of the *Albatross III* and the fleet prospered.

Top • 183: *Captain Hallas Foster at the helm of his charter boat KoKo. Hatteras, circa 1949.*

Bottom • 184: *The flybridge on the KoKo consisted of a seat, steering wheel and throttle controls. Hatteras, circa 1948.*

In the late 1940s and 1950s, Ernal's brother, Hallas Foster, also operated a charter boat out of Hatteras harbor adjacent to the Albatross fleet. His boat *KoKo* was one of the first vessels to be rigged with a "flybridge," which in this case was actually a chair mounted on the roof of the cabin complete with a simple throttle and steering controls. The *KoKo* was a close companion of the Albatross fleet.

In 1958, Ernal "Ernie" Foster, Jr. joined the fleet as a mate but he was already experienced, having accompanied his father on trips since he was three. In 1962, Captain Bill Foster and Ernie were involved in one of the unforgettable stories that abound in the history of the Albatross fleet. Onboard the *Albatross II* for a day of marlin fishing, Ernie tied on baits as Bill steered toward his favorite spot. One lure was a beat-up trolling plug with a bent hook a friend had sent from Hawaii, and the other bait was a beautiful large, white squid that Ernie had expertly rigged for giant marlin. Almost as soon as the baits went overboard, a blue marlin appeared under the squid. The huge fish trailed the bait and slapped it with his bill only to spin and strike the old bent hook bait. Both Fosters were sure they would lose the fish because it went on a tail-walking display like none they had ever seen. The marlin immediately sounded and the fight was on. After only about 20 minutes the exhausted marlin surfaced. Bill turned the controls of the *Albatross II* over to Ernie so he could help wire the giant before the hook completely straightened. After several frantic moments, the marlin was secure. Now what? A call to a nearby charter boat for help was quickly answered and the fish was safely loaded onboard. The marlin officially weighed 810 pounds, a new world record that stood until it was broken in 1974 at Oregon Inlet.

Top • 185: *Captain Bobby Scarborough, far left, watches as mate Allen Burrus unloads a marlin caught on the* Red Fin. *Hatteras, Marlin Club 1970.*

Bottom • 186: *Dr. Oury, right, poses with a nice marlin caught on the* Red Fin *with Captain Bobby Scarborough, standing left, and mate Allen Burrus, kneeling. Hatteras Marlin Club, 1970.*

In addition to once holding a world record, Captain Foster and the Albatross fleet claims the first blue marlin to be caught by a female angler north of Florida when Mrs. Betsy Walker landed a large blue marlin on the *Albatross* in 1951. Also, the first catch and release occurred on the *Albatross II* in 1958 when Jack Cleveland of Greenwich, Connecticut, pioneered this now common conservation practice.

Over the next several years, Captain Ernie Foster became one of the most accomplished and successful charter fishermen on the Outer Banks. Upon Ernal's death on January 8, 1996, Ernie shouldered the responsibility for operation of the fleet. He continues to run the three Albatross boats with the same enthusiasm and dedication that his father possessed. In addition, Ernie has added an extraordinary sense of history and tradition that he communicates to his lucky customers. Captain Ernie Foster fishes with a sincere reverence and respect for conservation and for the culture that brought the Albatross fleet into existence. Using the same Core Sounders

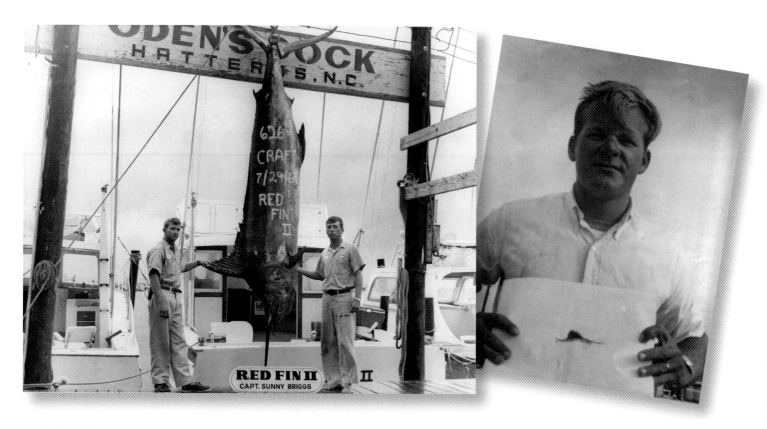

Left • 187: *Captain Sunny Briggs, right, and mate Billy McCaskill display a nice 626-pound marlin caught on the Redfin II. Oden's Dock, Hatteras, July 29, 1969.*

Right • 188: *Captain Bobby Scarborough holds a baby sailfish against a sheet of paper. A dolphin they landed on the Red Fin regurgitated the sailfish, so Captain Scarborough flew a sailfish flag back to the dock. Hatteras, 1967.*

that his father did before him, Captain Foster's clients experience a unique glimpse of sportfishing the way it was 60 years ago on the Outer Banks. Along with his wife Lynne, the Fosters embody a spirit and tenacity for protecting and preserving our coastal heritage. The future of the Albatross fleet is in good hands.

Just down the waterfront from Fosters Quay is Oden's Dock. Around 1960, a number of charter boats started docking here along with some of the finest captains on the Outer Banks. Included in this list are Albert Styron, *Kitty*; Edgar Styron, *Twins*; Freeman Stowe, *Twins II*; Tommy Littleston, *Lu-Mar*; Buster Hummer, *Skipper*; Tex Balance, *Escape*; Jerry Winters, *Ken Winn*; Tom Daughtry and Sunny Briggs, *Redfin II*; and the legendary Bobby Scarborough, *Twins* and *Redfin*.

The Hatteras Marlin Club

The Hatteras Marlin Club is one of the best fishing clubs on the East Coast and it holds an important place in the history of sportfishing on the Outer Banks. In the 1940s and early 1950s, a group of sportsmen operated a small waterfowl hunting club at Hatteras. The group owned several curtain blinds along with a string of stake blinds in the shallow waters of Pamlico Sound. Even though travel to Hatteras was difficult, the excellent duck hunting made the journey worthwhile.

In 1953, Edgar Styron opened the Blue Marlin Restaurant and Dock on the property adjacent to the small hunting club. Styron had the Rose Brothers on Harkers Island build *The Twins* and *Twins II,* charter boats named after his twin children Edgar and Sherry. These square-stern boats were docked at the restaurant and were popular with restaurant patrons. Styron operated the restaurant and charter boats until he retired in 1959.

With declining duck populations and growing interest in Hatteras as a sportfishing destination, owners of the hunting club contacted a small group of friends and influential North Carolina businessmen with the concept for a fishing club. From this idea, the Hatteras Marlin Club was formed. Early leaders included Willis Slane, Earl Phillips, Charles Johnson, and Governor Luther Hodges. On February 4, 1959, the official documents were filed establishing the Hatteras Marlin Club as a non-profit corporation dedicated to sportfishing, conservation, research and education. The bylaws limited participation to 125 members.

Top • 189:

Mrs. Kathleen Styron and children, Edgar, front left, and his twin sister, Sherry, held by Mrs. Styron along with Brenda Styron, back left, and Rhonda Styron, front right, pose with the first marlin caught at the Hatteras Marlin Club. The charter boats Twins *and* Twins II *are named after Edgar and Sherry Styron. Hatteras, May, 1959.*

Bottom • 190:

Aerial view of the Hatteras Marlin Club. Hatteras, circa 1965.

The formation of the Marlin Club fortuitously coincided with the opportunity to buy the hunting club property and the Blue Marlin Restaurant and Dock. The Marlin Club purchased the restaurant property and docks for $57,000 and hired Bounce Anderson as its first caretaker. The Marlin Club remodeled the existing structures on site and added other amenities to encourage family participation.

Charles Johnson, an internationally recognized sportfisherman, was elected as the first Commodore of the Hatteras Marlin Club in 1959. His fishing and boating exploits include landing 14 large bluefin tuna in a single day and winning the Miami to New York boat race. Johnson also purchased the first sportfishing boat made by the Rybovich family in Palm Beach, Florida. As Commodore of the Hatteras Marlin Club, Johnson's first priority was to host a billfish tournament. In 1960, the Marlin Club sponsored a marlin tournament

Top • 191: *Captain Buster Hummer, left, poses with a fishing party and a 423-pound marlin caught on the* Twins *at the Blue Marlin Fishing Center. Hatteras, May 21, 1958.*

Bottom • 192: *The* Twins *was one of a two-boat fleet owned and operated by Captain Edgar Styron. Hatteras, circa 1958.*

with participants from Venezuela, Mexico and Bermuda as well as from several states along the East Coast. The first winner was E.A. "Chilo" Bird from Puerto Rico, and the Hatteras Marlin Club was off to a great start.

After several years of claims and boasts about where the best marlin fishing occurred, the Hatteras Marlin Club and the Marlin Club of Puerto Rico organized a formal competition to settle the issue. The winner was to be awarded the official title of "Billfish Capital of the World." In 1961, the Hatteras Marlin Club easily landed the most billfish and won the title.

The Hatteras Marlin Club is also the site of a famous decision by one of its members, Willis Slane, to construct a vessel that could handle the rough inlets and waters around Cape Hatteras. In the spring of 1959, Slane and several other members of the

Marlin Club arrived for a few days of fishing. Unfortunately the weather was bad and the ocean was too rough for their Core Sound boats. This was becoming an all-too-frequent occurrence and since most of the anglers had traveled a great distance to get there, they were not in a very good mood. On the third day of playing cards and cussing the weather, Slane slammed his cards down and announced that he was going to build a boat big enough and strong enough to fish in any weather, and he was going to build it out of a new material called fiberglass. The others chided Slane about his idea and when he got mad he further vowed to have the boat ready in one year. The bets were placed.

Slane returned to High Point, assembled a team of architects, designers and fabricators, and formed a company called Hatteras Yachts. He began construction on a large sportfishing boat and 11 months later, in March 1960, his 41-foot fiberglass vessel was completed. Named *Knit Wits* for the group of hosiery executives that invested in his wild-eyed scheme, she was trucked from High Point to Morehead City where she was launched for her maiden voyage to the Hatteras Marlin Club. Slane had lived up to his promise and the success of the *Knit Wits* was the beginning of a major development in boatbuilding and sportfishing history.

Top • 193: *The* Knit Wits, *named after the hosiery executives that invested in the project, was the first sportfishing boat manufactured by Hatteras Yachts in High Point. 1960.* Bottom • 194: *Willis Slane, founder of Hatteras Yachts, built the* Knit Wits *on a challenge from fellow members at the Hatteras Marlin Club. Hatteras, 1959.*

Throughout the next decade, the Hatteras Marlin Club faced the same internal problems that most clubs encounter. An increasingly distant membership led to waning interest, diverse ideas about the direction of the club and financial challenges. Through these difficulties, strong leadership and a renewed commitment to its original purposes revived the Club. The caretaker for the Club is now Homer Styron, son of Edgar Styron. The Hatteras Marlin Club's annual billfish tournament is one of the best on the East Coast and the Hatteras Marlin Club continues to be an important part of sportfishing on the Outer Banks.

Top • 195: *A 379-pound marlin caught on the* Knit Wits, *the first Hatteras Yacht. Hatteras Marlin Club, 1960.*

Bottom • 196: *Postcard of the* Knit Wits *docked at the Hatteras Marlin Club. Hatteras, circa 1965.*

The Ocracoke Charter Fleet

While the sportfishing in Ocracoke was outstanding, there were simply not as many guides, boats or visitors to rival the fleets at Oregon Inlet or Hatteras. A journey to Ocracoke from the north was an adventure filled with ferry crossings, sand roads and oceanfront driving. Many visitors to Ocracoke preferred to catch the mail boat from Morehead City or to book passage on a freight boat from New Bern. Once on the island, guests were treated to a wonderful stay at the Pamlico Inn, a large and accommodating hotel on Silver Lake in the heart of the village. William and Annie Gaskill purchased this inn in 1915 and it became renowned for its hospitality and great food. Visitors to the inn paid $17.50 per week including meals. In addition to other amenities, guests could hire William or his son Thurston, for a day of fishing.

William "Captain Bill" Gaskill is one of the earliest sportfishing guides on the northern Outer Banks. He began taking inshore parties for channel bass and bluefish in 1910. Captain Bill was born in 1869 and even though he operated the Pamlico Inn, he was a first

Left • 197:

Poster

advertising

fishing trips

at Ocracoke.

Circa 1947.

and foremost a commercial fisherman. Tom Eaton, an avid sportfisherman, approached Captain Gaskill about a fishing trip to the Gulf Stream. Not wanting to waste time on this nonsense, Bill referred Eaton to his son Thurston who enjoyed sportfishing.

Top Left • 198:

Captain Thurston

Gaskill on one

of his last duck

hunting trips in

Pamlico Sound.

Ocracoke, circa 1985.

Top Right • 199:

The Southwind *and Captain*

Thurston Gaskill return to

the dock after a day of fishing.

Ocracoke, 1970. Bottom

Right • 200: *Business card*

for Captain Thurston Gaskill.

Circa 1950.

For Big Channel Bass,
Cobia, Blues and Mackerel

CAPT. THURSTON GASKILL

Cruiser "Southwind"

OCRACOKE, N. C.

DUCK AND GOOSE HUNTING

P. O. Box 277

Phone: WA 8-3851

Thurston was eager but he had never been to the Gulf Stream and his old boat, a locally made craft, was somewhat questionable. Eaton, however, was determined and young Thurston was willing, so the two left early for parts unknown. Thurston reported that they made it offshore just fine and caught six nice dolphin. The return trip was more eventful because Thurston didn't know that the Gulf Stream flowed north. When he got close to shore on his return trip, Thurston realized they were at Hatteras Inlet rather than Ocracoke Inlet. Embarrassed but safe, Captain Gaskill and Eaton returned through Pamlico Sound to the dock at Ocracoke where they were met by a group of worried family and friends. This was an inauspicious start to Captain Thurston Gaskill's long and remarkable career as an Ocracoke hunting and fishing guide.

CHAPTER FOUR

Origins of Charter Fishing on the Southern Outer Banks

BUNNY

MOREHEAD CITY

Origins of Charter Fishing on the Southern Outer Banks

In late 1945, a Merchant Marine ship from New England steamed toward the port of Morehead City carrying military personnel and supplies just as it had done many times during World War II. On this trip however the threat of German U-boats was gone and the vessel traversed "Torpedo Alley" with only winds and waves to impede its progress. The captain was relaxed and joking as a crewman watched the monotonously flat bottom on his depthfinder. An occasional shipwreck loomed up and then disappeared as they powered against the Gulf Stream. About 45 miles east of Cape Lookout, an unusual series of ledges and drop-offs echoed across the screen. The bottom rose up from 600 feet and peaked at around 250 feet.

The navigator made a comment about the structure to Ed Purifoy, a Morehead City native and charter boat fisherman who was on wheel watch. As Purifoy stepped over to take a look, the chart dipped up and down and leveled off before dropping back to very deep water. Purifoy thought this might be a good place to catch bottom fish and he began to draw a map of the area. Ed knew that none of the charter boats had electronics so he recorded the compass heading, marked the time on his watch and noted the speed as the large ship lumbered back to Buoy 14 off Cape Lookout Shoals. Once they passed the buoy, Purifoy made a few notes, thanked the navigator and returned to his duty station. He didn't think much about it.

Captain George Bedsworth was also just getting back from military duty in the Army and he was more than ready to pick up his charter fishing business. Before the War, Bedsworth worked with Captain Ottis Purifoy and his mate, Ed Purifoy, on the *Barracuda*. When the threesome decided to renew their association, Captain Bedsworth and Ed resumed charter fishing while Ottis pursued his seafood business and a grand idea for a fleet of charter boats.

That year, 1946, the inshore fishing was very good and the *Barracuda* had great success catching groupers and snappers around the wrecks as well as bluefish and Spanish mackerel around Cape Lookout. They occasionally ventured out to Buoy 14, known locally as the "Knuckle Buoy," for dolphin, King mackerel and amberjack, but no farther.

In the spring of 1947, Captain Bedsworth and Ed Purifoy were preparing for another season when Purifoy mentioned the underwater structure he had seen the year before. Captain Bedsworth was interested but it was a long run, probably four hours or more on the *Barracuda*, and they would have to plan for a trip like that.

The captain was relaxed and joking as a crewman watched the monotonously flat bottom on his depth-finder. An occasional shipwreck loomed up and then disappeared as they powered against the Gulf Stream.

Left • 201: *Captain George Bedsworth on the charter boat* Dolphin. *Morehead City, 1949.*

Right • 202: *Catch onboard the* Dolphin *with Captain George Bedsworth, seated left, and mate Ed Purifoy, kneeling far right. Morehead City, May 14, 1952.*

When the inshore fishing slowed in the middle of June, George and Ed decided to try their new spot. The weather was good and the *Barracuda* was loaded with fuel when they left the Morehead City dock. After two hours, zipping along at 10 knots, they arrived at the Knuckle Buoy and set their course, speed and time according to Ed's notes. After about two more hours, the *Barracuda* slipped into the blue waters of the Gulf Stream. Not too far now, Ed figured. By this time Captain Bedsworth was beginning to have doubts about this adventure. He had already stated that he was not going to waste much time looking for this bottom structure, but when Ed motioned for George to stop, both men were anxious to see what they would find.

As the party lowered their baits George guessed that they would not have enough line to reach the ocean floor. Much to his surprise, the water was only about 250 feet deep, just as Ed predicted. As soon as the first bait hit bottom, a nice snapper was hooked. After two hours of drifting and non-stop fishing action, George was convinced that this was indeed a special spot.

There was no place to hide when the *Barracuda* returned to port loaded with an exceptional catch of snappers and groupers. Everyone wanted to know where they caught the fish. In his characteristic Carteret County brogue, Bedsworth responded: "Why in the ocean, of course."

Still without divulging their location, Captain Bedsworth and Ed Purifoy returned several times to their offshore spot with the same results. In July 1947, George and Ed switched from the *Barracuda* to the *Dolphin,* a newer square-stern boat designed and built for sportfishing. This new boat was the first of several in Captain Ottis Purifoy's new fleet called the Lucky 7 Fishing Fleet, or sometimes, the Dolphin Fleet.

The new *Dolphin* was faster and had greater range than the *Barracuda,* so their secret offshore spot was more accessible. In August 1947, a charter party booked the *Dolphin* for a day of trolling and Captain Bedsworth decided it was a good time to try the rocky outcrop. Almost as soon as the lines went overboard, the group caught a nice dolphin. Before long they landed a few more and in mid-morning they boated a white marlin. By quitting time the boxes were full and Captain Bedsworth knew he had to tell the others about this place. When the *Dolphin* returned to Morehead City with the first recorded white marlin, the fleet was buzzing. The next morning when the charter captains gathered for coffee at Sonny's Restaurant, George told them about this rock formation and how Ed had found it. More important, he told them how to get there.

Although other boats fished in this location, it was September 14, 1957, when Captain Bill Olson, on the *Mary-Z,* landed the first documented blue marlin there. In reference to its underwater plateaus and hard bottoms, local captains began calling this place the "Big Rock."

Left • 203: Exceptional catch of five blue marlin landed in one day on the Dolphin *with Captain George Bedsworth. Anglers were Mr. and Mrs. John Adams of Raleigh and nephew Buddy Adams of Durham. Mr. Adams caught three marlin, the largest of which was 367 pounds, while Mrs. Adams and Buddy landed one apiece. Morehead City, June 15, 1959.*

Two years later, on June 15, 1959 while fishing at the Big Rock on the *Dolphin*, Captain Bedsworth set a new standard for marlin fishing along the Outer Banks. His party, Mr. and Mrs. John Adams of Raleigh along with nephew Buddy Adams of Durham, landed a record five blue marlin in one day, the largest of which weighed 367 pounds.

The Big Rock is now well known to offshore anglers. The underwater canyons and ridges provide an ideal habitat for many species of offshore gamefish. The Big Rock is readily accessible to today's charter fleet as well as private boats, and it remains one of the best places along the Atlantic seaboard for offshore big game fishing. Acknowledging the fishery resources at the Big Rock, Morehead City hosts one of the largest marlin tournaments in the world, the Big Rock Blue Marlin Tournament.

Overview

Top • 204: *Fishermen and their catch on the Greta D. with Captain Charles Webb Willis, back right. Morehead City, 1958.*

Bottom • 205: *Captains Charles "Long Charlie" Willis, left, and Abner Willis clean up the fish box on the Greta D. Morehead City, circa 1935.*

Charter fishing on the southern Outer Banks has a rich tradition that dates from the early 1900s, and it is still going strong. Lewis, Fulcher, Willis, Guthrie, Midgette, Gould, Day, Harker, Brown, Harris, Bedsworth, Davis, and Howland—the names of charter captains from this area are a roll call of legendary Outer Banks fishing families. Many other great anglers and boat captains led the way for the thriving charter business that exists today.

The Morehead City fleet was the largest and most visible collection of charter boats on the southern Outer Banks. Among the most recognizable was the famous Lucky 7 Fleet that operated from the Morehead City waterfront from the late 1930s through the 1970s. Captain Ottis Purifoy made an indelible impact on sportfishing in North Carolina. Likewise, Captains Tony Seamon and Ted Garner created a lasting legacy by focusing much publicity and attention on the local charter industry.

Fleets located at Harkers Island and Marshallberg were also important in the sportfishing heritage of the Outer Banks. Captains such as Claude Brown, Myron and Buddy Harris, Jimmy and Woo Woo Harker, Ray and Edward Davis and the Jones brothers provided many people with wonderful fishing experiences and Down East hospitality.

Early Charter Fishing

Sportfishing parties began chartering local guides around 1910 along the southern Outer Banks. In Morehead City, Captain Garland Gilliken offered charter fishing from his sailing sharpie docked at the Atlantic Hotel. His trips were inside the inlet and the catch consisted of trout, flounder, croakers and spot. Captains Charles Webb "Long Charlie" Willis, so named because he was tall and skinny, and Abner Parker Willis took parties fishing on a Core Sounder, *Greta D.* Captain Ottis Purifoy followed by Captain Steve Roberts, began taking parties in 1933 on the *Violet*, a round-stern Core Sounder built by Alden Guthrie. Both the *Greta D.* and the *Violet* were inshore boats that fished mostly for bluefish and mackerel.

Captains Darcy Willis, *Joy*; Charlie Bennett, *Pal*; George R. Lewis, *Squeaky*; William R. Willis, *Sylvia II* and *Gerald*; Esmond Brock, *Jean B.*; Sam H. Curtis, *Stella Mae*; Arthur Midgette, *Delma M;* and George Willis, *Jean* were early charter fishermen in Morehead City. Most of their boats were round-stern Core Sounders that docked at the Atlantic Hotel and fished in the sounds near Beaufort Inlet or around Cape Lookout.

One of the earliest and most respected captains from Morehead City was Captain Joe H. "Pappy Joe" Fulcher. Pappy Joe was born in 1876 and started charter fishing in 1910 on a boat called the *Lualma.* He carried parties to deep holes behind the inlet and in the channel where they anchored for black sea bass, flounder, trout and croakers. Pappy Joe's grandson and namesake, Joe Fulcher, tells of working as a mate on the *Lualma* and he

Top • 206: *Charter boats and private yachts docked at the Morehead City Yacht Basin. The first boat in the foreground is the charter boat* Jean B. *skippered by Captain Esmond Brock. Morehead City, circa 1950.* Bottom • 207: *Captain Charlie Bennett at the helm of the charter boat* Pal. *Morehead City, circa 1948.*

vividly describes how they found their fishing holes. Joe said Pappy Joe positioned the *Lualma* using three reference points and then calculated the wind and current before setting the anchor. Pappy Joe wouldn't let anyone fish until he dropped a baited hand line into the hole and, if he caught a fish big enough, then the party could fish. If not, Joe had to re-position the anchor until Pappy Joe was satisfied. This might take three or four tries but when they were over the spot, they caught fish.

Top • 208: *The charter boat* Lualma *is docked beside the* Blue Water. *Morehead City, 1953.* Bottom • 209: *Captain Pappy Joe Fulcher, right, with an inshore fishing party on his sailboat. Pappy Joe chartered from the dock behind the Atlantic Hotel. Morehead City, circa 1915.*

When Pappy Joe figured they had caught enough they moved to another hole and the process started over. Joe reports that they went to four or five places around the sound on a full day trip.

Joe describes the *Lualma* as an unusual boat that was

built around 1900 for commercial fishing. She had a square, uplifted stern and she was equipped with a unique rudder system that included two large foot pedals for steering: one for port and the other for starboard. Pappy Joe, not being very tall, often stood on these pedals because he could see better and he could steer the boat just by shifting his weight from side to side.

Joe recalls one day when his party didn't catch many fish and Pappy Joe was frustrated. As they returned to the dock, young Joe was in his usual position on the bow of the *Lualma* ready to catch a piling and secure the dock line. He noticed that they were coming in a little faster than normal and when he turned to see what was wrong, Pappy Joe wasn't there. In an untimely slip, he had fallen off the pedals, lost control of the throttle and everything onboard was awry. Joe hollered just as the *Lualma* glanced off one piling and then another. The unexpected force threw the party forward and almost pitched Joe overboard. When Pappy Joe regained control, he yelled at Joe as if it was his fault. "Why didn't you catch that piling like you were supposed to?" Pappy Joe screamed. Not knowing what to say or do, Joe decided that his best bet was to keep quiet.

Pappy Joe made a big loop and came back to the dock, this time under control. Joe caught the piling as planned and everything was fine. While reminiscing about this event, Joe said he has seen other captains yell at deck hands when their boats came in too fast and out of control. He figures it is an inherent trait of all captains to blame someone else, but he is convinced that keeping his mouth shut was one of the best decisions he ever made.

Top • 210: *When fishing was slow, Pappy Joe Fulcher sold conch shells to tourists. The* Lualma *and* Blue Water *are docked behind him. Morehead City, 1956.* Bottom • 211: *The charter boats* Lualma *and* Blue Water *docked beside the Sanitary Fish Market and Restaurant. A rainbow is captured across the sky. Morehead City, circa 1954.*

Text continued on page 108

Top Left • 212: *Three generations of fishermen pose on the cabin of the Lualma.*

Pappy Joe, right, his son Hubert, left, and grandson Joe, front, represent many years of charter fishing experience. Morehead City, circa 1960. Top Right • 213: *Charter captains and friends gather for lemonade and to celebrate Captain Pappy Joe Fulcher's 83rd birthday. Back row left to right are Abram Davis, Mick Lewis, Stamey Davis, Pappy Joe Fulcher, Bill Henry, Ottis Purifoy, John Smith and Ted Garner, Sr. Front row left to right are Dave Gould, Leroy Gould and Moody Lewis. Morehead City, 1959.*

Bottom Left • 214: *Captain Hubert Fulcher, center, takes the* Blue Water *past the aviation fuel storage tanks toward Beaufort Inlet. Reginald Lewis painted the sailfish on the flybridge. Morehead City, 1953.*

Bottom Right • 215: *Captain Hubert Fulcher with a catch on his charter boat* Blue Water. *1953.*

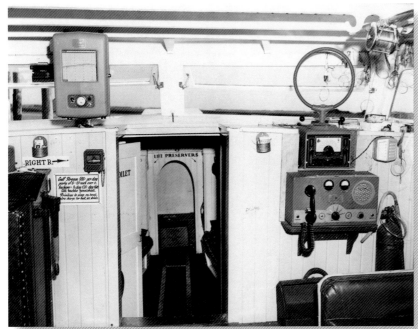

Top Left • 216: *Interior of the charter boat* Blue Water *with its state of the art electronics. The ship to shore radio, bottom right, was the largest in the fleet and Captain Fulcher was regularly called on to transfer messages from other boats. Morehead City, 1951.*

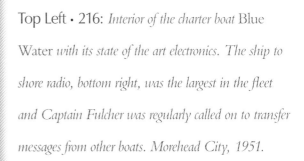

Top Right • 217: *Nice catch of King mackerel on the* Monnie M. *Captain Tony Seamon, right, and mate Guion Lewis, third from right, help hold the fish. Morehead City, September 25, 1935.* Bottom Left • 218: *Captain Tony Seamon, right, and mate Guion Lewis, left, hold a day's catch on the* Monnie M. *Morehead City, 1935.* Bottom Right • 219: *The charter boat* Monnie M. *was captained by Tony Seamon and Ted Garner, Sr. They offered overnight accommodations on the boat as well as meals. Morehead City, 1938.*

The Morehead City Charter Fleet

Origins of the Morehead City charter fleet can be traced to several key people and developments in the mid-1930s. Among the first promoters of charter fishing on the southern Outer Banks were Captains Tony Seamon and Ted Garner who began a charter fishing business in 1934 on a boat named *Mary Ethel*. In 1935, they purchased the *Monnie M.*, a larger vessel with a flybridge, beds and a kitchen. The pair quickly became known not only for fishing but also for the fresh seafood that they cooked onboard.

Left • 220: *Captains Ted Garner, Sr., left, and Tony Seamon pose with King mackerel. Morehead City, 1937.* Right • 221: *The Sanitary Fish Market was a combination fish market and restaurant. A large rod and reel was mounted over the entrance. Morehead City, 1938.*

Unlike charter fleets on the northern Outer Banks, southern charter captains advertised fishing packages that included onboard sleeping accommodations and meals. A typical charter trip on the *Monnie M.* started in the late afternoon when the party arrived at the Morehead City waterfront. Captain Seamon and mate Guion Lewis greeted the party and got them loaded before heading to Cape Lookout Bight where they anchored for the evening. Once secure, Captain Seamon used a small gas cooker to prepare fresh fish with all the trimmings. At sunset, the meal was served on the stern of the boat and afterwards the party told stories and relaxed until bedtime. Fishing started early the next morning and by mid-afternoon the boat returned to the docks, restocked supplies and started over with a new party. At that time, the rate for a full day trip was $10 per person including one overnight on the boat and three meals.

After a couple of years, Seamon and Garner decided to stop offering room and board as a part of their fishing package. Instead they expanded their onshore business to include a fish market and restaurant to better serve their clients. The partners leased a small building on the Morehead

City waterfront from Charles S. Wallace for $25 per month. Wallace imposed several restrictions on the lease. The sale of alcoholic beverages was prohibited and, because of the threat of fire, only minimal cooking was allowed. In addition, Wallace demanded that the premises be kept neat and clean and he checked for compliance every week. On February 10, 1938, captains Tony Seamon and Ted Garner opened their fish market-restaurant and, in an attempt to accommodate all the requirements of the lease, they simply called their business the Sanitary Fish Market.

Ted Garner assumed responsibility for operating the market and restaurant while Tony Seamon continued the charter fishing portion of the business. Even though the restaurant opened with only 12 barstools and a serving counter, the Sanitary Fish Market quickly gained a reputation for outstanding seafood and the demand soon overwhelmed their capacity.

Captain Seamon continued to charter fish until 1942 when he decided to enter the market and restaurant on a full-time basis. In 1949, Garner and Seamon purchased an additional piece of property on the waterfront and built a new facility called the Sanitary Fish Market and Restaurant. In 1969, the restaurant was expanded and in 1980, Ted Garner Jr. purchased the business. The Sanitary Fish Market and Restaurant continues to serve fresh local seafood on the Morehead City waterfront.

Left • 222: *Captain Tony Seamon, left, with Tony Seamon, Jr. and his first blue marlin. Morehead City, 1958.*

Right • 223: *On their 20th Anniversary, Captains Tony Seamon, left, and Ted Garner pose with their first stove from the Sanitary Fish Market. Morehead City, 1958.*

Another pioneer of the Morehead City charter fleet is Captain Ottis Purifoy. Born in 1911, Captain Purifoy began helping out on the Morehead City docks as a fish cleaner and deck hand in the early 1920s. He started commercial fishing in the 1930s but he quickly realized the potential for sportfishing. In the late 1930s, Captain Purifoy opened a wholesale market where commercial fishermen could bring their catch for distribution to restaurants and seafood markets throughout North Carolina. He also operated a retail fish market on the Morehead City waterfront.

Left • 224: *Captain Ottis Purifoy poses in front of the sign for his Lucky 7 Fishing Fleet. Morehead City, 1952.*

Right • 225: *Captain Francis Purifoy at the helm of his charter boat the* Red Snapper. *Morehead City, 1958.*

In addition to his commercial interests, Captain Purifoy assembled a fleet of charter boats known throughout the region as the Lucky 7 Fishing Fleet. He hired some of the most experienced boat captains and fishermen along the southern Outer Banks to operate his boats. Among these talented fishermen were three of his brothers, George, Ed and Francis Purifoy. These noted captains earned a reputation and following that is legendary among North Carolina sportfishing enthusiasts.

The Lucky 7 Fishing Fleet originated with Captain Purifoy's own charter boat, the *Barracuda*. In 1946, Purifoy contracted with Bill Pittman from the South River section of Carteret County to construct the *Dolphin*. Captain Purifoy proceeded to expand his fleet until it reached a high of 14 boats. These vessels docked at the Morehead City waterfront near Captain Purifoy's seafood market.

In an unusual mix of Roman numerals, numbers and names, the Lucky 7 Fishing Fleet at one time included the *Dolphin, Dolphin One, Dolphin II, Dolphin III, Dolphin*

IV, Dolphin V, Dolphin VI, Dolphin 7,
Barracuda, Gulf Breeze, Shearwater, Sea
Raven, Little Sister and *Beth.* Even though
the charter captains primarily fished
on one boat, they were often called on
to take another vessel for a day or to
change boats for a season depending on
the needs of the fleet.

    All of the charter captains in the
Lucky 7 Fishing Fleet were well-known
and respected. They included "Little"
George Bedsworth and Herman Gibson,
Dolphin and *Dolphin One;* Jack Lewis
and Kemp Wickizer, *Dolphin II;* Ottie
Russell and Francis Purifoy, *Dolphin III;*
Buddy Mizelle, Bob Ballou, *Dolphin IV;*
Pete Midgette, Doyle L. Taylor, Jr., M.L.
Marinus Snipes, C.H. Willis, *Dolphin V;*
Wallace Guthrie, *Dolphin VI;* Jack Lewis,
Dolphin 7; Boose Lewis and Ed Purifoy, *Barracuda;* Willard Lewis and Willie Bedsworth,
Gulf Breeze; Donnie Mason, Aubrey Willis, Bill Williams and Percy Howland, *Shearwater;*
Earl Holt, George Purifoy and Kenneth Ball, *Sea Raven;* Clyde Willis and Percy Howland,
Little Sister; and Ottis Purifoy, *Beth.*

    In addition to being an outstanding fisherman, Captain Purifoy also effectively
promoted this assemblage of charter boats. He was one of the first to
advertise amenities for fishermen including on-site
fish cleaning, packing, freezing,
photography and taxidermy.
When the *Barracuda* was retired
from daily charters, Captain
Purifoy positioned her on blocks
across the street from his seafood
market where she remained for
several years as an advertisement for
the Fleet. The death of Captain Ottis
Purifoy in 1981 brought an end to
the Lucky 7 Fishing Fleet and to an
extraordinary period of charter fishing
on the southern Outer Banks.

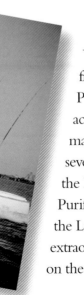

Top • 226: *Bradley*
McIntosh stands ready for a
fishing party in the doorway
of the booking headquarters
for the Lucky 7 Fishing
Fleet. Morehead City, 1955.
Bottom • 227: *The* Red
Snapper *heads for Beaufort*
Inlet. Morehead City, 1959.

Text continued on page 116

Top Right • 228: *The Dolphin prepares to leave the docks for a family cruise. Morehead City, circa 1959.* Top Left • 229: *Captain Ottis Purifoy checks the daily catch records for each boat in the Lucky 7 Fishing Fleet. Morehead City, 1961.*

Bottom Left • 230: *The Dolphin One returns to the docks. Morehead City, 1950.*

Bottom Right • 231 *Catch on the Dolphin One with Captain George Bedsworth, kneeling second from left. Morehead City, circa 1966.*

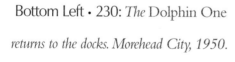

Top Left • 232: *Lucky fishermen display seven marlin caught in one day on the* Dolphin *with Captain George Bedsworth. Morehead City, 1965.* Top Right • 233: *The* Dolphin II *unloads its catch beside the booking headquarters. Morehead City, circa 1961.* Bottom Left • 234: *Anglers on the* Shearwater *with Captain Bill Williams, back row in open shirt, and mate Harrison Guthrie, back row right. Morehead City, 1961.* Bottom Right • 235: *The* Dolphin VI *cruises down the waterfront after a day of offshore trolling. Morehead City, circa 1958.*

Top • 236: *The charter boat* Gulf Breeze *trolls off Cape Lookout with Captain Willard Lewis at the helm. The mate often is called on to climb up the tower and search for fish or floating debris. Morehead City, circa 1954.*

Middle Left • 237: *Built in the late 1930s by Asa Buck, the charter boat* Little Sister *is a typical Core Sounder adapted for charter fishing. She was captained by Clyde Willis. Morehead City, 1956.*

Middle Right • 238: *Captain Ottis Purifoy retired his charter boat* Barracuda *to the "hill" where she advertised for the Lucky 7 Fishing Fleet. Morehead City, circa 1960.* Bottom • 239: *The* Gulf Breeze *trolling at Cape Lookout. Morehead City, circa 1954.*

Top • 240: *Sailfish caught onboard the* Victory *with Captain Bill Ballou, back left. Morehead City, 1948.*

Bottom Left • 241: *Fishermen pose with catch in front of Captain Bill's Sport Fishing Fleet sign. Morehead City, 1950.*

Bottom Right • 242: *Fish coming over the transom of the charter boat* Mermaid II *with Captain A.A. "Pop" Whiticar. Morehead City, 1950.*

Top • 243:

The round-stern charter

boats Mattie G., *left,*

and Harriet L., *right,*

return to Morehead City

with Captains Leroy

Gould and Dave Gould.

1952. Bottom • 244:

Captain Dave Gould,

standing on the stern of the

Harriet L., *holds a King*

mackerel caught near Cape

Lookout. 1947.

Beginning in 1936, Captain Headen "Bill" Ballou operated a small seafood restaurant on Arendell Street in Morehead City. He also skippered a charter boat called the *Victory*. In 1941, Captain Ballou moved his restaurant to the waterfront where he combined both operations under the name Waterfront Café and Fish Market. In the late 1940s he changed the name to Captain Bill and Bob's and then to Captain Bill's Waterfront Restaurant. Captain Bill Ballou, on the *Victory,* and Captain A.A. "Pop" Whiticar, on the *Mermaid II* and *Gannett,* became known as the Captain Bill's Sport Fishing Fleet. Captain Bill's Waterfront Restaurant is the oldest continuously operated restaurant in Morehead City.

Many other captains and charter boats operated from the Morehead City docks. Among the most noted are Captains Dave, Leroy and Terrell Gould. Captain Dave Gould began charter fishing in 1938 when he commissioned Cagie Adams to build his first charter boat, the *Harriet L*. His son, Captain Leroy Gould, joined the charter business in 1950 and he had Cagie Adams build his charter boat called the *Mattie G.* In 1958, Asa Buck built the *Harriet L. II* for Captain Dave Gould and, two years later, the *Mattie G. II* for Captain Leroy Gould.

Top • 245: *The* Harriet L. *waits silently in the snow along the Morehead City waterfront. 1948.* Bottom • 246: *Charter boats* Mattie G. II, *left, and* Harriet L. II *return to the docks. Morehead City, circa 1961.*

In 1975, Terrell Gould became the third generation of charter fishermen in the Gould family. In 1976, he had Lloyd and Alex Willis on Harkers Island build the *Harriet L.*, named in honor of his grandfather. Captain Terrell Gould continues to offer sportfishing charters with the same enthusiasm and expertise that his father and grandfather did before him.

The Day family also represents three generations of charter fishing experience. Captains Leland Day, *Empress*; Gordon Day, *Corsair*; Leslie Day, *Wunderlust*; Ben Day, *Marlin II*; and, David Day, *Marlin Too* are well-known charter fishermen.

In the late 1940s, more than 30 charter boats dotted the Morehead City waterfront. This group of sportfishing pioneers includes Captains Darcy Willis, *Joy II* and *Moonglow*; Theodore Lewis, *Sylvia II*; John C. Guthrie, *Nancy Max*; Dave Strickland, *Carribean*; and Alfred Pittman, *Lois Nancy II*.

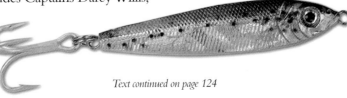

Text continued on page 124

Top Left • 247 *The* Carribean, *with Captain Dave Strickland,*
returns to the docks after a day's fishing at Cape Lookout. 1959.
Top Right • 248: *Captain Strickland, right, relaxes on the*
Carribean. *Morehead City, 1958.* Bottom Left • 249: *Captain*
Johnny Styron, left rear, poses with a fishing party on the Sylvia I.
Morehead City, 1956. Bottom Right • 250:
The charter boat Lois Nancy II *returns to port*
with Captain Alfred Pittman at the
helm. Morehead City, 1957.

Top Left • 251: *The A.M. Willis II returns to the dock with a fishing party. Morehead City, 1955.* Middle Left • 252: *The charter boat* Judy Linda *and Captain Bill Howland heads for Beaufort Inlet. 1957.* Middle Right • 253: *A fishing party poses with their catch after a successful day on the A.M. Willis II. Morehead City, 1959.*

Bottom • 254: *The charter boat Bill-N-Jim, with Captain Jim Howland, recorded the first documented sailfish caught by a woman angler in North Carolina when Mrs. Glennie Howland boated one on August 7, 1947. The Bill-N-Jim gets a few repairs and new paint. Morehead City, 1956.*

Top Left • 255: *Fishermen Gregory Poole, Sr., left, and Gordon Vaughan, right, pose with marlin they caught on the Bunny Too. Morehead City, June 6, 1963.* Top Right • 256: *Captain Delmas Willis heads the charter boat Bunny toward Beaufort Inlet and a day of trolling around the Cape. Morehead City, circa 1959.*

Above • 257: *Captain Arthur Lewis checks his instruments onboard the Bunny Too. Morehead City, 1966.* Bottom Left • 258: *Captain Arthur Lewis brings the noted charter boat Bunny Too back to port after a day of fishing. Morehead City, circa 1964.*

Top Left • 259: *The* Judy Linda *leaves the docks behind the Sanitary Restaurant. Morehead City, circa 1958.* Top Right • 260: *The charter boat* Jeanne II, *with Captain Bruce Tapscott at the helm, prepares to dock. Morehead City, circa 1964.* Middle Right • 261: *The* Cottonwood, *with Captain Roy Lewis at the helm, motors up the channel towards Beaufort Inlet. Circa 1955.*

Bottom • 262: *The charter boat* Tommy LuLu, *captained by John C. Guthrie, rests at her berth on the Morehead City waterfront. 1959.*

Top Left • 263: *Nice King mackerel landed on the* New Moon II *with Captain Franklin Guthrie, right. Morehead City, circa 1958.*

Top Right • 264: *A big marlin is unloaded from the charter boat* Dreamo Lu *with Captain Jim Talton. Morehead City, circa 1962.*

Bottom Left • 265: *The charter boat* Tom 'n Jerry *with Captain Tom Talton, second from left in the cabin, shows off 5 marlin and a wahoo caught on a fishing trip to the Big Rock. Morehead City, circa 1965.*

Bottom Right • 266: *Captain Ray Coats, back right, with a fishing party that landed a nice blue marlin on the charter boat* Blue Marlin. *Morehead City, circa 1960.*

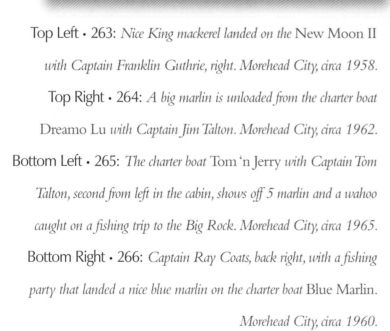

Top Left · 267: *The charter boat* Rock-a-Long, *with Captain Rock Hardison, fishes off Cape Lookout with several other boats. Morehead City, circa 1964.* Middle Left · 268: *The charter boat C-Oats, captained by Don Coats, rests in her Morehead City berth. Circa 1965.* Bottom Left · 269: *The Mako, with Captain Frank Johnson, waits for a fishing party. Morehead City, circa 1965.* Top Right · 270: *A 391-pound marlin caught on the Rock-a-Long is displayed. Captain Rock Hardison, kneeling left, and mate David Day, kneeling center, are well-known fishermen on the southern Outer Banks. Morehead City, 1965.*

Contemporaries of these great fishermen, many of whom fished from the 1940s through the 1960s, include captains Stacy Willis, *A.M. Willis*; Jim Howland, *Bill-N-Jim*; William Howland, *Judy Linda*; Delmas Willis and Arthur Lewis, *Bunny* and *Bunny Too*; Moody Lewis and John C. Guthrie, *Tommy Lulu*; Roy Lewis and Joe Rose III, *Cottonwood*; Bruce Tapscott, *Jeannie II*; Franklin Guthrie, *New Moon II*; Jim Talton, *Dreamo Lu*; Tom Talton, *Tom'n Jerry*; Rock

Top • 271: *The party boat* Danco *prepares for a day of offshore bottom fishing. Morehead City, circa 1959.*

Bottom • 272: *The* Carolina Queen *returns from a cruise around the waterfront. Morehead City, circa 1958.*

Hardison, *Rock-a-long*; and Frank Johnson, *Mako*. Many other charter fishermen are recognized on a memorial to the fleet, the Skipper's Roster, located on the Morehead City waterfront.

Early charter fishing on the southern Outer Banks also included several large party

fishing vessels capable of carrying 90 passengers or more. In the 1950s, the *Danco, Carolina Queen* and *Carolina Princess* were all operating from Morehead City.

The *Danco* was built as a PT boat in 1945 and retrofitted for party fishing in 1952.

On June 21, 1953, the *Danco* carried her first party of 20 fishermen for a day of offshore bottom fishing. The price was $6 for adults and $3 for children. Captains on the *Danco* included Kemp Wickizer, R.A. Merrell and Gordon "Red" Willis.

The original *Carolina Queen* was an Army rescue boat used in World War II that was later replaced by a larger and faster steel-hulled vessel. Captains of the *Carolina Queen* included Lloyd Smith, Homer Fulcher, Frank Grantham and George Hall.

The *Carolina Princess* was originally a military patrol boat. In 1970, Will Guthrie built the second *Carolina Princess,* a wooden-hulled boat, for Captain Woo Woo Harker. Jeff Drake and Lloyd Reed also served as captains on the *Carolina Princess*. These well-known party boats provided offshore fishing opportunities to many anglers who could not afford a private charter.

In addition to the waterfront charter boats, the Morehead City Yacht Basin also included several charter vessels and a host of private sportfishing boats and sailboats. Founded in 1947, the Morehead City Yacht Basin was originally owned and operated by Charlie North Bennett and Warren Lorenzo "Bump" Styron with dockmaster James Hester. Bump Styron and James Hester were fixtures at the Yacht Basin through 1960 when Styron died. Hester continued until the late 1990s and was an integral part of the early years of sportfishing and boating in Morehead City.

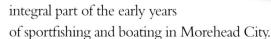

Top • 273: *The party boat* Carolina Princess *is ready for an offshore fishing trip. Morehead City, circa 1964.* Middle • 274: *Private and charter boats docked at the Morehead City Yacht Basin. Circa 1962.* Bottom • 275: *Aerial view of the Morehead City Yacht Basin. Circa 1960.*

Top Left •
276: *Captain*
Stacy W. Davis
poses in front
of a sign on
Harkers Island
advertising
his charter business.
The party boat Capt.
Stacy *was named in his*
honor. Harkers Island,
1945. Top Right •
277: *Captain Stacy M.*
"Bertram" Davis poses
on his charter boat The
Kids. *Harkers Island,*
1949. Bottom • 278:

Captain Benny Brooks rests

onboard his charter boat the

Ocean Spray. Harkers Island,

circa 1949.

The Harkers Island
Charter Fleet

Harkers Island
had a small but thriving
charter fleet from the
1930s through the 1960s.
This fleet included the
famous fishing family of
Captain Stacy W. Davis
and his sons Clark, Jack,
Sunnie and Stacy M.
"Bertram" Davis. In 1935,
Captain Stacy, as he is
respectfully known, had

Brady Lewis build the *Leona*, a commercial boat that he later adapted for charter fishing. Under the experienced tutelage of Captain Stacy, his sons Jack and Sunnie began their fishing careers as mates on this vessel.

In 1947, Captain Clark Davis built and operated the *Captain Vic*, a square-stern boat used for sport and commercial fishing. A year later, in 1948, Bernie Gillikin built Captain Bertram Davis a 45-foot charter boat called *The Kids* that was capable of fishing offshore. Captain Davis operated from Harkers Island until 1950 when he went to work with the state ferry system.

In 1954, Captain Sunnie Davis had the Rose Brothers on Harkers Island build

his first wooden vessel, a party boat called the *Capt. Stacy* in honor of his father. Under the direction of Captain Davis, the *Capt. Stacy* is a part of the sportfishing legacy along the southern Outer Banks.

Captains Benny "Red" Brooks, *Ocean Spray*; Jimmy Harker, *Eleanor* and *Gale Ann*; Jimmy "Woo Woo" Harker, *Shell Point*; George Perry Willis, *Mariner*; and Blaine Johnson, *C.J.* were among the many charter fishermen who carried parties from the docks at Harkers Island.

The Marshallberg Charter Fleet

The boatbuilding community of Marshallberg was also home to a small but capable fleet of charter boats. Beginning in the early 1920s, Captain Charlie Willis operated a boat called *Flirt*, taking parties to Cape Lookout for a day of inshore bottom fishing. Captain Dick Salter owned a charter boat named *Mildred* that did not have an engine. He "shoved" his party to Cape Lookout using nothing more than a push pole.

Sam Harris charter fished from Marshallberg during the 1930s and 1940s on a boat called the *Cora Lee*, a 30-foot Core Sounder. Since Marshallberg was somewhat isolated from the major tourist population in Morehead City, charter captains had to be

Top Left • 279: *Fishing party poses with their catch on the charter boat* The Kids. *Captain Bertram Davis, left rear in checkered shirt, fished from Harkers Island. 1949.* Top Right • 280: *Captain Jimmy Harker and his son, "Woo Woo" Harker, enjoyed a day of fishing on their Harkers Island charter boat. Circa 1949.* Bottom • 281: *Docked in front of Carl Lewis' motel, Captain Benny Brooks readies his Harkers Island charter boat* Ocean Spray *for a fishing party. 1958.*

Top · 282: *The Claudia Sue was both a commercial craft and a charter boat for Captain Claude Brown. Marshallberg, 1950.*

Bottom · 283: *Captain Dick Salter poles his charter boat* Mildred *from Marshallberg to Cape Lookout. He also ferried passengers to the Cape for a day at the beach. Circa 1910.*

creative in order to get "walk-up" fishing parties. On days that he did not have a scheduled group, Captain Sam Harris reportedly hitched a ride on the first car going from Marshallberg to Morehead City. He hung around the docks talking to people about fishing and usually managed to scrape up a party for that day, price negotiable. The only condition was they had to have a car so he could catch a ride back to Marshallberg.

From the 1930s through the 1950s, several other charter boats fished from the Marshallberg waterfront. Captains Myron "Ace" Harris, Claude Brown, Archie Jones, Neal Jones, Edward Davis and Charles Newkirk all carried charter parties. Like their Harkers Island and Morehead City neighbors, the Marshallberg fleet offered overnight stays and meals either on the boat, at the home of the captain or in a local residence.

One of the most noted and respected captains was Claude Brown. Born in 1913, Captain Brown commissioned his first charter boat, the *Claudia Sue*, from Bernie Gillikin in 1949. This boat was named for his two daughters Claudia and Sue. Brown built his second charter boat, *Miss Belle*, in 1956 with assistance from Brady Lewis, Jimmy Jones and Charlie Claude Jones of Harkers Island. Eugene, Dale and Kenny Chadwick built his third charter boat, *Miss Belle II*, and James M. Taylor and Lorrie Moore built his last charter boat, the *Mama Belle*, in 1988.

Captain Brown and long-time mate Elbert Clinton Gaskill carried parties through Barden's Inlet to the eastern side of Cape Lookout. They trolled around the wreck of the *Atlas*, known to fishermen as the *Atlas* tanker, for King mackerel, amberjack, dolphin and occasionally a sailfish. In the late 1950s the fee for such a trip was $14 per person including room and board.

Captain Brown quit fishing in 1980 and died in 1998. Throughout his career he was widely esteemed in the community both as an accomplished fisherman and as a gentleman. Captain Claude Brown epitomized the character, generosity and kindness that is common along the Outer Banks.

In the 1954, Myron Harris built his first charter boat, the *Sammy H.* He was a math teacher during the school year, but Myron loved the water and he operated his charter boat out of Marshallberg during summer break. Myron proceeded to open Harris Boatworks in Marshallberg and, along with his son, charter fisherman and boatbuilder Buddy Harris, they became renowned for their talents in both areas.

Top Left • 284:
Captain Claude Brown cleans up his charter boat Miss Belle *at Marshallberg. 1958.*

Top Right • 285:
Captain Brown stands in front of the framing for his charter boat, Miss Belle. *Marshallberg, 1956.*

Bottom • 286: *Captain Brown poses with a sailfish caught onboard the* Miss Belle. *Marshallberg, August 10, 1963.*

The Jones brothers also operated a charter service at Marshallberg. Archie Jones and Neal Jones took parties on the *Downeaster* and Pelham Jones ran the *Judy*. Pelham Jones was also the principal of the school in Marshallberg so he only worked during the summer as a charter captain.

Captain Ray Davis was both a charter captain and an accomplished boat-builder. Ray charter fished and commercial fished from a boat called the *Sally D.* Captain Davis and Mildon Willis built this round-stern Core Sounder in 1946.

Top • 287: *Claude Brown sits on the stern of his charter boat the* Miss Belle II *while she is under construction in Marshallberg. 1974.*

Bottom • 288: *Business card for Captain Claude Brown. Marshallberg, circa 1958.*

Captain Edward Davis worked with his father Ray Davis and brother Bernie Davis to build his own Marshallberg charter boat. They worked on the project during their spare time and at night. When Edward finished his boat in 1967 and aptly named her *Moonlighter*, he started carrying charter parties from Marshallberg.

The charter fleets in Carteret County included many great fishermen and classic fishing boats. They are an important part of the boatbuilding and sportfishing heritage on the Outer Banks.

[CHAPTER FIVE]

The Dawn of Sportfishing Boats

The Dawn of Sportfishing Boats

*I*n 1968, the Oregon Inlet charter fleet was going strong, attracting fishermen from around the country for a chance to catch dolphin, tuna, wahoo and maybe even a billfish. One North Carolina group may not have come as far as others, but their trip was still a memorable one.

These anglers drove from deep in the mountains all the way to the Outer Banks to catch some fish. The mountain men had been to Oregon Inlet the year before and they had their adventure all planned out. They would leave home early in the morning, drive 500 miles across North Carolina and arrive at the Fishing Center just after dark. They planned to fish all the next day and then start back home the same night. Frugal by nature, they would bring enough food and drinks for the entire trip and sleep in the car.

After a long day's drive, the fishermen arrived at Oregon Inlet right on schedule. They parked their old station wagon directly behind the *Erma Queen*, the same boat they chartered the previous year. Six big men crawled out of the car and immediately broke out sandwiches and soft drinks in the parking lot. After a stroll around the dock, the men drew straws to see where they would sleep. Before long, the mountaineers had rolled out their blankets and prepared for the evening that lay ahead. Two were on the front seat, two on the back seat and the two lucky winners had the bed of the station wagon.

During the night, a low-pressure system formed off the coast and a strong northeast wind kicked up. By the time the first captain arrived at the Fishing Center, the station wagon was rocking from wind gusts that measured over 20 knots. Undaunted, the relentless fishermen piled out of their quarters and prepared for an eventful fishing trip. When the last man finally stood upright, a blast of wind whisked the cap off his head, hurling it into the dark waters of the turning basin. The baldheaded mountain man ran over to a mate standing nearby as if he had lost a child, and the two fished his cap out with a long-handled gaff. A small disaster had been averted, but a bigger one awaited.

H.T. Gaskins, veteran captain of the *Erma Queen*, arrived to dispatch the bad news to his fishing party. The wind was predicted to increase throughout the day and the charter fleet was not going out. Either wait until tomorrow or try again next year, he told them. For this group, however, neither option was acceptable. These were hearty souls who were here to go fishing and, by gosh, they were going fishing.

During the night, a low-pressure system formed off the coast and a strong northeast wind kicked up. By the time the first captain arrived at the Fishing Center, the station wagon was rocking from wind gusts that measured over 20 knots. Undaunted, the relentless fishermen piled out of their quarters and prepared for an eventful fishing trip.

RED FIN

Left • 289: *The* Erma Queen, *pictured here with Captain Billy Brown, backs into her berth at the Oregon Inlet Fishing Center. 1973.*

Right • 290: *Captain Bob Scarborough, rear, watches as mate Allen Burrus prepares to hoist a marlin to the scales. Hatteras. 1970.*

The men tried to talk Captain Gaskins into making the trip but he would have none of it. Feeling sorry for their plight, H.T. offered a suggestion. They could drive to Oden's Dock at Hatteras and ask Bobby Scarborough if he would take them fishing on the *Red Fin*. Gaskins knew that Bobby was famous for going when no one else would and he also wanted to pay him back for several practical jokes that Scarborough had pulled. This could be the perfect solution.

Without hesitation, the fishing party concurred with the plan and they piled into the station wagon for their trip to Hatteras. They arrived at Oden's Dock in about an hour and located the *Red Fin* in a line of charter boats still tied to the dock. Captain Scarborough, grandson of Wanchese boatbuilder Bob Scarborough, had already sent his mate home for the day and was preparing to leave himself when the six big men, each dressed in a red flannel shirt, bib overalls and brogans, showed up behind his boat. Surely they didn't want to go fishing.

In a dialect he had never heard, one man asked Bobby if he would take them out. Captain Scarborough replied in his best "hoi toide" accent, "I think so. I just had a quitter for tomorrow and you can fill in."

"No, not tomorrow. *Today!*" came the response in unison. There was a long, long pause and before Bobby decided, one of the men said, "We figured you'd be too scared to take us."

That did it. Without hesitation Bobby responded, "Okay, but we're coming in when you get sick." Everyone agreed and Scarborough called his mate, Allen Burrus, to return to the dock. This would be an easy $150 because the winds were increasing, now clocked at over 25 knots, and waves would be breaking over the bar. Bobby figured they wouldn't even get offshore before this mountain party gave up.

As the group made preparations for the big day, Bobby and Allen exchanged snide glances. The men loaded a bag of sandwiches, some apples and an old rusty washtub filled with soft drinks and ice. These guys didn't even have a cooler. This was too easy.

The *Red Fin* headed around the breakwater and up the channel to Hatteras Inlet. White water broke all the way across the inlet and the waves were at least 8 feet tall. Rain squalls added to the misery as Captain Scarborough carefully navigated past the sea buoy.

Above • 291: *Legendary charter fisherman, Captain Bobby Scarborough, checks his tackle. Sunny Briggs, a famous charter captain and boatbuilder who docked at Oden's beside Scarborough, said fishing against him is like pitching to Babe Ruth every day. Hatteras, 1968.*

Once in the ocean they headed toward the light tower at the tip of Diamond Shoals. Bobby was expecting someone to call it quits at any moment. When the *Red Fin* took a couple of waves over her bow, Bobby glanced back to make sure that the cabin was draining. To his astonishment, all six big men in their wet, red flannel shirts, bib overalls and brogans, were laughing and drinking sodas. Good grief, how could that be?

For two and a half hours the *Red Fin* labored into a massive head sea. As they neared the shoals, the waves grew to over 10 feet and the rain beat down even harder. Captain Scarborough had sized up the mountain men and if they could make it, so could he. Bobby motioned for Burrus, who was hanging on for dear life, to put some lines out. Allen managed to get two spoons overboard and as soon as the lines straightened, two fish were hooked. Giant bluefish, each weighing over 15 pounds, were landed and thrown into the fish box. The spoons went back overboard and quickly returned with the same results: two more huge bluefish and two more happy anglers. One of the smallest men in the group latched on to something big, a 55-pound amberjack. In his typical mountain drawl he hollered out to his friends that this fish was really "a-feudin'" with him and it was going to take some "doin's" to get him in.

Above • 292:

Lucky fisherman poses with a

585-pound marlin caught on

the Red Fin *with Captain*

Bobby Scarborough, right, and

mate Allen Burrus, kneeling.

Hatteras, June 28, 1968.

Soon the box was full but the fishing hadn't slacked off one bit. Burrus was bringing fish in so quickly that all he could do was pull the hook and let them flop on the deck. Over the next three hours, the party caught one after another and by 2 p.m. they were knee-deep in fish. Everyone, including Allen, had fallen into the slimy mess. Bobby couldn't control his laughter. What a sight! Big fish, big waves and big mountain men—how could anything be more fun than this?

At 2:30, Captain Scarborough turned the *Red Fin* for home. He still had to get everyone safely back to shore and the weather had not let up. After a couple of hours through the slop, Bobby eased into Hatteras and backed into his berth. Allen threw the fish onto the dock and counted them: 67 big bluefish, 10 albacore and 6 amberjack.

The mountain men threw their empty washtub up on the dock alongside the fish and backed their car as close as possible. One man opened the hatch and the rest began launching fish right into the back of the station wagon. They packed fish into every square inch leaving only enough room for three men in the front seat and three in the back seat. When they realized that all of the fish wouldn't fit inside, they stacked the remainder on top of the car. Then, they lashed the whole mess down.

The mountain men profusely thanked Captain Scarborough and Allen Burrus for a great trip. They paid the captain and headed for the car when they noticed their old washtub. After a brief huddle, one man eased over to Bobby and whispered that since they didn't have room to take the tub home, they wanted Allen to keep it as a reward for his hard work.

The men thanked Bobby again and crammed into the car. Their wet, slimy clothes hardly dampened their enthusiasm. They were clearly excited about heading back to the mountains and figured if they could get there before daybreak, they'd have enough time to show off their catch before the community fish cleaning. They had enough fish to last another year and they were already planning their return. Bobby and Allen silently prayed for good weather.

Bluefish tails were fluttering in the wind as the station wagon headed up Highway 12. In a moment of reflection, Captain Scarborough realized that these mountain men were just like him: determined, enthusiastic and adventurous. The only difference was, "My Lordy, they sure did talk funny."

Overview

Private sportfishing boats dawned in the late 1940s and 1950s along the North Carolina Outer Banks. The post–World War II economy was growing and people had more money to spend on recreation and leisure-time activities. Gasoline and diesel engines had improved and boats were safer, faster and had more range. The highway system was better and the Outer Banks were more accessible to inland population centers. All these factors contributed to an increasing interest in offshore sportfishing.

The earliest sportfishing boats on the northern Outer Banks evolved from shad boats and on the southern Outer Banks they emerged from sharpies and Core Sounders. Local fishermen took fishing charters when the opportunity arose just to supplement their income. Few saw sportfishing as a way to make a living, and some even viewed it as a waste of time. But as the charter fleets grew and the demand for fishing opportunities increased, boatbuilders responded by constructing more sophisticated sportfishing vessels. They started focusing on the sportsman and their boats were designed exclusively for offshore fishing.

The great boatbuilders who led the transition from charter boats into the dawn of private sportfishing boats on the northern Outer Banks include Wilton Walker, Allen Hayman, Worden Dough, Lee Dough and Bob Scarborough. The transition on the southern Outer Banks included respected boatbuilders Ray Davis, Charlie Alligood, Ray LeMay, Nat Lee Smith and Asa Cannon.

These fine boatbuilders took the shad boat and the Core Sounder and made them sportfishing vessels. Even though many of their boats were built from the late 1940s through the 1960s, some of them are still in use today. The talents and skills of these boatbuilders and fishermen started a legacy along the Outer Banks, and they were instrumental in the early years of the new industry.

Above • 293:

The Connie Dionne *with charter captains Matt Spivey, back left, Moon Tillett, back center, Delton Dowdy, back right, and Jack Hoffler, back kneeling. The* Connie Dionne *was the first sportfishing boat on the northern Outer Banks to be equipped with a diesel engine. Oregon Inlet Fishing Center, circa 1954.*

Left • 294: The Deepwater was built by John Wilson, Warren O'Neal and Roy Etheridge in 1953 and she is one of the boats that exemplifies the transition from charter boat construction to better finishes and amenities for private sportfishing. Oregon Inlet Fishing Center, 1954.

Right • 295: Captain Belove Tillett built the original Lollypop in 1935. In 1953, Captain Chick Craddock and Joe Stewart Midgett rebuilt the boat specifically for sportfishing and moved her to the Oregon Inlet Fishing Center. Captain Craddock charter fished until 1978 on the Lollypop. She is an example of the transition to modern sportfishing boats. Oregon Inlet, 1954.

Dawn of Sportfishing Boats on the Northern Outer Banks

Currituck County, the northernmost stretch of the North Carolina Outer Banks, is home to several outstanding boatbuilders. Many Currituck craftsmen also made decoys as well as small skiffs for duck hunting. One such artisan is Wilton Walker, noted for his stylish decoys and hunting skiffs. Walker is also well known for his square-stern cabin boats that were constructed in the late 1940s through the 1950s.

Wilton Walker lived in the Tulls Creek area on the mainland of Currituck County. He started building boats in the 1930s and his reputation for building sleek, fast boats that could navigate shallow waters spread throughout the region. During the early 1950s, Walker began building "sport cruisers" that were used for inshore bottom-fishing charters and touring. Many of these boats were made for clients in Virginia and Maryland.

Among the first to recognize Walker's talents was a group of bootleggers who purchased one of his boats, modified the engine and turned it into a "rum runner." Local law enforcement officers did not have a boat fast enough to catch the band so they contracted with Walker to build a sistership and they soon captured the men.

This same scenario was repeated when wildlife officers encountered a group of game poachers who kept eluding officials in one of Walker's boats. Walker jokingly said that he had stumbled onto the only way to make money in the boatbuilding business—work both sides of the law.

Farther down the Currituck County mainland is Point Harbor and the home of Allen Hayman. Born in 1899, Hayman began building boats with his father, Tom Hayman. Allen completed his first boat, an 18-foot commercial fishing skiff, in 1916. In the 1920s, Hayman built boats for fishermen and hunters to use in Currituck Sound.

In the 1930s, when gasoline motors became popular, Hayman began the transition to sport cruisers and "runabouts." In the 1940s and 1950s, he began constructing sportfishing boats for local charter captains. Allen Hayman, unlike many of the early boatbuilders, made half-models that guided his construction. His boats were made using the plank-on-frame method and he was such a perfectionist that he rarely used glue.

Noted boatbuilder and charter captain Bobby Sullivan, grandson of Allen Hayman, learned his craft under Hayman's watchful eye. Bobby said that a charter boat captain once asked them to replace a few deck boards damaged during a storm. Hayman and Sullivan ripped out the entire deck and cleaned the bilge before starting the replacement. When Bobby asked about the extra work where no one would ever see it, Allen replied, "Do it right, whatever it takes. You wouldn't wear dirty underwear, would you?"

Top • 296: *Wilton Walker, standing in the water, readies his sport cruiser for a day of fishing. Currituck Sound, circa 1950.*

Bottom • 297: *A party boat destined for charter fishing at Virginia Beach sits at Wilton Walker's dock. Tulls Creek, circa 1948.*

One of the most notable boats built by Allen Hayman was the *Carrov*. Completed in 1952 for Captain Carson Stallings, and named for Carson and his wife Rovina, the *Carrov* was an important member of the Oregon Inlet charter fleet. In 1962, legendary charter boat captain Tony Tillett purchased the *Carrov* from Stallings and changed her name to the *Carolinian*. She became the first of four world-famous Oregon Inlet charter boats with the same name. The *Carrov* was also the boat on which Bobby Sullivan started his boatbuilding career as an apprentice to Allen Hayman.

In 1959, Allen Hayman moved his boatbuilding shop to Kitty Hawk on the Outer Banks. There he built sportfishing boats that were popular as charter boats. The *Ponjola*, built in 1962, was the first sportfishing boat built at his Kitty Hawk shop. Allen Hayman retired in 1975 and died in 1983. With more than 250 boats to his credit, Allen Hayman was an important boatbuilder in the transition from charter boats to private sportfishing boats.

Text continued on page 142

Right • 298: *Wilton Walker was known for his sporty fishing and cruising boats. This vessel is running in Currituck Sound. Circa 1949.* Middle Left • 299: *Noted boatbuilder, Allen Hayman, leaves his workshop in Point Harbor. 1962.*

Middle Right • 300: *A private sportfishing boat built by Wilton Walker is being delivered to Manteo. Circa 1952.*

Bottom • 301: *Allen Hayman built private sportfishing boats at his Point Harbor shop in Currituck County. This vessel is almost finished and ready for delivery. 1947.*

Top Left • 302: *Allen Hayman working on the* Carrov. *This boat was built for Captain Carson Stallings and was purchased in 1962 by Captain Tony Tillett. The* Carrov *represents the transition from round-stern commercial boats to sportfishing boats. Point Harbor, 1952.*

Top Right • 303: *An Allen Haymen sportfishing boat awaits its owner at the harbor on the Elizabeth City waterfront. 1948.* Middle • 304: *The* Carrov *heads for launching in Currituck Sound. Point Harbor, 1952.*

Bottom • 305: *Allen Hayman, with the help of Bobby Sullivan, built the sportfishing boat* Follow the Sun. *Hayman incorporated many of the yacht finishes and amenities into this vessel. Point Harbor, 1963.*

Left • 306: *Worden Dough*

standing in the path that led to

his backyard boatworks on the

north end of Roanoke Island.

Circa 1928. Right • 307:

The private sportfishing boat

Ponjola *is almost complete at*

Allen Hayman's boat shed in

Kitty Hawk. This was the first

private boat built at the Kitty

Hawk location. 1962.

The Dough family on Roanoke Island had successfully built shad boats for more than 40 years when Worden and Lee Dough began to add cabins and fishing amenities to them. By the late 1940s and into the 1950s, Worden and Lee designed and built their boats to accommodate larger engines with more storage for fishing tackle and gear. The two developed a reputation for quality workmanship and were highly acclaimed for their stylish and functional fishing boats. The Dough brothers were also noted for their ability to adapt commercial boats to sportfishing, sometimes even taking an old boat down to the keel before rebuilding it.

Every community has its characters and on Roanoke Island one such legend is Worden Dough. Tales of his exploits rank high among the many stories told by local boatbuilders.

In addition to his reputation as a craftsman, Worden Dough was also noted for his salty language. Very salty. One spring a local school group had scheduled a tour of the Dough boatyard. Horrified at the thought of Worden unleashing a string of profanities in front of the children, the carpenters secretly concocted a scheme to distract him while the group was touring.

Their plan called for a lookout to greet the kids before Dough could get there. Another worker was poised to intercept Worden and create a distraction by asking a few questions until the tour was well underway. It was a great plan, but unfortunately two classes arrived instead of one. The group was so large that it required the efforts of all the carpenters. The plan was quickly modified and was still working until Worden noticed the two teachers just standing around. He thought they looked bored so he offered to take them on a personal tour.

The children asked the carpenters a lot of questions and obviously had a great time. After they departed, one carpenter snickered and asked Worden how the wide-eyed teachers liked his tour. In a quick retort he replied: "All I can say is they know a lot more now than they did when they got here." Everyone was sure of that but no one dared ask for an explanation.

Worden's brother, Lee Dough, was also a very talented boatbuilder and a respected charter captain. Lee and Worden shared the same propensity for detail and structure, so much so that some believe Worden lived three years longer just to keep people from messing with his tools.

Like Worden, Lee Dough seemed to be an easy target for pranksters. In 1947, when the charter boats docked at Dykstra's canal, Lee had a meticulous daily routine that included arriving an hour before daylight, firing up his engine, pumping water out of the bilge and visiting the bathroom on his charter boat, *Libby-D*. This ritual was repeated every day.

Early one morning on his way to Dykstra's, Captain Ken Ward spotted an opossum on the road and decided it would make a good fishing partner for Lee. He jumped out of his car and captured the critter in a dip net. When he got to the dock, he threw the opossum into the cabin of the *Libby-D* and slammed the door. Captain Dough arrived right on cue and proceeded to fire up the engine and pump the bilge. By the time he eased into the cabin, Ken Ward had assembled the other captains and they were in on the prank.

Top • 308: *Worden Dough rests in front of one of his beautifully styled shad boats. Roanoke Island, circa 1939.* Bottom • 309: *A round-stern boat built by Worden Dough was used for commercial fishing and for sportfishing. The trawling gear is still onboard while a sportfishing party is trolling. Oregon Inlet, circa 1947.*

Left • 310: *Captain Lee Dough works on the* Libby-D *at the Oregon Inlet Fishing Center docks. 1955.* Right • 311: *Worden Dough started construction of the sportfishing boat* Germel *and she was completed by Bob Scarborough. This boat was built for Walter Davis of Elizabeth City. Oregon Inlet Fishing Center, 1964.*

After a few minutes, a loud hissing sound shattered the darkness and Captain Dough came screaming out of the cabin with his pants bunched around his ankles. Seems as though the opossum had crawled into the bathroom and was hiding on a shelf in front of the toilet. When Lee sat down, they were face to face in the darkness. As soon as each realized the other was there, a horrible commotion erupted and the opossum won. It's a good thing Lee couldn't give chase at that particular moment because the pranksters would never have escaped with their lives.

Another local boatbuilder and renowned craftsman was Bob Scarborough of Wanchese. Born in 1894, Bob had a well-deserved reputation for his intellect as well as his superior carpentry skills. Scarborough received training as an architect during World War I, and he was one of the few boatbuilders in the area who could read blueprints.

In addition to building boats, Scarborough operated a cannery for channel bass in Wanchese under the name R.E. Scarborough and Son. Known as Cape Hatteras Brand Channel Bass, the cannery thrived until the late 1940s when channel bass were designated as game fish and the commercial harvest was restricted. The cannery was then adapted for processing crabs until 1960 when it closed.

In the late 1940s and early 1950s, Bob Scarborough built the sportfishing boats *Carrie* and *Chee Chee* for Captain Will Etheridge, Jr. Bob also built the charter boat *Andrea* for Charles Scarborough and he adapted more than 30 boats from commercial use to sportfishing. Bob Scarborough died in 1966 and he will be remembered as an important part of the Outer Banks boatbuilding heritage. Ricky Scarborough, one of North Carolina's most widely known and respected builders of custom sportfishing boats, is the grandson of Bob Scarborough, and he is continuing the family's proud boatbuilding tradition.

Dawn of Sportfishing Boats on the Southern Outer Banks

Ray Davis of Marshallberg was among the most talented and prolific boatbuilders on the southern Outer Banks. Born in 1913, Ray began his career working with M. W. Willis in 1946. That year, Ray built his first boat, the *Sally D.*, for commercial use and for charter fishing. Mildon Willis recognized the potential in Ray Davis and nurtured his boatbuilding talents. In 1950, Davis started Ray Davis Boat Works in his backyard near the Marshallberg waterfront. He soon built a shop and began building sportfishing boats that were important in the metamorphosis from round-stern Core Sounders to square-stern boats. These sportfishing boats included the *Cecelia Marie, Moonstruck, Sea Filly, Fiesta, Shady Lady* and the *Nansea*.

Text continued on page 148

Top • 312:

Captain Herbert Perry, left, relaxes on the cabin of his charter boat Mildred I, *named after his wife Mildred Irene. Circa 1946.*

Bottom • 313: *Captain Ray Davis stands in front of the private sportfishing boat* Cecelia Marie *at his Marshallberg boat shop. June, 1951.*

Top • 314: *A 45-foot sportfishing boat is under construction at Ray Davis Boat Works. Marshallberg, 1950.* Middle Left • 315: *A private sportfishing boat,* Sea Filly, *overshadows a smaller skiff at the boat yard of Ray Davis. Marshallberg, 1959.* Middle Right • 316: *The private sportfishing boat* Moonstruck *is under construction. Marshallberg, 1957.*

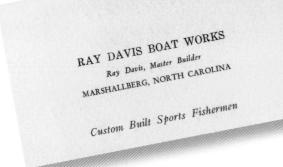

RAY DAVIS BOAT WORKS
Ray Davis, Master Builder
MARSHALLBERG, NORTH CAROLINA

Custom Built Sports Fishermen

Bottom Left • 317: *Business card for Ray Davis Boat Works and Captain Ray Davis. 1950.*

Bottom Right • 318: *The* Moonstruck *is pulled into the water. Marshallberg. 1957.*

Top Left • 319: *Captain Ray Davis prepares for the launch of the* Nansea. *Marshallberg, 1970.*

Top Right • 320: *The* Shady Lady *is outfitted at the Marshallberg dock of Captain Ray Davis. 1966.*

Middle • 321: *The* Nansea *rests on the calm waters of Core Sound before heading to Hatteras. Marshallberg, 1970.* Bottom • 322: *The* Moonlighter *was a charter boat built by Ray and Edward Davis. Marshallberg, 1967.*

Edward Davis joined his father in the boatbuilding business during the mid-1960s and his younger brother Bernie Davis helped out for two years during the late 1960s. They built square-stern charter boats including the *Moonlighter, Lisa* and *Mako*. Bernie's son, Gary Davis, also worked with the family in their Marshallberg shop as he honed his boatbuilding skills. Together this family produced some of the earliest sportfishing vessels on the southern Outer Banks.

Captain Ray Davis retired in 1978 after a 32-year career and more than 100 sportfishing boats to his credit. Ray Davis was a respected and important boatbuilder during the dawn of sportfishing vessels. He died in 1997 but his legacy on the southern Outer Banks continues.

Top • 323: The North Carolina Fisheries research boat is tied up at Morehead City. Captain Nat Lee Smith of Gloucester built this large vessel. Circa 1937.

Charlie Alligood and Ray LeMay built sportfishing boats from their boat shop in the Carteret County community of Davis. Alligood started the business in the 1940s when most of their vessels were for commercial fishing. With the arrival of Ray LeMay in 1954, the shop started constructing square-stern sportfishing boats.

The Alligood and LeMay team produced many finely crafted sportfishing vessels. According to coastal historian Ed Pond, two carpenters who worked with Ray LeMay were a talented father-son team. The "old-man" was in his eighties while his son was in his sixties and they were still going strong. One day the father was working inside the hull and he asked his son to cut a board "about this long," as he held up two fingers to show him the length.

His son called back, "Daddy, how many times do I have to say it, you need to learn how to read a tape measure!"

Bottom • 324: Nat Lee Smith in front of a small skiff and a sportfishing boat. Gloucester, 1955.

To which his father replied, "Son, I can't. All those lines just confuse me. I know the big ones, they're inches, and I can get the half inches and the quarter inches. But, what about all them little lines?"

Without hesitation, his son shot back, "Daddy, they're called eighth inches and there's twelve of 'em in one inch."

Nathaniel Leecraft "Nat Lee" Smith of Gloucester built commercial boats, sportfishing boats and research

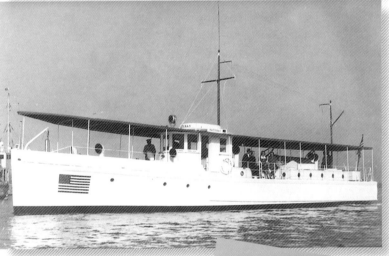

Top • 325: *Captain Nat Lee Smith planes a juniper board for one of his sportfishing boats. Gloucester, 1955.* Middle • 326: *The North Carolina Fisheries research vessel* Hatteras *with dignitaries onboard. This boat is the third vessel built by Captain Smith for the Fisheries Division. Circa 1946.*

Bottom • 327: *A new Fisheries research vessel is dedicated along the waterfront in Morehead City. Captain Nat Lee Smith, standing in the rear with a Captain's hat, built this vessel. Circa 1949.*

vessels for the State of North Carolina during his long boatbuilding career. He did not like the flare that Brady Lewis developed, preferring instead to build boats with a more Vee-shaped bow.

Nat Lee built mostly small cruisers and charter vessels but he did build several large research boats for the North Carolina Department of Conservation and Development. During his boatbuilding years, Nat Lee Smith is credited with helping in the transition from commercial vessels to sportfishing boats. His style boat, with a Vee-shaped bow and flat stern was popular with many sportfishermen, especially ones that trolled in near-shore waters.

Top Left • 328: *Tookie Willis works on a private sportfishing boat along the Harkers Island waterfront. Circa 1954.*

Top Right • 329: *Asa Cannon planks a large sportfishing vessel. Morehead City, circa 1962.* Bottom • 330: *The Manaru "on the rail" at Asa Cannon's boat yard. Morehead City, circa 1962.*

Other boatbuilders on the southern Outer Banks who influenced the transition from commercial to sport boats included Tookie Willis on Harkers Island and Asa Cannon in Morehead City.

Willis built sportfishing boats along the Harkers Island waterfront much like his predecessors did. He incorporated the flared bow and square stern with a sweeping sheer line and trunk cabin. Willis was a very capable boatbuilder who adapted his boats to the changing needs of sportfishermen.

Asa Cannon built sportfishing boats from his Morehead City boat shop. He was especially noted for his finish work and was contracted by Hatteras Yachts to customize the interiors of their molded fiberglass boats. Cannon also was respected for his repair work. He gradually stopped building boats to concentrate on custom repairs and interiors.

The conversion from commercial boats to charter boats was a big step, but the transition from charter boats to sportfishing boats was even bigger. With the dawn of sportfishing boats during the late 1940s through the 1950s, the stage was set for the transformation to the modern Carolina-style sportfishing boats.

CHAPTER SIX

Pioneers of the Carolina Style

Pioneers of the Carolina Style

Lee Perry began his charter fishing career in the early 1950s on a small boat called the *Jinny B* that he operated out of the Oregon Inlet Fishing Center. Perry later became captain of the charter boat *Deepwater* and he was acknowledged as one of the most intense, excitable and passionate fishermen in the fleet. Having worked for years along side Warren O'Neal and Omie Tillett, Lee Perry was also recognized as one of the most talented and experienced boat carpenters on Roanoke Island. Captain Perry was very well liked and respected by his peers.

But Lee Perry was easily duped—very easily—and so he was the target of many devious and dastardly practical jokes. Like the time Lee and Omie Tillett were working with Warren O'Neal on the construction of the *Sea Byrd*. When they broke for lunch, Omie alerted Warren to watch carefully but gave no further indication of what he had in mind.

As work resumed that afternoon, Lee and Omie crawled into the bow of the *Sea Byrd* to begin framing the cabin. After only a few moments, Warren heard a loud thump. Then he heard it again. After half dozen or so loud smacks, Lee crawled out of the boat and silently walked over to the work bench where he dumped the contents of his nail pouch. He went over to a window and held the empty pouch up in the light to check for holes. Finding none, he refilled his pouch with nails and crawled back into the boat. A few minutes passed before Warren heard the bang again. This time it was followed by a few expletives. Loud stammering followed the next wallop and Lee climbed out of the hull. He stomped over to his workbench, removed his nail belt and reached down to pick up his toolbox. In anger, he jerked up on the toolbox but it wouldn't budge. Lee mumbled a few words, gave the box a swift kick and hobbled out of the shop.

Omie climbed out of the *Sea Byrd* almost in tears. He confessed to Warren that as they crawled around the cabin, he secretly dropped a few nails in front of Lee. Every time his knee came down on one, Lee jerked up and bumped his head on the ceiling. He had also glued Lee's toolbox to the floor because he knew exactly what Lee would do.

Omie had his number. Throughout their years together and as much as Lee tried, he never caught Omie at his game.

In the mid-1970s, when epoxy glue became popular with boatbuilders, the timing was right for Lee Perry to be tricked again. One morning at Sportsman Boatworks, Sunny Briggs and Allen Foreman mixed glue and talked about how good it looked; in fact, it looked almost good enough to eat. Lee admonished them and warned of its dangers.

He stomped over to his workbench, removed his nail belt and reached down to pick up his toolbox. In anger, he jerked up on the toolbox but it wouldn't budge. Lee mumbled a few words, gave the box a swift kick and hobbled out of the shop.

Top • 331: *Nice catch on the* Deepwater *with Captain Lee Perry, kneeling left, and mate Billy Holton, kneeling right. Oregon Inlet Fishing Center, 1962.* Bottom • 332: *Captain Lee Perry at the helm of the* Deepwater. *Oregon Inlet, 1960.*

Sunny and Allen hatched a plan and at lunch they drove into Manteo with a single purpose in mind: to pick up some vanilla pudding.

When they returned to work, Allen slipped the pudding into a clean coffee can just like the one they used for mixing glue. Sunny found a stick and he whipped the pudding as if he was stirring up another batch of glue.

Right away Allen began talking about how good it looked and Sunny offered a challenge: if Allen would try it, then so would he. Right in front of Lee, Allen ate a big bite of pudding. He chewed, swallowed, waited a moment and then bragged about its taste. Sunny also took a mouthful and commented about how good it was.

Lee's glasses slid down his nose as he watched in disbelief. He called Omie over and offered an expressive report much like one child tattling on another: "Omie, they ate the glue, they ate the glue."

Although tempting, no one laughed and after a long silence, Lee reached in his wallet, pulled out a five-dollar bill and slammed it on the table. He stammered and stuttered but he finally got it out: "I bet you five-dollars you won't do that again."

Sunny and Allen looked at each other and both reached for the cup of "glue" at the same time. They hungrily slurped down the remaining pudding while Lee pointed and said, "See, Omie, I told you, I told you. They ate some glue and they gonna die."

No one died but after a couple of minutes, Allen gasped and grabbed his throat. Lee ran over and, rather than offering to help, he shook his finger and shouted, "I told you so, I told you so. I knew if you ate that stuff that it was going to kill you!"

This time they couldn't hold back and when they broke down and told Lee what they had done, he got so mad he didn't speak for two days.

Lee Perry also brought on many extraordinary situations

Left • 333: *Mate Buddy Davis, left, and Captain Lee Perry, center, pose with a marlin caught on the* Deepwater. *Oregon Inlet Fishing Center, August 12, 1966.*

all by himself. Once when he was about 20 miles offshore he hollered to his mate Wayne "Snookie" Johnson that the *Deepwater* felt sluggish. He slowed and stopped the engine. As if on cue, Lee slipped while climbing off the flybridge but he caught the gin pole. In a move that would have embarrassed an exotic dancer but make Inspector Clouseau smile, Lee magically twirled around the pole, flipped over and slid headfirst onto the cabin floor.

When he regained his composure and assured everyone that he was okay, Lee opened the engine box to find that the exhaust hose had worked loose and the bilge was filled with water. In a spontaneous reaction that did little to instill confidence among his fishing party, Lee stammered, "Oh my gosh Snookie, we're sinking, we're sinking!"

Snookie calmed the party and reconnected the hose. He pumped all of the water from the bilge and convinced the reluctant group to continue their trip. This was just another day fishing with Lee Perry.

A couple of years before Captain Perry retired, he replaced the engine in the *Deepwater* with a larger, more powerful diesel. He was very proud of his new found speed and he often chided other captains whose boats were not as fast. One day Lee was fishing off Cape Hatteras with most of the boats in the charter fleet. That afternoon the wind picked up and Captain Omie Tillett had worked inshore to fish in calmer waters along the beach. At quitting time, Lee decided to race the other boats back to the dock, unload his party and get to the fuel dock first so he wouldn't have to wait in line.

Lee pushed the *Deepwater* into attack mode and after an hour he was well ahead of the fleet. Captain Perry radioed Omie to gloat about how fast he was running. "*Sportsman*, I wish you were out here with the rest of us," he confidently declared.

Omie already knew the answer but he responded anyway, "Why is that *Deepwater*?"

"So I could run by you too," snorted Lee with a big laugh.

The *Deepwater* made it to the docks first followed by the *Sportsman*. Lee backed the *Deepwater* into her slip and his mate Snookie Johnson wrapped the dock line around one piling on their finger pier just to hold the boat while everyone unloaded. When Lee saw that the party was safely on the pier with all of their gear, he yelled, "Clear?" just to make sure Snookie had untied the dock line.

At that same moment, Omie was backing the *Sportsman* into a nearby slip and Omie's mate hollered, "Clear," in a signal to Omie that the dock line on the *Sportsman* was secure.

Clear to one person may not be clear to another. In his rush to the fuel dock, Lee heard someone yell "Clear" and, thinking it was Snookie, he gave the *Deepwater* a hard throttle. Unfortunately, his dock line was still tied to the piling and when it snapped taut, the finger pier lurched over tossing the party and all of their gear into the water. The group was fished out and everyone was okay, but Lee had done it again.

Despite his gullibility and awkwardness, Lee Perry was a beloved and respected member of the Oregon Inlet charter fleet. His exploits are legendary and he is an important part of the Outer Banks sportfishing heritage.

Despite his gullibility and awkwardness, Lee Perry was a beloved and respected member of the Oregon Inlet charter fleet. His exploits are legendary and he is an important part of the Outer Banks sportfishing heritage.

Overview

From the late 1950s through the 1970s, a new era in boatbuilding was ushered in along the Outer Banks. The transition from commercial boats to the development of offshore recreational boats had already begun and sportfishing was more popular than ever. Recreational anglers demanded larger and faster boats and they wanted amenities that had never been imagined on the old charter vessels. In addition, new materials and construction techniques emerged that made construction of these new vessels possible. Boatbuilders responded and the Carolina style began to evolve.

Many Outer Banks boatbuilders and fishermen were pioneers in the development of sportfishing and boatbuilding. On the northern Outer Banks innovators were Warren O'Neal, the Tilletts—Sam, Omie and Tony—and Sheldon Midgett. On the southern Outer Banks, Julian and Will Guthrie, James T. and Paul Gillikin, and James and Earl Rose each left a lasting mark on the Carolina-style sportfishing boat and our offshore sportfishing heritage.

Pioneers on the Northern Outer Banks

Warren O'Neal is acknowledged as the father of the Carolina-style sportfishing boat. He is recognized among his peers for his design innovations, construction techniques and skill as a master craftsman. O'Neal is also noted for his attention to detail and his ability to transfer his experience on the water to the design and construction of sportfishing boats. Perhaps most important, Warren O'Neal is acclaimed as a teacher. He guided many of the contemporary boatbuilders as they started their careers, and he influenced the early years of custom boatbuilding and offshore sportfishing on the northern Outer Banks.

Buddy Davis, a renowned boatbuilder and charter boat captain sums up the feeling of most craftsmen on Roanoke Island: "Captain Warren started it all and the rest of us just picked up the ball and ran with it. He deserves all the credit." Likewise, Sunny Briggs, also a well-known Outer Banks fisherman and boatbuilder, described Warren O'Neal as "a uniquely talented boat designer coupled with unmatched skills as a craftsman. He was our mentor."

Warren O'Neal was born in Manteo in 1909 and, like most other young men living on the Outer Banks, he began commercial fishing at an early age. O'Neal built his first boat in 1925 because he "needed one." It was a small, flat-bottomed skiff used for crabbing and fishing. Warren honed his skills as a waterman and he learned to use a wide range of boats and commercial fishing gear. These experiences would prove invaluable later in his boatbuilding career.

In the mid-1940s, Captain O'Neal spent his time commercial fishing in Pamlico Sound and the near-shore ocean waters on a round-stern shad boat. His boat was rigged

Above • 334: *The original round-stern* Pearl *was built by Otis Dough and Warren O'Neal and used for commercial and sportfishing. Manteo, 1949.*

for commercial fishing although Warren occasionally took it out for a little speckled trout fishing. It was during this era that Warren and other local commercial fishermen began to see a growing public interest in sportfishing.

In 1949, Otis Dough and Warren O'Neal completed construction on a round-stern juniper boat designed for commercial use. Warren decided to purchase the boat and he named her *Pearl*, after his wife Pearl Daniels O'Neal. In typical fashion he fished the *Pearl* for a couple of seasons at Dykstra's canal and then at the Oregon Inlet Fishing Center. In 1951, he decided to make some modifications that would improve her versatility. He added 5 feet to her length, squared the stern and changed the interior to better accommodate sportfishermen. Captain O'Neal described the *Pearl's* conversion from commercial to sportfishing: "I had her rigged for shrimping and when that was over, I'd take the mast out, mount some chairs and run parties." After a few more fishing seasons with the *Pearl* and ever increasing requests for sportfishing charters, O'Neal made another transition that set the stage for the entire boatbuilding industry on the Outer Banks.

Top • 335: The Pearl after Warren O'Neal modified her for sportfishing. She was lengthened by five feet and the stern was squared. Oregon Inlet Fishing Center, circa 1956. Bottom • 336: *The Sportsman with Captain Omie Tillett at the helm, backs into her slip at the Oregon Inlet Fishing Center. This boat was built by Captain Warren O'Neal and is the predecessor of the Carolina-style sportfishing boat. 1961.*

During the late 1950s, Warren was encouraged by other charter fishermen to build a boat using the new design and building techniques that were coming out of Florida. In 1959, Warren opened O'Neal Boatworks on the Manteo waterfront and his first client was good friend and fellow fisherman Captain Omie Tillett.

While charter fishing in Florida during the winter, Captain Tillett visited Rybovich Boatworks and was very impressed with their sportfishing vessels. Their boats featured a broken sheer line and sleek inset cabin. Rybovich was also using the

Left • 337: *Captain Warren O'Neal stands in front of the Mel-O-Dee on the Manteo waterfront. 1962.*

S-frame in the hull to provide shape and more interior room for the cabin.

Captain Tillett described the design to Warren and the two made a trip to Norfolk to look at a Rybovich sportfishing boat. Captain O'Neal also liked the new style and he started preparations for Omie's new boat called *Sportsman*.

Acknowledged as the first local boat builder to "put his boat on paper," Warren drew sketches, plans and even built scale-models of the hull to make sure the lines and proportions were correct. Most other boat builders used the "rack-of-the-eye" method. In his customary humble manner, Warren explained that he had to see how a boat was going to look before he built her because he was not as smart or talented as other boatbuilders.

Among the design innovations utilized by Captain O'Neal in the *Sportsman* were a broken sheer line, deep-Vee forward, S-frame, and inset cabin. He also added a Harkers Island flared bow and an exaggerated tumblehome.

Unlike most of the other boatbuilders of that era, Warren preferred the sharp entry, or deep-Vee forward hull. In a 1987 interview, O'Neal reflected on this innovation: "The first boats I built were all flat-bottomed. I started putting a deep-Vee into the hulls of the bigger boats because it just seemed to me like they needed it. I had been running boats all my life and I knew what it took to make them efficient."

Along with a deep-Vee, O'Neal's boats flattened toward the stern to accommodate the weight of larger engines and to handle better in following seas. "You sort of flatten out the Vee as you move aft. You don't want too much Vee at the stern of a big boat or she won't run right. It takes a lot of power to push a deep-Vee hull," O'Neal said.

Text continued on page 164

Right • 338: *The Mel-O-Dee was the charter boat of Captain Buddy Cannady. She is showing off her new name behind Warren O'Neal's boat shop on the Manteo waterfront. 1962.*

Top • 339: *Warren O'Neal poses in front of the* Jersey Devil *at his Manteo shop. 1968.* Middle Left • 340: *An IGFA world record marlin, 1,128 pounds, is hoisted onto the* Jersey Devil. *Hatteras, June 5, 1975.* Middle Right • 341: *Warren O'Neal and his wife Pearl after a day's fishing at Wimble Shoals on the* Pearl II. *Oregon Inlet Fishing Center, September 20, 1965.* Bottom • 342: *Captain Omie Tillett takes the* Olive E III *out for her maiden voyage with Warren O'Neal in the cockpit. Manteo, 1964.*

Top Left • 343: *Bettie Kellogg christens the* Sea Byrd *as Captain Warren O'Neal looks on. Manteo, 1963.* Top Right • 344: *Two Warren O'Neal boats run side by side. The Pee Wee, top, and Pee Wee, Jr. are excellent examples of Captain O'Neal's work. Manteo, circa, 1967.* Bottom Left • 345: *Captain Warren O'Neal works on a skiff in his Manteo boat shed. Circa 1970.*

Bottom Right • 346: *The Nat II takes her maiden voyage down the Manteo waterfront. Circa 1972.*

Top Left • 347: *Warren O'Neal works on a model of the* Nat II *at his home in Manteo. Circa 1970.* Top Right • 348 *Captain Warren O'Neal at the helm of his charter boat the* Pearl II. *Oregon Inlet, circa 1968.* Bottom Right • 349: *A fishing party with two marlin caught on the* Pearl II *with Captain Warren O'Neal, back right. Oregon Inlet Fishing Center, September 4, 1967.* Bottom Left • 350: *Captain Warren O'Neal, center, peeks between two marlin caught on the* Pearl. *Oregon Inlet Fishing Center, circa 1957.*

Top • 351: *Captain O'Neal returns to the Oregon Inlet Fishing Center on the* Pearl II. *Circa 1968.* Middle Left • 352: *Father of the Carolina-style sportfishing boat, Warren O'Neal. Manteo, circa 1980.* Middle Right • 353: *Captain O'Neal leaves his Manteo workshop with his tools in hand. Circa 1976.* Bottom • 354: *Warren O'Neal considered the 46-foot sportfishing boat* Lady B *to be one of his best hulls. Manteo, circa 1975.*

In the fall of 1960, Warren O'Neal began construction on the *Sportsman* with the help of Omie Tillett and Lee Perry. She was launched in the spring of 1961 and a new standard for Carolina sportfishing boats was established. Omie recounts that some even called the *Sportsman* an "O'Nealovich" because it was Warren's adaptation of a Rybovich.

After the *Sportsman*, Warren built a 37-foot charter boat for Captain Buddy Cannady called *Mel-O-Dee,* as well as a number of other boats including *Olive E III, Olive E IV, Olive E V, Nat II, Rebel, Pee Wee, Little Jeanie, Islander, Mini Pearl*, and his favorite, *Lady B.* Warren O'Neal also built the *Jersey Devil* that once held the 80-pound line class IGFA World Record blue marlin, a 1,128-pounder, caught at Hatteras.

In 1964, Warren built his own charter boat, *Pearl II,* and he continued to charter fish at Oregon Inlet until his retirement in 1976. Captain O'Neal died in 2000 at the age of 90. In all, he built more than 25 magnificent boats from 1959 until 1976 at his little boat shop on the Manteo waterfront. Captain Warren O'Neal is remembered as the "father of the Carolina style," but he is equally respected for his character and integrity.

Top • 355: *Noted captain Sambo Tillett cleans a channel bass on the stern of his charter boat,* Waterwitch. *Wanchese, circa 1939.* Bottom • 356: *The Tillett family includes, left to right, Omie, Tony, Sarah Wynne and Sam. Manteo, circa 1948.*

Among the most legendary sportfishing and boatbuilding families on the Outer Banks are the Tillets—Sam, Omie and Tony. There's even a saying around the docks at the Oregon Inlet Fishing Center, "If you ain't fishing with a Tillett, then you ain't fishing." The facts support this claim since the collective sportfishing experience of Sam, Omie and Tony Tillett totals more than 150 years and counting. This respected threesome has been an integral part of the Outer Banks sportfishing and boatbuilding heritage since the mid-1920s.

Sam "Sambo" Tillett, the family patriarch, was born in 1907 and began commercial fishing in Pamlico Sound during the mid-1920s. In the 1930s, Sam adapted his shad boat so he could carry sportfishing parties to Oregon Inlet. A group of six fishermen paid a total of $10 per day to catch large channel bass, up to 60 pounds, and bluefish, up to 18 pounds, on hand lines and simple reels with no drags. As sportfishing began to expand in the late 1930s, Sam increased his fee to $15 per day for a party of six and his reputation continued to spread. He was recognized among his peers as one of the premier fishing guides on the northern Outer Banks.

Omie Tillett was born in 1929 and, like his father, he showed an interest in sport-fishing at an early age. When he was 10 years old, Omie began to rig baits, tend lines and clean fish on Sam's charter boat, the *Spur*. In 1949, at the age of 20, Omie became captain of his first charter boat, *Jerry Jr.* Charter fishing was becoming a viable seasonal business and a charter fleet began to develop. Sam and Omie helped lead the transition from a loosely formed assemblage of boats docked in Dykstra's canal to an organized fleet at the Oregon Inlet Fishing Center.

Top • 357: Captain Omie Tillett, left, and mate Sunny Briggs, right, with a day's catch on the Sportsman. *Oregon Inlet Fishing Center, 1965.* Bottom *• 358: Captain Omie Tillett backs the* Sportsman *into her slip beside Captain Sam Tillett's charter boat* Tony. *Oregon Inlet Fishing Center, 1962.*

Since charter fishing was seasonal, many captains moved their boats to Florida and chartered there in the winter. Omie spent several years fishing in Florida until 1960 when he decided to stay home and work with Warren O'Neal on his new boat. This collaboration that resulted in many of the design innovations that are incorporated into today's Carolina-style sportfishing boat.

Omie continued to work for Warren O'Neal through the winter of 1973. The following year, he ventured out on his own with the formation of Sportsman Boatworks. His first boat was *Miss Boo* followed by *Gal-O-Mine, Skylark, Sportsman, Temptation, Carolinian, Brothers Pride* and *Mary I.*

Top • 359: Omie Tillett and the famous charter boat Carolinian *at Sportsman Boatworks in Manteo. 1978.*

Bottom • 360: Omie Tillett, back left, and Tom Daughtry, pose with a school group in front of the Carolinian. *Manteo, 1979.*

Unfortunately, Omie developed a severe allergic reaction to the new epoxies and resins used in boatbuilding, and in 1981 he sold Sportsman Boat-works to long-time employee Tom Daughtry. The shop was moved from Manteo to Wanchese where Daughtry built several boats including *Pescador* and *Never A Doubt* under the Sportsman Boatworks name. Daughtry closed Sportsman in 1990 and a boatbuilding legacy came to an end.

Omie continued to charter fish from Oregon Inlet where he became a mentor and role model to many of the younger captains. He started a tradition of blessing the fleet every morning just as the boats cleared the inlet. The charter captains slowed and waited for Omie's invocation before proceeding for their day of fishing. Even though the prayer included a different message every day, it always contained a reference to our abundant natural resources, good weather, great fishing and the safety of families back on shore. This tradition has spread around the world and Omie is still called on to lead prayers at tournaments and other special events where fishermen gather.

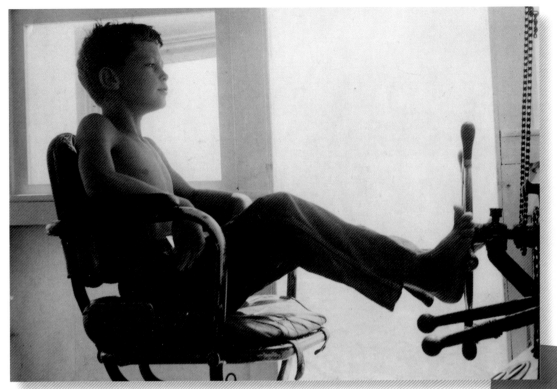

Text continued on page 172

Top • 361: *"Captain" Tony Tillett runs the charter boat* Jerry Jr. *with a fishing party headed for Oregon Inlet. 1949.*

Bottom • 362: *Tony Tillett, age 7, struggles to hold a dolphin as brother Omie helps from behind. Dykstra's canal, 1947.*

Tony Tillett, Omie's younger brother, was born in 1940. At the age of 8, Tony began helping his father Sam Tillett at Dykstra's canal on a boat named the *Spur.* When he was 9, Tony carried his first fishing party to Oregon Inlet for channel bass. Standing on a drink crate to see over the wheel, Tony followed Sam closely all day. By the time he was 12, Tony was guiding fishing parties to the inlet by himself.

During his teenage years, Tony fished with Omie and his uncle Chester on one of Sambo's boats named for him, the *Tony.* He continued to hone his fishing skills under the tutelage of Sam and Omie until he became a full-time charter captain in 1962 when he purchased the *Carrov* from Carson Stallings.

Tony wanted to rename his boat calling her the *Carolinian.* He had bought the letters for the stern and had already removed *Carrov* but he hadn't gotten around to nailing the new letters in place, a practice the Coast Guard was enforcing at the time. As a cutter approached one day, Tony was forced to dive overboard and nail the name *Carolinian* to the stern. Although he was 30 miles offshore when this happened, he did get the name changed in time and Tony embarked on a celebrated charter fishing career.

Many of the great charter captains in today's Oregon Inlet charter fleet, as well as several more around the world, were nurtured as mates under the guidance of Captain Tony Tillett. Few fishermen will ever match his experience or fishing prowess.

Top Left • 363: *The Carolinian, with Omie Tillett, kneeling on the bow, and Tony Tillett, at the stern, on the road from Manteo to Wanchese where she will be launched. May, 1979.* Bottom Left • 364: *Captain Tony Tillett with his charter boat Carrov just before changing her name to*

the Carolinian. Oregon Inlet Fishing Center, 1962. Top Right • 365: *Omie Tillett, left, and Tony Tillett pose with the Carolinian just before she goes overboard. Wanchese, 1979.* Bottom Right • 366: *The father and son fishing team, Captain Sambo Tillett and Captain Tony Tillett, display two marlin. Oregon Inlet Fishing Center, 1957.*

Top Left • 367: *The charter boat* Miss Boo II, *built for Captain Arvin "Porky" Midgett, was the first boat built by Sportsman Boatworks. Wanchese, 1974.*

Middle Left • 368: *The charter boat* Gal-O-Mine *was built for Captain Allen Foreman by Omie Tillett. She returns to the Oregon Inlet Fishing Center after a successful day of fishing. 1975.*

Bottom Left • 369: *The* Mary I, *now the* Barbara B, *was the last boat built by Captain Omie Tillett. Manteo, 1974.* Right • 370: *One of Captain Omie Tillett's most famous charter boats was the* Temptation. *She prepares for launch in Wanchese. 1978.*

Top Left • 371:

Captain Tony Tillett

backs the Carolinian

to the fuel docks at the

Oregon Inlet Fishing

Center. Captain Bobby

Sullivan on the Wahoo

is just pulling away.

1973.

Top Right • 372: *The Carolinian returns to the Oregon Inlet Fishing Center. 1964.* Bottom Left • 373: *The Carolinian returns with 17 release flags after a great day offshore. 1979.* Bottom Right • 374: *Captain Tony Tillett, kneeling left, and brother Captain Omie Tillett, kneeling right, each landed a marlin. Oregon Inlet Fishing Center, June 8, 1972.*

Top Left • 375: *The Cherokee with Captain Sheldon Midgett, left, and a catch of striped bass. Manns Harbor, circa 1973.* Bottom Left • 376: *Captain Sheldon Midgett, left, and son/mate Mike Midgett, second from left, pose with fishing party and marlin caught on the Fish-N-Fool. Oregon Inlet Fishing Center, 1975.*

Bottom Right • 377: *Captain Sheldon Midgett on the* first *Fish-N-Fool returns to the Oregon Inlet Fishing Center. 1972.*

Another colorful and respected charter captain and boatbuilder on the northern Outer Banks is Sheldon Midgett. Born in 1929 at Manns Harbor, Sheldon began commercial fishing as a teenager. He fished pound nets and gill nets around Roanoke Island using an old shad boat until he was old enough to join the Merchant Marine. During this service, Sheldon's deep appreciation and

Left • 378: *Captain Sheldon Midgett, standing left, and son Mike Midgett, kneeling, with a fisherman and marlin caught on the* Fish-N-Fool II. *Oregon Inlet Fishing Center, September 2, 1977.* Right • 379: *Captain Midgett on the third* Fish-N-Fool. *Oregon Inlet Fishing Center, circa 1988.*

love for the ocean intensified. Upon his return to Roanoke Island, Sheldon resumed his work on the water as a commercial fisherman.

In 1961, Midgett decided it was time to return to the ocean and he acquired a boat slip at the Oregon Inlet Fishing Center. He started carrying inshore charters for rockfish, bluefish and channel bass on his first boat, the 26-foot *Baby Duck.* Captain Midgett quickly became accepted as a member of the Oregon Inlet fleet and he started filling in on offshore charters. Sheldon soon was able to purchase a well-known charter boat, the *Cherokee,* and he fished aboard her for several years. Sheldon then purchased the *Kay* and he captained this vessel for a couple of more years.

Like many of the other charter captains, Sheldon Midgett worked during the winter months in local boatbuilding shops where he easily mastered carpentry skills. He struggled, however, with the conceptual aspects of boat design until a chance meeting on Harkers Island.

Midgett was returning from a vacation when he decided to swing by Harkers Island to see where the fabled backyard boatbuilders worked. As he drove around, he noticed an old man working on a beautifully proportioned skiff under a tree in his yard. Sheldon stopped, introduced himself and the two men fell easily into talk of boatbuilding.

Captain Midgett worked his way over to the skiff and decided that the lines and proportions were superb but the workmanship was some of

Top • 380: *The charter boat* Stormy Dutchess, *built by Sheldon Midgett, is launched at a ramp beside the airport on Roanoke Island.* 1974. Bottom • 381: The Fish-N-Fool *with Captain Buddy Davis at the helm and mate Dean Johnson, on the bow, returns to the Oregon Inlet Fishing Center with nine release flags. Circa 1973.*

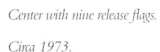

the worst he had ever seen. Soon the discussion got around to how to "lay out a boat." The old man took a stick and drew some figures in the dirt to explain how he set up battens and frames to get the right proportions. Captain Midgett sat in amazement since this was the first time he really understood how to build a boat. He reportedly said that he learned more about boatbuilding in 30 minutes, from drawings in the dirt, than he had in 20 years of building boats.

The old boatbuilder was Captain Stacy Guthrie, and he was almost blind when he met Sheldon. Even though his carpentry skills had failed, his enthusiasm and expertise were as sharp as ever and he made a tremendous impact on Captain Midgett. Armed with a new understanding, Sheldon returned to Roanoke Island where he started construction on a small fishing boat named the *Tilley B.*

Sheldon Midgett then constructed his famous charter boat, the *Fish-N-Fool.* He followed this boat with the *Fish-N-Fool II* and then, on his third charter boat, he returned to the first name, *Fish-N-Fool.* Captain Midgett was noted for construc-tion innovations that saved time and materials. His boats were also known for their strength and ride.

Top Left • 382:

Captain Sheldon

Midgett on the

flybridge of the Fish–

N-Fool. *Oregon Inlet*

Fishing Center, 1989.

Top Right • 383:

The Fish-N-Fool II

with Captain Sheldon

Midgett, returns

through Oregon Inlet.

Circa 1987. Bottom • 384:

Captain Sunny Briggs on the

Sea Fever. *This boat was*

built by Sheldon Midgett.

Oregon Inlet, 1973.

Captain Midgett was a mentor to many of the famous contemporary boatbuilders on the northern Outer Banks including Buddy Davis, Billy Holton and Paul Spencer. One of Sheldon's last boats was the 55-foot charter boat *Sizzler* that he built with his son-in-law Paul Spencer.

Sheldon Midgett is affectionately known as "Papa Shel" even though he was a stout, burly man with a rough exterior. He was fearsome to his mates but he was highly regarded as a boatbuilder and fisherman. He is one of many boatbuilders who have not received the recognition they deserve.

Captain Midgett died in 2004 at the age of 75. His career on the water was marked by many years as a charter captain at the Oregon Inlet Fishing Center and as a Roanoke Island boatbuilder. Papa Shel represents the best characteristics of a generation past.

Pioneers on the Southern Outer Banks

Julian C. Guthrie is among the most accomplished and widely known builders of sportfishing boats on the southern Outer Banks. Julian was born in 1914 on Harkers Island. His father is John Henry Guthrie and his grandfather is William Henry Guthrie, both boatbuilders and commercial fishermen.

Julian grew up on Harkers Island at a time when boatbuilding was at its zenith. He learned to efficiently use a hatchet, saw, adz and hammer as tools of the trade, and he became so successful that he was in demand even at a young age. Just to prove that he could build a boat, Julian constructed his first vessel in 1926 at the age of 12. This craft was a small wooden sailing skiff the family used to reach their fishing camp at Cape Lookout and for transportation around Harkers Island.

Julian also had a special talent for selecting just the right trees for fashioning the keel, frames, ribs and planks. He looked for wood that had a straight grain without many knots or splits, called "wind shakes." Since the wood used for boatbuilding grew locally on Shackleford Banks, Harkers Island or in the mainland swamps, Guthrie was often chosen by other boatbuilders to search out just the right trees.

Julian Guthrie worked with, and was trained by, the most talented craftsmen on the southern Outer Banks. Among this list of boatbuilders are Brady Lewis, Stacy Guthrie, Clem Willis, Lloyd Willis, Earl and Aredell Rose, and James T. Gillikin.

Top • 385: *Hi-Tide Boatworks with a commercial vessel under construction and a sportfishing boat being outfitted. Williston, circa 1960.*

Bottom • 386: *Captain Julian Guthrie in his Hi-Tide Boatworks shop. Williston, circa 1985.*

In the late 1940s, Joe Whitley formed West End Boatworks on Harkers Island and he employed the best builders from the community. Brady Lewis was hired as the manager, and other craftsmen included Julian Guthrie, Chauncey Guthrie, Clem Willis and Cletus Rose. Whitley also owned a lumberyard so he had access to the juniper, cypress and pine used by boatbuilders. West End Boatworks primarily built commercial vessels but they also built sportfishing boats including the *Mary-Z* that in 1957 landed the first blue marlin caught from Morehead City.

In 1951, Julian Guthrie recruited his 17-year-old nephew Will Guthrie to work at West End Boatworks. Will quickly acquired the necessary carpentry skills and he

Top • 387: *Sportfishing boat under construction at Hi-Tide Boatworks. Williston, 1961.*

Bottom • 388: *Interior of Julian Guthrie's boat shed with a sportfishing boat under construction. Williston, circa 1961.*

became an outstanding boatbuilder. Will Guthrie is now one of the most widely known and respected of all the boatbuilders on the southern Outer Banks.

Julian Guthrie started Hi-Tide Boatworks in 1958 on the waterfront in Williston shortly after West End Boatworks went out of business. Among the talented boatbuilders who worked at Hi-Tide Boatworks were Terry

"Tuck" Guthrie, Woody Hancock, William Reed Willis, Earl Rose, Lonnie Gillikin, Heber Guthrie, Chauncey Guthrie, and "Danny Boy" Lewis. The first sportfishing boat they built was a Morehead City charter boat, the *Bunny*, for Delmas Lewis. More than

30 sportfishing boats and even more commercial boats were built at Hi-Tide Boatworks from 1958 through 1985, when Julian retired. The 72-foot *Allison* was the largest sportfishing boat built by Julian Guthrie and was one of three boats with that name constructed for Wesley Wilson of Tampa, Florida. The last sportfishing boat Julian built was the *Blue Marlin* in 1984.

In 1993, the North Carolina Arts Council Folk Heritage Award was presented to Julian Guthrie in recognition for his contributions to the boatbuilding heritage of North Carolina. Julian died in 1998, but his legacy lives on through the many craftsmen who learned the trade from this legendary boatbuilder.

Will Guthrie operated his own boat shop, Will's Boatworks, on Harkers Island from 1966 until 1986. He built more than 30 sportfishing, commercial and party boats during that time and he implemented many new design and construction techniques. Examples of boats Will Guthrie built include the party boat *Carolina Princess* for Woo Woo Harker in 1970, charter boats *Sea Whisper* and *Sea Wife IV* and a private sportfisherman, *Atlantus*. With a lifetime of experience and an outstanding reputation in boatbuilding, Will Guthrie has served as a consultant for boatbuilders from around the country.

Text continued on page 180

Top Left • 389: *The private sportfishing boat* Miss Complexion *leaves Williston on her maiden voyage. Circa 1967.* Top Right • 390: *The interior of the* Miss Complexion *included the latest technology and custom fabrication. Circa 1976.* Bottom • 391: *The Morehead City charter boat* Bunny *was built by Hi-Tide Boatworks. Circa 1958.*

Top Left • 392: *Will Guthrie works on the stern of a sportfishing boat at the Hi-Tide Boatworks shop. Circa 1984.*

Top Right • 393: *Noted boatbuilder Will Guthrie checks on the fabrication of a sportfishing boat. Circa 1990.*

Bottom Left • 394: *Standing on the bow of the Bob-N-Tim, Will Guthrie oversees her launch. Williston, circa 1965.* Bottom Right • 395: *The* Bob-N-Tim *overshadows a commercial fishing skiff. Williston, circa 1965.*

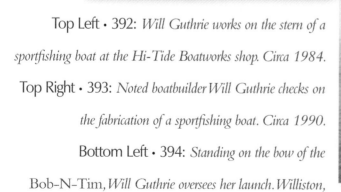

Top Left • 396: *Will Guthrie launches the sportfishing boat* Capt. Buck *from Will's Boatworks. Harkers Island, 1968.* Top Right • 397: *The charter boat Sea Whisper was built by Will Guthrie for Captain Arnold Tolson at Hatteras. Harkers Island, 1972.* Middle Left • 398: *The Miss Jill is launched on Harkers Island. She was built by Will Guthrie at Will's Boatworks. 1974.* Middle Right • 399: *Will Guthrie launches the Sea Foam from Will's Boatworks. Harkers Island, 1970.* Bottom • 400: *The charter boat Sea Wife IV, built by Will Guthrie, heads offshore with a fishing party. Circa 1978.*

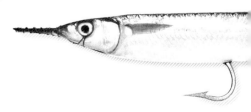

Another family of boatbuilding pioneers on Harkers Island, the Gillikin brothers, were legendary in the early development of sportfishing boats. James T. and Paul Gillikin began a family tradition of building sportfishing boats and world-renowned party boats that continues today.

Top • 401: View of Gillikin Brothers Boat Yard on Harkers Island. 1957. Bottom • 402: The Morehead City charter boat Cottonwood *was built at Gillikin Brothers Boat Yard. Harkers Island, 1954.*

James T. Gillikin was born in 1920 and began building boats in 1946 with Brady Lewis, pioneer of the flared-bow boat. Together they constructed quality commercial vessels made of heart pine, juniper and mahogany ranging in length from 28 feet to more than 50 feet. During a six-year period, Gillikin and Lewis built approximately 40 boats, many of which are still in use by local commercial fishermen.

In 1951, James T. Gillikin was joined by Clem Willis, another exceptional boatbuilder, and together they built commercial vessels for two years. In 1953, James T. and Paul Gillikin formed the Gillikin Brothers Boat Yard on Harkers Island. The era of private sportfishing boats was just beginning and the Gillikin brothers were among the first local builders to enter this market. They were contracted to build 12 recreational fishing boats during their first two years of operation, one of which was the Morehead City charter boat *Cottonwood*, built in 1954.

With a new surge of business, James T. and Paul Gillikin hired Brady Lewis as the yard foreman and brother Vance Gillikin as a boatbuilder. Other local carpenters who worked at Gillikin Brothers Boat Yard include Lonnie Fulcher, Alvie Fulcher, Ralph

Left • 403: *Gillikin Brothers Boat Yard prepares to launch a sportfishing boat. On Harkers Island a boat launching was so important that school classes often attended. Over 200 people witnessed this event. 1955.*

Hamilton, Mervin Rose, Hallas Rose, George Rose, James Allen Rose, Sam Salter, Harold Guthrie, David Lewis and Terrell Scott. Gillikin Brothers Boat Yard continued to build boats until James T. Gillikin's retirement in 1971. With as many as six party boats under construction at one time, James T. Gillikin estimated that more than 100 boats were built at the Harkers Island boat yard during his 18-year tenure.

During the 1950s and 1960s, Gillikin Brothers Boat Yard was especially noted for their custom party boats, many of which are still in use. Among these vessels are the *Viking*, 1960; *Teal*, 1961; *Miss Regnilles*, 1961; *Ranger III*, 1963; *Capt. Joe II*, 1964; and *Captain Ben Litwin*, 1965. They also built custom sportfishing vessels on Radio Island in Beaufort with the name Gillikin Craft. Fishermen around the world are still enjoying their use.

The Gillikin Boat Yard overcame several tragedies including the electrocution of Paul in 1961, two devastating fires and a flood. James T. Gillikin died in 2004 and a generation recognized for building some of the most notable sportfishing vessels and party boats in the world had passed on. Their legacy will be long remembered and celebrated. The family boatbuilding traditions are being continued by a new generation of Gillikin craftsmen on Harkers Island.

Text continued on page 186

Top Right • 404: *The Gillikin Brothers Boat Yard crew poses with a sportfishing boat. Standing, left to right is: Vance Gillikin, Ralph Hamilton, an unidentified worker and Clem Willis. Kneeling left to right is: Paul Gillikin, Mervin Rose, James T. Gillikin and Hallas Rose. These great craftsmen built many classic Carolina-style sportfishing boats. Harkers Island, 1956.*

Below • 405: *The* Jon-Lee II *on her maiden voyage to the Morehead City waterfront. 1955.*

Middle Right • 406: *A young boy is selected from the group to christen the* Jon-Lee II. *Harkers Island, 1955.*

Bottom • 407: *The water flies as the* Jon-Lee II *slides down the rail. Harkers Island, 1955.*

Top Left • 408: *A sportfishing boat is framed up inside Gillikin Brothers Boat Yard. Harkers Island, circa 1972.* Middle Left • 409: *Interior of Gillikin Brothers Boat Yard with three party boats under construction. The Gillikin's made some of the most beautiful party boats in the world. Many are still in use today. Harkers Island, circa 1965.*

Above • 410: *The Gillikin Boat Yard crew pulls another sportfishing boat into the water at Harkers Island. 1956.* Bottom • 411: *A classic Harkers Island sportfishing boat is launched at Gillikin Brothers Boat Yard. 1956.*

Top • 412: *The party boat* Ranger III *on her maiden voyage from Harkers Island. Circa 1963.*

Middle Left • 413: *The Sea Dragon is under construction. This party vessel shows the plank-on-frame construction technique used at the Gillikin Brothers Boat Yard. Harkers Island, 1962.*

Middle Right • 414: *The party boat* Capt. Stacy *is almost ready for launch from the Gillikin Brothers Boat Yard. Harkers Island, 1971.*

Bottom Left • 415: *The maiden voyage of the* Capt. Stacy *as she heads to Morehead City. 1971.*

Bottom Right • 416: *The party boat* Dolphin *is launched from Gillikin Brothers Boat Yard. Harkers Island, 1957.*

Top Left • 417: *James Rose stands in front of the famous Rose Brothers Boatworks shop on Harkers Island. 1967.* Top Right • 418: *Earl Rose working at his band saw in the Rose Brothers Boatworks yard. Harkers Island, circa 1959.* Bottom Left • 419: *A sportfishing boat is launched from Rose Brothers Boatworks. Harkers Island, circa 1960.* Bottom Right • 420: *The sportfishing boat Roc-Lo is under construction at Rose Brothers Boatworks on Harkers Island. Circa 1956.*

Top • 421: Earl Rose and Robert Rose work on the Miss Rose, a commercial boat. Harkers Island, circa 1974. Bottom • 422: A Rose Brothers sportfishing boat cruises in Florida. Their sportfishing boats were popular with fishermen along the entire East Coast. Circa 1965.

Earl and James Rose were also boatbuilding pioneers on Harkers Island during the dawn of sportfishing boats. Earl was born in 1908 at Salter Path in Carteret County. His family moved to Cape Lookout in 1909 and on to Harkers Island in 1918. James was born three years later in 1921.

Earl began building sail skiffs and workboats with his father, Aredell, in 1928 and he served as an assistant to Brady Lewis. James Rose also started boatbuilding at an early age and the two brothers formed a partnership in 1946 called Rose Brothers Boatworks. In 1948, they built their first private sportfishing

Top • 423: *Earl Rose works on the bow stem of a boat in his backyard boat shed. Harkers Island, circa 1972.* Bottom • 424:

The 63-foot sportfishing boat Virginia Lady *was built by the Rose Brothers on Harkers Island. 1973.*

boat for Allan C. Smith, an advertising executive from West Palm Beach, Florida. They went on to build the 74-foot yacht *Atlas,* the 56-foot party boat *Caralan,* the 42-foot sportfishing boat *White Porpoise,* the 65-foot *Virginia Lady,* and the Morehead City charter boat *Dreamo Lu,* among many others. In all, James Rose reported that the Rose Brothers Boatworks built more than 500 boats of all types during its 33-year history.

Calvin and Halsie Rose joined Earl and James at Rose Brothers Boatworks during the 1960s, and in 1972, they branched off and started Rosecraft Boatworks on Harkers Island. Rosecraft was noted for its fine sportcruisers and fishing boats.

Top • 425: *The crew at Rose Brothers Boatworks poses in front of their shop. From left to right are: Peter Willis, Calvin Rose, James Rose, Halsie "Fin Boy" Rose, and Earl Rose. Circa 1969.* Bottom • 426: *The charter boat Twins was built by the Rose Brothers for Homer Styron at Hatteras. The Twins was one of the boats that marked the transition from commercial craft to sportfishing vessels. Hatteras, 1958.*

When James died in 1979 at the age of 58, Earl lost interest in the business and only built one more boat, a 39-foot round-stern trawler for his son Robert. Earl Rose died in 1981 at the age of 72. The Rose brothers are key figures in the heritage of boatbuilding on the North Carolina Outer Banks. Their talents and skills are evident in their boats and they were pioneers in the early years of sportfishing boats.

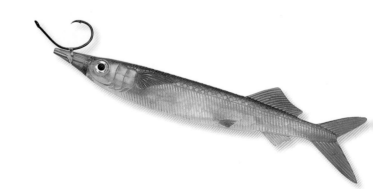

[CHAPTER SEVEN]

Building a Legacy

Building a Legacy

Given enough time on the water, the right location, the necessary angling skills and a lot of luck, an avid marlin fisherman may be fortunate enough to encounter a giant fish once in a lifetime. Much as they had for Santiago in Ernest Hemingway's *The Old Man and the Sea*, these factors came together for Sam Stokes off Oregon Inlet in the "Graveyard of the Atlantic" on August 8, 1978. An epic battle ensued.

Stokes, captain of the charter boat *Fight-N-Lady*, did not experience Santiago's string of bad luck, 84 days without a fish, but he had not boated a marlin over 400 pounds all summer and he didn't like it. Some big ones had been caught, but none on the *Fight-N-Lady*. To make matters worse, Sam's reputation was at stake. He had always been recognized as a serious fisherman with an innate talent for catching fish, so much so that he was nicknamed "Goldfinger" by the other charter boat captains. His luck was bad enough that summer that some even kidded about having his nickname revoked. Not exactly words of encouragement.

With most of the charter fleet heading to the southeast toward Cape Hatteras, Captain Stokes and Captain Nevin Wescott Jr., on the *Sundancer*, decided to take a chance and fish northeast of Oregon Inlet. Like Santiago, they wanted to try a little farther offshore than usual, to the 100-fathom line, and maybe find a big one in waters not often fished.

It was a perfect morning as the *Fight-N-Lady* and *Sundancer* cleared the sea buoy and Sam wondered if this might be the day that his luck would change. The ride offshore was a little longer than usual but still uneventful. Captain Stokes and Captain Wescott slowed when they found a temperature change and they put their lines overboard. They decided to troll close to each other in hopes of raising more commotion and maybe more fish. They were so close, less than 100 yards apart, that mates John Bayliss on the *Fight-N-Lady* and Marty Brill on the *Sundancer* could almost talk to each other. The breeze was calm out of the northeast and the ocean was flat. It was going to be a great day of day fishing whether they caught anything or not.

By 9 o'clock, the *Fight-N-Lady* had settled in to a routine when Captain Stokes spotted a large, dark shadow behind the starboard teaser. He yelled for John to get ready. It was a marlin, a big marlin. The big blue followed the teaser for what seemed like an eternity without making a move. Her huge fins were so far out of the water that Captain Wescott and Marty Brill could see them from the *Sundancer*. Sam jerked on the teaser and the marlin disappeared. After a few long seconds, a terrific spray of water erupted behind the starboard bait, a skirted ballyhoo rigged on a 50-pound class reel and number 10-wire leader. The reel was screaming as John grabbed the rod from its holder and set the hook.

It was a perfect morning as the Fight-N-Lady *and* Sundancer *cleared the sea buoy and Sam wondered if this might be the day that his luck would change. The ride offshore was a little longer than usual but still uneventful.*

Like all great captains, Sam immediately began directing traffic and John was doing exactly the right things. The angler, an Air Force fighter pilot just back from military duty, was in the chair and he had control of the rod. So far, so good. Now it was time to settle down for a battle, and with a fish this big, Sam guessed it might be a long one.

After an hour, Sam radioed Nevin and the two talked about the size of the marlin. Captain Stokes didn't get a good look but he knew it was big and he guessed that the marlin was more than 800 pounds, maybe a lot more. Since the fish didn't jump right away, neither captain could be sure. By one o'clock, and still no sighting of the fish, the estimates started to grow. Now it was wait and see.

At 2:30, the marlin was still deep and not giving an inch. Captain Stokes had tried every trick he knew. Backing down, running side to side, more pressure, less pressure—nothing was working. Captain Wescott radioed to Captain Stokes that it was time to head for shore but he didn't want to leave the *Fight-N-Lady*. Sam reassured Nevin that they had plenty of fuel, the weather was perfect

Above • 427: *Captain Sam Stokes, left, and mate John Bayliss, right, pose with a fisherman and a sailfish caught on the* Fight-N-Lady. *Oregon Inlet Fishing Center, 1978.*

and they would be in shortly, so the *Sundancer* headed off to the west leaving the Sam and his fish all alone in the ocean.

The marlin was heading east and all the *Fight-N-Lady* could do was follow. They were now in very deep water over 12 miles from where the giant was hooked. After two hours, the fish turned back to the west and headed for shallower waters. Soon Sam found the *Fight-N-Lady* in 17-fathoms of water over 10 miles west of where the marlin was hooked. Ridges and canyons dot the bottom along this stretch and the marlin took advantage of the rips by tailing along in the current and saving her strength.

The angler, on the other hand, was fatigued and the muscles in his arm knotted up under the strain, but he refused to let anyone else have the rod. This was his fish. The equipment seemed to be holding up well but everyone on board was clearly tired.

By six o'clock, the fleet was back at the Oregon Inlet Fishing Center and most of the crowd had dispersed. Marty Brill, mate on the *Sundancer*, was eager to find out about the big marlin so he waited at the docks for the *Fight-N-Lady* to return. At nine o'clock, Marty raised Captain Stokes on the radio to check on their status. He was still hooked up and doing fine but there was no sign of the fish so they didn't know how big it was.

As Captain Stokes had not done much night fishing, this was a new experience. He had his lights on and he tried to keep the party focused on the fish, not on the eerie darkness and the quiet that surrounded them. Almost precisely at 11 p.m., the marlin stopped moving. Sam and John figured the giant was dead and they were bringing her up.

In no time, the fish appeared about 10 feet behind the transom and, as the light of a full-moon reflected off the marlin, everyone on the *Fight-N-Lady* saw for the first time what a giant they had tangled with.

When John Bayliss grabbed the leader, the marlin responded with ten or twelve of the most spectacular leaps that Captain Stokes has ever witnessed. He vividly describes the moonlight reflecting off the tremendous marlin as she tail-walked over a perfectly calm sea. Fortunately, the angler was ready and the fish remained on the line.

At 2 a.m., the 50-pound class reel finally had enough and seized up. In an instant, John Bayliss snipped the line, re-tied the marlin to an 80-pound class reel and the fight was renewed. Now the fish had worked the *Fight-N-Lady* almost back to the exact spot where they started this battle.

At 5 a.m., Captain Stokes radioed to the Fishing Center that they were still hooked up and finally seemed to be gaining ground. The anticipation grew among the other captains and they offered encouragement to the *Fight-N-Lady*. Sam's voice seemed to reflect a renewed confidence.

Around 7:30 a.m., the tired marlin came up alongside the boat. This was the first time that Captain Stokes had a glimpse of the fish in the daylight and he was staggered. He estimated the marlin's weight at 1,200 pounds or more. Sam radioed the fleet about his estimate and everyone was ecstatic.

The *Sundancer* was headed straight for the *Fight-N-Lady* to offer assistance and support, just as they had done the day before. Captain Wescott arrived around 8 a.m. and he too spotted the fish. Nevin agreed with Sam—the fish was over 1,200 pounds.

At 8:30 a.m., twenty-three and a half hours after the giant was hooked, the *Fight-N-Lady* had the marlin alongside. Just as John Bayliss grabbed the leader, the marlin made a great lunge. As if in slow motion, the number 10-wire leader separated and in an instant the blue marlin was free. A few strokes of her giant tail fin and the great marlin disappeared into the depths.

The *Fight-N-Lady* was silent. What could be said? The angler, crew and marlin had fought a good fight and, this time, the marlin won. Sam returned to the docks as Santiago returned to his village: without his quarry and possibly without ever having another opportunity to land such a magnificent fish. He had, however, regained his confidence and restored his reputation. Sam Stokes was "Goldfinger" once again.

Above • 428: *The* Fight-N-Lady, *with Captain Sam Stokes at the helm and mate John Bayliss, standing right, returns to her slip at the Oregon Inlet Fishing Center, 1978.*

Overview

The period from 1970 through 1985 marked the rapid growth and development of the Carolina-style sportfishing boat along the Outer Banks. During this time many innovations occurred both in construction techniques and in boat design. Fabrication using jigs became popular, cold-molding using plywood with glues and epoxies evolved, hulls were modified to generate greater speeds, interiors were designed with more space and amenities and electronics took a significant leap forward.

Top • 429: *Mate Buddy Davis, kneeling left, and Captain Omie Tillett, kneeling right, pose with a fishing party and their catch on the* Sportsman. *Oregon Inlet Fishing Center, August 8, 1965.* Bottom • 430: *Captain Buddy Davis at the helm of the Sheldon Midgett built charter boat* Fish-N-Fool. *Oregon Inlet Fishing Center, 1975.*

Many legendary boatbuilders emerged during this period. On the northern Outer Banks were Buddy Davis, Billy Holton, Buddy Cannady, Bobby Sullivan, Ricky Scarborough, Sunny Briggs, Paul Mann and Irving Forbes. The southern Outer Banks also produced many legendary boatbuilders

including Vance, Ricky and James Gillikin, Lloyd and Alex Willis, Terry Guthrie, Jamie and Houston Lewis, and Myron and Buddy Harris.

The construction of Carolina-style boats during this period also shifted away from building sportfishing boats with a charter boat finish to building sportfishing yachts. The reputation of Carolina boats was enhanced and the boatbuilders of this era brought quality to the forefront of their work.

Northern Outer Banks

One of the most widely known and accomplished of all North Carolina boatbuilders is Buddy Davis. Born in 1948 on Roanoke Island, Davis began working on a charter boat at the Oregon Inlet Fishing Center in 1962 when he was 14 years old. During his apprenticeship, Buddy learned the art of rigging baits, tying knots and working lines. He also became proficient at reading the water, putting out a spread of baits, fighting and gaffing fish and especially dealing with fishermen. He credits his teachers, some of the best captains in the Oregon Inlet fleet, with patiently sharing their knowledge and skills during his learning process. Davis worked with many of the great captains including Omie Tillett, Lee Perry and Warren O'Neal.

With an innate passion for fishing and a strong desire to learn the art of boatbuilding, Buddy Davis convinced Warren O'Neal to let him serve as an apprentice. On the northern Outer Banks, winter was boatbuilding time and Davis started with O'Neal in the winter of 1967. At first he was only allowed to clean the shop and pass materials to the carpenters but he was quick to absorb the why's and how's of boatbuilding. Even during his time off, Buddy Davis would come to the shop and watch for hours as O'Neal neatly cut and fitted juniper boards.

Warren O'Neal recognized the potential in Buddy Davis and he began to nurture his talents. Davis and fellow apprentice Stuart Bell, O'Neal's grandson, steadily progressed in the boat shop until they were bestowed with the honor and title of "Official Boat Sanders." And sand they did. All day, every day, they hand-sanded the wide juniper boards on a boat large enough to fill the entire shop. They sanded until

Top • 431: *The charter boat Capt. B.C. travels through Manteo on her way to launch. This was the first sportfishing boat built by Buddy Davis. Manteo, 1973.* Bottom • 432: *Captain Buddy Davis, left, and a fisherman display a marlin caught on the charter boat* Sportfisher. *Oregon Inlet Fishing Center, 1968.*

the boards were perfectly smooth and just when they thought they were through, Warren made them sand some more. Finally, after what seemed like weeks of sanding, O'Neal decided it was time to apply the first coat of paint. Then another coat was added and the Official Sanders had to start all over again.

Top • 433: *The* Pisces IV *is a contemporary sportfishing boat built by Buddy Davis. Oregon Inlet, 2005.*

Bottom • 434: *Two boats built by Buddy Davis running offshore. Oregon Inlet, 2004.*

After the third coat of paint was applied, the hull was finished and the two apprentices had learned a fundamental requirement of boatbuilding—hard work. Bell believes that this was Warren's subtle way to make sure that he and Davis understood the value of staying in college. They did.

Buddy Davis continued to work summers at the Oregon Inlet Fishing Center and in 1968 he became captain of his first boat, the *Sportfisher*. He worked for two more winters with Warren O'Neal before taking a job with Sheldon Midgett in the winter of 1970. During his tenure with Midgett, Buddy Davis learned the carpentry skills and construction techniques that provided a foundation for his extensive boatbuilding expertise. He credits Sheldon Midgett for teaching him how to efficiently build boats.

In 1973, Buddy Davis started Davis Boatworks in Manteo and like his mentors, he built boats only in the winter. His first boat, the *Capt. B.C.*, was built for charter captain Buddy Cannady. This 46-foot charter boat had a juniper hull and was built using the traditional plank-on-frame method. In 1974, Davis moved his boat shed to Wanchese where he built the *Bishop 2* with Billy Holton and Sunny Briggs.

During this time, Buddy continued to operate a charter boat at the Oregon Inlet Fishing Center and he honed his skills on the water. With a passion for boats, Davis studied how each boat in the fleet performed under a variety of sea conditions, and he learned from his fellow captains about the most desirable sea-keeping characteristics of each.

After the *Sportfisher*, Davis purchased the *Skipper* from Buster Hummer in Hatteras and he fished on this boat until 1975 when he sold her to fellow Oregon Inlet charter captain Charles Midgett. Davis then became captain of the *Fish-N- Fool*, built by Sheldon Midgett. He chartered on this boat

Top • 435: *The sportfishing boat* Tetelestai *cruises in the ocean just after clearing Oregon Inlet, 2005.*

through the summer of 1976 when he started building boats full-time.

In 1977, Buddy Davis was among the first North Carolina boatbuilders to experiment with diagonal juniper plank boats covered with fiberglass. In 1978, he switched to diagonal mahogany plywood covered with a fiberglass skin instead of juniper planks. A year later Davis changed to diagonal plywood covered with fiberglass and he achieved the strength and durability he was seeking at a better cost. Davis credits both Rybovich and Merritt, famous boatbuilders in Florida, with pioneering these techniques, and he acknowledges their significant influence on his boats.

In 1981, Buddy Davis began building boats using jigs instead of the traditional plank-on-frame construction techniques. Craig Blackwell, now a noted custom boatbuilder in Manns Harbor, was hired to help with the jig design. Soon Davis started using epoxy resins and glues common in cold-molded construction. In 1983, another transformation occurred as Davis entered the era of fiberglass molded, semi-custom sportfishing boats.

Bottom • 436: *Three Buddy Davis boats run along together. Oregon Inlet, 2005.*

Buddy Davis continues his tradition as a North Carolina boatbuilding pioneer with the fabrication of semi-custom sportfishing boats at his Wanchese plant. He has recently expanded his line to include a 28-foot and a 34-foot fiberglass sportfishing boat.

Since 1973, Buddy Davis has built more than 300 sportfishing boats ranging from 28 feet to over 80 feet, and he has introduced the Carolina flare to fishermen around the world. His skill as a boatbuilder and an innovator makes him one of the legends in the boatbuilding industry. Warren O'Neal paid Davis a noteworthy tribute in 1987 when he said: "Buddy is doing things with boats that we only dreamed about." Another local boatbuilder aptly measured Davis's impact and influence when he said, "As Buddy Davis goes, so we all go." Buddy Davis is a pioneer who has made a lasting impact on the Outer Banks boatbuilding and sportfishing heritage.

Billy Holton is another well-known and respected boatbuilder in Wanchese. Born on the north end of Roanoke Island in 1947, Holton began working on a charter boat at the

Top • 437: *Captain Moon Tillett, kneeling left, his son Billy Carl Tillett, kneeling right, and mate Billy Holton, standing, display bluefish caught on the charter boat* Ranger. *Oregon Inlet Fishing Center, 1961.*

Bottom • 438: *Mate Billy Holton, kneeling right, and Captain Buddy Cannady, kneeling beside Holton, pose with fishermen and their catch on the* Mel-O-Dee. *Oregon Inlet Fishing Center, June 28, 1963.*

age of 13. He served as a mate for six years working with captains Moon Tillett on the *Ranger*, Lee Perry on the *Deepwater* and Buddy Cannady on the *Mel-O-Dee*. In 1966, at the age of 19, Holton became captain on the charter boat *Sea Star*, formerly the *Chee Chee*. Billy operated the *Sea Star* from the Oregon Inlet Fishing Center during the summers and he worked with local boatbuilders during the winter.

In 1973, Billy Holton started Holton Boatworks and he constructed a famous Oregon Inlet charter boat, *Fireball*. In 1977, Holton built the first plywood jig boat built on Roanoke Island with the completion of *Fired Up*. Since jig boats are built "upside down," or with the keel up, rather than the traditional "right side up," or keel down, Billy expressed frustration with this new approach. He admitted that on occasion, when his workers were not around, he even stood on his head so he could visualize how the boat was coming along.

Billy Holton continued to captain a charter boat until 1980 when he purchased the workshop of Sheldon Midgett and started building boats full-time. He changed the name of his business from Holton Boatworks to Holton Custom Yachts, and he proceeded to build 35 offshore sportfishing boats. Billy Holton describes his boats as "stout and heavy, with extra bulkheads and stringers, in order to withstand the punishment of higher speeds in heavy seas." He recently completed construction of the new *Carolinian* for Captain Tony Tillett, the *Playmate* for Captain Billy Baum and the *TFB* for a private owner.

To get the precise shape, proportions and hull characteristics, Billy Holton and Greg Bell collaborate to create their own computerized designs that are customized for each boat and owner. Billy is involved in the construction process from start to finish and the result is a classic, custom Carolina offshore fishing boat. He has obviously mastered the ability to picture how an upside-down hull will look as evidenced by the sleek lines and stylish appearance of his boats.

Another of the renowned charter boat captains and boatbuilders on Roanoke Island is Buddy Cannady, respectfully known as "Captain B.C." Born in 1932, Cannady has been a charter boat captain at the Oregon Inlet Fishing Center for 52 years. He is an integral part of the sportfishing and boatbuilding heritage of the northern Outer Banks.

Buddy Cannady acquired his first charter boat in 1954, a vessel built by Bob Scarborough called the *Snot*, and he built his first boat that same year, a flat-bottomed skiff used for duck hunting around Roanoke Island. Soon his juniper skiffs were in demand among other hunters and commercial fishermen and a boatbuilding business evolved. In 1960, Cannady began working with Warren O'Neal on large sportfishing boats and, like many others, he learned the art of boatbuilding from the master.

In 1962, O'Neal built a beautifully designed and crafted charter boat for Buddy Cannady called the *Mel-O-Dee*, named after Cannady's daughter. He hired sign painter R.O. Givens from Elizabeth City to paint her name on the stern. One Sunday, Givens, known for his creativity and artistic abilities, scrolled *Mel-O-Dee* across the transom and then added musical notes and bars. It was so different from the simple, traditional style of lettering that word quickly spread in the community about the unique painting. By the time Givens finished, a crowd of more than 50 people had gathered behind O'Neal's workshop just to see this work of art.

Text continued on page 202

Top • 439: *Boatbuilders Buddy Davis, left, and Billy Holton, right, in front of the sportfishing boat* Bishop 2. *Davis and Holton teamed with Sunny Briggs to construct this vessel. Wanchese, 1974.*

Bottom • 440: *The first boat built by Billy Holton,* Fireball, *returns to the Oregon Inlet Fishing Center with 13 release flags. 1973.*

Top • 441: *The Carolinian was built by Billy Holton for Captain Tony Tillett. Wanchese, 2005.*

Middle Left • 442: *Group photograph of three Holton Custom Yachts running together. 2005.*

Middle Right • 443: *Captain Buddy Cannady, center, with mates Billy Holton, left, and Jack Hoffler, right, pose with a blue marlin caught on the Mel-O-Dee. Oregon Inlet, July 5, 1963.* Bottom • 444: *This private sportfishing boat, TFB, was built by Billy Holton at Holton Custom Yachts. Wanchese, 2004.*

Top Left • 445: *Buddy Cannady works on the bow of a small sportfishing boat at his Manteo boat shed. Circa 1969.* Top Right • 446: *The yellow* Capt. B.C. *with Buddy Cannady at the helm displays 10 release flags. Oregon Inlet Fishing Center, circa 2000.*

Bottom Left • 447: *The sportfishing boat* Aggressor *appears from the boat shed of Captain Buddy Cannady. Manteo, 2003.* Bottom Right • 448: *The charter boat* Calcutta *was built by Buddy Cannady. Manteo, circa 1996.*

Left • 449: *Captain Bobby Sullivan poses with a marlin caught on his charter boat, the* Wahoo. *Oregon Inlet Fishing Center, August 2, 1971.* Right • 450: *Captain Bobby Sullivan, left, and Allen Hayman stand beside* Follow the Sun, *a sportfishing boat they built. Point Harbor, 1963.*

In 1973, Buddy Davis built a new charter boat for Buddy Cannady named the *Capt. B.C.* In 1974, Cannady opened Cannady Boatworks and began building sportfishing boats. His first boat was the 52-foot *Capt. B.C. II.* Buddy Davis, Sunny Briggs, Billy Holton and Rudolph Peele all pitched in to help with Cannady's boat. Cannady went on to build several boats with the same name that he used for a year or two and then sold. In the process, he learned from each one and made modifications if the boat did not perform as he thought it should. Now Cannady is working on hull number 29, all custom sportfishing boats over 52 feet in length. He has always used, and continues to use, the traditional juniper plank-on-frame methods that he learned from Warren O'Neal. In addition, Buddy Cannady has built more than 100 small hunting and fishing skiffs over the past 50 years. Capt. B.C. is one of the legends of boatbuilding and charter fishing and his reputation continues to grow.

Captain Bob Sullivan is an embodiment of the folk stories and legends surrounding boatbuilding and sportfishing on the northern Outer Banks. Not only is Sullivan an outstanding boatbuilder, but he is also a very well-liked and respected fisherman with a knack for helping people have a good time.

Born in 1940, Sullivan is the grandson of legendary boatbuilder Allen Hayman. In 1952, at the age of 12, Bobby started helping around Hayman's workshop as the charter boat *Carrov* was being built. Sullivan continued to work with his grandfather every day after school and during the summers, learning the skills necessary to build great sportfishing boats.

Bobby Sullivan also had a passion for offshore fishing. In 1968, he became captain of the charter boat *Wahoo* that he and Allen Hayman built. Sullivan continued to fish and build boats until Hayman retired in 1975.

Top • 451: *The* Miss Boo *is towed past Jockey's Ridge in Nags Head on her way from Point Harbor to Wanchese. 1989.* Middle • 452: *Bobby Sullivan built the charter boat* Smoker. *Oregon Inlet, circa 1990.* Bottom • 453: *The* Marlin Fever *was one of three boats with this name built by Captain Bobby Sullivan. Oregon Inlet, 1994.*

Sullivan then took over Hayman's old workshop at Point Harbor in Currituck County and began building boats on his own.

Sullivan uses the traditional juniper plank-on-frame techniques. His boats are stylish, functional and very well-constructed. Bobby has built 28 sportfishing boats from 46 to 62 feet, including noted charter boats *Marlin Fever, Temptress, Smoker, Sea Breeze* and *Miss Boo*. Captain Sullivan continues to charter fish, build boats and enjoy people. He ably carries on the family legacy and he is an important part of the North Carolina boatbuilding and sportfishing heritage.

Another legendary boatbuilder on the northern Outer Banks with a well-deserved worldwide reputation is Ricky Scarborough. Ricky is known for his beautifully designed and crafted custom sportfishing boats that exemplify the Carolina style. In recognition of his skill and talent, he is acknowledged among his peers as "a boatbuilder's boatbuilder."

Top • 454: *Ricky Scarborough, right, and Ricky Scarborough, Jr. work on a sportfishing boat at their boat shed in Wanchese. 2004.* Bottom Left • 455: *One of Ricky Scarborough's sportfishing boats, the* Inger, *runs toward the Gulf Stream. Oregon Inlet, 2004.* Bottom Right • 456: *The* Billfisher, *with lines overboard, settles in for a day of trolling. Oregon Inlet, 2005.*

Ricky was born in 1947 on the southern end of Roanoke Island in Wanchese. He grew up duck hunting and fishing in the marshes around his home where he nurtured an intense appreciation for the natural resources of the region. His grandfather, Bob Scarborough, was a noted boatbuilder and carpenter who was among the most prominent boatbuilders and craftsmen on the northern Outer Banks.

Ricky Scarborough started work as a commercial crabber and duck hunting guide at the Duck Island Club. The first boats he built were flat-bottomed skiffs used for crabbing and fishing and his own 17-foot tunnel boat for duck hunting in shallow water. Ricky's skiffs became very popular and were in great demand. In all, he built more than 100 of these stylish boats for commercial fishermen and hunters throughout the region. Ricky continued commercial fishing while pursuing his passion for duck hunting and boatbuilding. Unlike most of the other boatbuilders, he did not get involved in charter fishing.

Scarborough worked for Omie Tillett in the winter of 1976 and credits Captain Tillett as a major influence on his boatbuilding techniques. In 1977, Ricky founded Scarborough Boat Works in Wanchese. He began constructing 22- to 30-foot center console boats for sportfishing and hunting. These boats were juniper plank-on-frame and covered in fiberglass. In 1981, Scarborough built his first large sportfishing boat, a 44-footer named the *Poor Girl*, using the same techniques. Since that time, Ricky has built more than 80 custom boats that are prized by offshore sportfishermen around the world.

Ricky Scarborough has always used juniper for his boats, but he has adapted the construction techniques employed by his mentors to provide extra strength to the keel, ribs and stringers. Ricky now covers the juniper planks with diagonal plywood and fiberglass to make a strong, solid boat that has proven itself for more than 25 years in all kind of sea conditions.

Top • 457: *Ricky Scarborough built the sportfishing boat* Reel Affair. *2000.* Bottom • 458: *The private sportfishing boat the* Natural *running offshore. Ricky Scarborough boats are noted for their ride as well as their graceful lines. 1999.*

Fiercely independent and very astute, Ricky has charted his own course as a boatbuilder and has rightly earned the respect and acclaim that has followed. The accolades for boats built by Ricky Scarborough are lengthy but what might summarize them best is a comment made by a fellow boatbuilder when asked to describe the characteristics of a classic Carolina-style sportfishing boat. Without hesitation, he simply said, "It's a Ricky boat."

Top Left • 459: *Mate Sunny Briggs, right, with Captain Lee Perry on the charter boat* Deepwater. *Oregon Inlet Fishing Center, 1961.* Top Right • 460: *Captain Sunny Briggs, right, displays a 613-pound marlin caught on the* Bishop 2. *Oregon Inlet Fishing Center, September 24, 1975.* Bottom • 461: *The* Bishop 2 *with Captain Sunny Briggs on the bridge prepares for launch at Wanchese. 1974.*

Among all of the North Carolina boatbuilders, Sunny Briggs stands out as a link between the past and the future. He has been actively involved in every aspect of boatbuilding and sportfishing on the northern Outer Banks for almost four decades, and he has done so with great respect, even reverence, for the people and traditions that preceded him. Sunny is both a student and historian who easily talks of boats and boatbuilders, fish and fishermen. A sign over the entrance to his boat shop, a quote from Sunny's mentor, Captain Omie Tillett, sums up his philosophy: "There's a big difference between just getting a boat out and getting a good boat out... remember that."

Sunny Briggs was born in Elizabeth City in 1943 and moved to Manteo in 1954. He began working on the charter boat *Jinny B* with Captain Lee Perry at the age of 12, and continued to work during the summer as a mate with Captain Perry on the *Ponjola*, a boat built by Allen Hayman. Sunny also worked as a mate for Captain Omie Tillett and with captains Tony Tillett and Billy Baum. In 1965, Sunny became captain of his first charter boat, the *Jerry, Jr.,* with Marty Snow and Buddy Davis sharing time as his mate. This boat was originally a round-stern boat built by Jerry Turner of Wanchese and fished at Dykstra's canal by Captain Omie Tillett. In 1964, Bob Scarborough cut the transom out, squared the stern and made some cabin modifications so she would be better suited for charter fishing.

In 1968, Sunny became captain of the *Red Fin II,* which he fished from Oden's Dock in Hatteras from April through mid-July, and then from the Oregon Inlet Fishing Center until November. In 1970, Captain Briggs had Sheldon Midgett build the *Sea Fever,* which he operated until 1974 when he worked with Buddy Davis and Billy Holton to build the *Bishop 2.* In 1983 and 1984, Sunny captained the *Betcha* at the Oregon Inlet Fishing Center.

Throughout his charter fishing years, Sunny Briggs helped Omie Tillett and Sheldon Midgett build sportfishing boats in the winter. Sunny also constructed small skiffs, from 18 to 25 feet long, in his backyard. Equipped with an extensive knowledge of boats, boatbuilding and fishing, Sunny Briggs started Briggs Boatworks in 1985. His first boats were plank-on-frame sportfishing boats that ranged from 28 to 40 feet in length and were of exceptional quality and workmanship.

In 1993, Sunny Briggs ushered in a new era in boatbuilding when he became the first on Roanoke Island, and among the first anywhere, to construct a computer-designed

Above • 462: *The* Unexpected *displays the classic Carolina styling that Captain Sunny Briggs incorporates into his boats. 2002.* Bottom Left • 463: *The stylish* Smooth Operator, *built by Sunny Briggs, shows her Carolina flared bow and graceful lines. 2003.* Bottom Right • 464: *The* Ann Warrick *runs offshore. Built by Sunny Briggs, this private sportfisherman incorporates the latest technology and electronics in the industry. Pirates Cove, 2004.*

and router-cut sportfishing vessel. This development opened the door for custom boats designed and fabricated to precise measurements and strict tolerances. Computer-cut jigs eliminate what Omie Tillett describes as the saving grace for a boatbuilder: "The customer can't see both sides of a boat at the same time."

Sunny Briggs has built more than 50 offshore sportfishing boats since 1985, and he constructs each one with the care and attention that comes from taking pride in his work. Sunny has a deep appreciation for the heritage and culture of the Outer Banks, and he embodies the values and principles of the legendary fishermen and boatbuilders who came before him. Sunny Briggs has created his own legacy and he continues to be an important part of North Carolina's boatbuilding and sportfishing history.

Top • 465: *Paul Mann, left, worked as a mate on the charter boat* Sportsman *with Captain Omie Tillett, right. Oregon Inlet Fishing Center, 1975.*

Bottom • 466: *Paul Mann, center, checks the level on a large sportfishing boat. Manns Harbor, 2004.*

Paul Mann is another of the great boatbuilders on the northern Outer Banks with fishing in his blood. Born in 1959, Paul tagged along as a youngster with his grandfather, father and uncles who were all passionate fishermen. In 1972, Paul moved from Virginia to Nags Head and two years later, at age 15, he began working as a mate on a the charter boat *Playboy* at the Oregon Inlet Fishing Center. By 1977, Paul had become a capable fisherman, taking over as captain of his first vessel, the 32-foot *Lijo* at the Salty Dawg Marina in Manteo. In the winter of 1985, Paul worked with Sunny Briggs to build a sportfishing boat called the *Diamond Lady*. Mann continued to work with Briggs during the winter months until he started charter fishing full-time on a 42-foot Hatteras Yacht named the *Madd Hatter*.

In the winter of 1986, Paul assisted Captain Bobby Sullivan on his second charter boat with the name *Marlin Fever*. A year later, in 1987, Mann used Sullivan's workshop to build his first charter boat, appropriately called the *Madd Hatter*. With the success of

this vessel, Paul started Paul Mann Custom Boats in 1988 and built a workshop on his family homestead in Manns Harbor. Paul describes how he symbolically built his workshop

Top Left • 467: *The private sportfishing boat* Izzer, *with Captain Paul Mann at the helm, goes out for a trial run before delivery. Oregon Inlet, 2002.*

Top Right • 468: *Captain Paul Mann takes the* Line Dancer *out for a shakedown cruise. Oregon Inlet, 2001.*

Bottom • 469: *The* Hunter *was built by Paul Mann for Captain Walt Spruill. This sportfisherman is 72 feet long and she has the classic Carolina style. Pirates Cove, 2005.*

in seven days and on the eighth day he started building a boat, a 53-foot charter vessel named *Gannett*. Mann proceeded to build four more charter boats in a row: *Grand Slam*, *Tarheel*, *Outer Limits* and *Hog Wild*. Paul then built two private sportfishing boats—the *Blue Magic* and the first large sportfishing boat from the area to exceed 40 knots, the *Quintiki*. Since 1988, Paul has built 34 boats over 53 feet in length with the last two measuring just over 70 feet.

Paul Mann constructs his boats using the traditional juniper plank-on-frame techniques, but he takes this approach to another level. Mann builds his own battens, stations and frames for setting up the hull so he can customize the dimensions and shape of each boat. Then he builds the keel and ribs, attaches juniper planks with screws and epoxy, adds a layer of fiberglass, covers this with premium plywood, adds another layer of fiberglass and finishes with another layer of plywood. The hull is then faired with compound and painted with several coats of top-quality marine paint. The result is an exceptionally strong sportfishing boat with the traditional Carolina style.

Text continued on page 211

Top Left • 470: *Mate Irving Forbes, kneeling left, and Captain Omie Tillett, kneeling right, pose with two blue marlin each weighing over 400 pounds. Oregon Inlet Fishing Center, July 11, 1969.* Top Right • 471: *The sportfishing boat* Billfisher *was built by Captain Irving Forbes at his boat shed in Manteo. 1987.* Bottom • 472: *Mate Irving Forbes, kneeling, poses with Captain Omie Tillett, standing left, and an angler with a marlin caught on the* Sportsman. *Oregon Inlet Fishing Center, July 8, 1970.*

Every great boatbuilder has an extraordinary skill, and for Paul Mann it is his attention to the details of design and construction. Paul is a master at following the curves of windows, rounding steps and matching trim. He checks to see how water flows off surfaces so he can put drip moldings in just the right places, and he analyzes the ergonomics of fish boxes, tackle stations and helm pods for function and style. Paul constantly works to make the interiors of his custom boats tasteful and efficient. This attention to detail carries throughout the boat, from the engine room to the helm, and it demonstrates Paul's commitment to building a high-quality boat. Spend a few minutes with Paul Mann and it is easy to feel his passion for fishing and boatbuilding. It shows in his boats.

Another boatbuilder and fisherman who followed in the footsteps of his mentors is Irving Forbes. Born in 1951, Forbes moved to Wanchese in 1955 and started fishing with Captain Wayland Baum in 1960 on the charter boat *Mar-Anna* at the Oregon Inlet Fishing Center. Forbes also mated for Captain Chester Tillett on the *Tony* and for Captain Omie Tillett on the *Sportsman*.

Top • 473: *The old and new run side by side. The* Albatross II *and the* Fintastic, *built by Irving Forbes.* Hatteras, 1988. Bottom • 474: *The* My Boy IV *was built by Captain Irving Forbes in Manteo. 1993.*

After a five-year stint in the Coast Guard from 1970 to 1975, Forbes helped Omie Tillett finish the *Gal-O-Mine* at Sportsman Boatworks. That same year, 1975, Irving became captain of the *Gal-O-Mine* and worked at the Oregon Inlet Fishing Center. After the summer fishing season, Forbes went to work for Buddy Davis and built boats for 10 years.

In 1985, Irving Forbes started Forbes Custom Boats in the Manteo workshop of Warren O'Neal. He built many large sportfishing boats during this period, including the *Top Billin, Billfisher, Fintastic, My Boy IV* and *Southern Comfort*. Irving Forbes closed his shop in 1995 and collaborated with Paul Spencer at Spencer Yachts in Wanchese. Forbes continues to oversee the production at this prestigious boat yard.

Southern Outer Banks

Vance, Ricky and James Gillikin have carried on the family tradition of building outstanding sportfishing boats on Harkers Island since 1953. Vance began working with his brothers James T. and Paul Gillikin at Gillikin Brothers Boat Yard in 1954. Alongside a crew of outstanding carpenters and boatbuilders, Vance

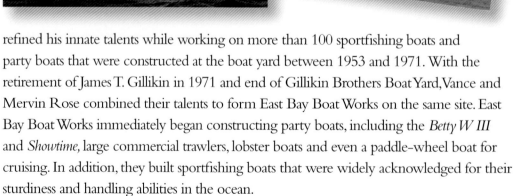

Top • 475: *Noted boatbuilder Ricky Gillikin stands atop a sportfishing boat at his East Bay Boatworks shop on Harkers Island. 1995.*

Bottom Left • 476: *The* Reel Dizzy *returns to Morehead City after a day of Gulf Stream fishing. Circa 2002.* Bottom Right • 477: *The East Bay Boatworks sportfishing boat* Sea Mistress *comes off a wave in rough seas. Cape Lookout, circa 2001.*

refined his innate talents while working on more than 100 sportfishing boats and party boats that were constructed at the boat yard between 1953 and 1971. With the retirement of James T. Gillikin in 1971 and end of Gillikin Brothers Boat Yard, Vance and Mervin Rose combined their talents to form East Bay Boat Works on the same site. East Bay Boat Works immediately began constructing party boats, including the *Betty W III* and *Showtime,* large commercial trawlers, lobster boats and even a paddle-wheel boat for cruising. In addition, they built sportfishing boats that were widely acknowledged for their sturdiness and handling abilities in the ocean.

Vance's sons, James and Ricky, joined him and Mervin Rose at East Bay Boat Works as soon as they were old enough. With the retirement of Mervin Rose, East Bay began to specialize in custom sportfishing boats. Ricky Gillikin led the design functions with Vance and James working in construction and fabrication. This team produced some of the most outstanding sportfishing boats on the southern Outer Banks. East Bay Boat Works built more than 200 boats during its 35-year history, and it is still constructing quality sportfishing vessels the Harkers Island way. Examples of their vessels include *Reel Dizzy*, *Thunder*, *Sea Mistress* and *True Grit*. Ricky developed a reputation for innovative designs that spread throughout the boatbuilding industry. Unfortunately, this very talented boatbuilder suffered an untimely death in 2004 at the age of 50.

In 2002, James Gillikin branched out and started another boatbuilding arm of the business called Gillikin Custom Boats. James builds 24- to 67-foot sportfishing boats using plank-on-frame techniques or cold-molded construction, depending on the request of the customer. His boats are crafted with the same expertise and proficiency carried by the Gillikin name.

Willis is another famous name in the history of boatbuilding on the southern Outer Banks. Lloyd Willis and his son Alex "Verl" Willis have enhanced a family boatbuilding tradition that started with Brady Lewis in the 1927. Lloyd Willis started building boats in the mid-1950s along the waterfront on Harkers Island. He built commercial fishing boats, skiffs and small fishing boats. Lloyd's son, Alex Willis, began helping out around the boat yard in 1960 when he was 11 years old. He described the early years working for his father in a workshop "as big as all outdoors, because it was." Like many other Harkers Island boatbuilders, out in the open was fine and the closer to the water, the better.

Top • 478: *The* True Grit *is a classic sportfishing boat built by Ricky Gillikin at East Bay Boatworks. Harkers Island, circa 1996.*

Bottom • 479: *James Gillikin stands beside his 26-foot sportfishing boat at Gillikin Custom Boats. Harkers Island, 2002.*

Lloyd taught by example and he was a great influence on Alex as he learned boatbuilding. They worked together for six years until Lloyd retired. Among the boats Lloyd Willis built was the *Harriet L.* for Captain Terrell Gould, a Morehead City charter captain.

Text continued on page 216

Top • 480: *A beautiful sportfishing boat leaves the Gillikin shop. Harkers Island, 2003.* Middle Left • 481: *James Gillikin checks the measurements on a sportfishing boat under construction. Harkers Island, 2002.* Middle Right • 482: *Lloyd Willis works on a small skiff at Willis Boatworks on Harkers Island. Circa 1978.*

Bottom • 483: *The charter boat* Harriet L. *is transported through Morehead City from Harkers Island. This boat was made for Captain Terrell Gould by Lloyd Willis. Morehead City, 1976.*

Top · 484: *Alex "Verl" Willis lays out a pattern for one of his sportfishing boats. Harkers Island, circa 1998.* Middle · 485: *Interior of Alex Willis Boat Construction shows the strip-plank construction that has made Harkers Island famous. Circa 1998.* Bottom · 486: *The Miss Caroline prepares for launch. She was built by Alex Willis. Harkers Island, circa 2001.*

Above · 487: *The Boss Lady is launched on Harkers Island. She will be outfitted by some of the best craftsmen on the Outer Banks. 1998.*

Top Left • 488: *Done Diggin was built by Alex Willis in his Harkers Island boat shed. Circa 1997.*

Top Right • 489: *The party boat* Lady Faye *was built by Alex Willis Boat Construction on Harkers Island. Circa 1994.*

Bottom • 490: *The plank-on-frame technique is used by Terry Guthrie in constructing his sportfishing boats. The blue tarp signifies that his boat is bigger than his shed. Harkers Island, 1998.*

Alex Willis founded Alex Willis Boat Construction and continues to build boats. He completed 13 party boats, including the *Lady Faye, Gulf Lady* and *Beverly B.,* and more than 80 custom sportfishing boats, including *Miss Caroline, Reel Attitude, Sea Bird* and *Enticer.* He has also built more than 40 commercial vessels. Alex Willis constructs his boats with cypress frames, juniper strips, fiberglass overlay and modern epoxies, glues and finishes. He continues to build traditional strip-planked boats that are both sturdy and functional.

One of the Harkers Island backyard boatbuilders who has been involved in constructing quality fishing boats for more than four decades is Terry "Tuck" Guthrie. His family lineage on the southern Outer Banks dates to Devine Guthrie, a whaler and boatbuilder from the 1800s.

Tuck was born in 1940 on Harkers Island and he started working at Hi-Tide Boatworks with legendary boatbuilder Julian Guthrie in 1960. Julian had already made the transition to sportfishing boats and Tuck was an important member of the crew who helped with the development of the "Guthrie sportfishing boat."

In addition to boatbuilding, Tuck worked as a mate on several charter boats during the summer until he started working at Hi-Tide Boatworks full-time. Tuck worked with Julian Guthrie for 27 years and together they built more than 50 large sportfishing boats and numerous commercial vessels.

From 1988 through 1999, Tuck worked in construction and at Parker Marine but continued to build boats in his spare time. In 2000, he returned to boatbuilding full-time when he started Guthrie Boatworks, still in his backyard on Harkers Island. He uses juniper framing and planking with traditional Harkers Island boatbuilding techniques while incorporating new materials into the exterior finishes of the hull. Tuck provides insight into his theory of boatbuilding when he says, "If your boat is not bigger than the shed, then your boat is too small." This is evidenced by the tarp attached to his workshop and remnants of trees he cut down just to get a new boat out of his yard.

In addition to the boats he built with Julian Guthrie, Terry Guthrie has built five private sportfishing and charter vessels since 2000. These include *Oodles*, *Point Runner* and *Virginian*. Now he just builds the hull and cabin, leaving the engines and finish work to others.

Guthrie's years of experience and his knowledge of boats are evident in his designs and craftsmanship. Terry Guthrie has taken "backyard boatbuilding" to another level.

Text continued on page 219

Top • 491:

Terry Guthrie, right, works amid the framing on a sportfishing boat. Harkers Island, 1998. Middle • 492: *Thank goodness for the Carolina flare. Terry Guthrie wriggles a large sportfishing boat out of his backyard. Harkers Island, 1998.* Bottom • 493: *The* Oodles *cruises down Bogue Sound on her maiden voyage. Morehead City, 2002.*

Top Right • 494: *Houston Lewis, left, Jamie Lewis, center, and James Lewis, right, work on the framing of a sportfishing boat. Harkers Island, 2002.* Below • 495: *A small sportfishing boat is ready for delivery in front of the Lewis Brothers Boatworks shop on Harkers Island. 2001.*

Middle Right • 496: *The Lewis Brothers Boatworks launches the sportfishing boat Southwind at Harkers Island. 1971.* Bottom • 497: *Houston Lewis, left, and Jamie Lewis, right, at work on a sportfishing boat. The Lewis brothers are master boatbuilders and craftsmen. Harkers Island, 2000.*

Left • 498: *Jamie Lewis shows the flare to an interested couple in his Harkers Island boat shed. 2001.*

Jamie and Houston Lewis, builders of classic Harkers Island style sportfishing boats, also carry on a family boatbuilding tradition. Their father, Burgess Lewis, was a well-known craftsman who built commercial fishing vessels along the shoreline with Brady Lewis, Stacy Guthrie and Clem Willis. Burgess was noted for construction techniques that provided some of the sturdiest and tightest boats ever built on the Island. Jamie and Houston learned these methods well. Their reputation for high-quality construction is widespread.

Jamie, born in 1939, and Houston, in 1944, were building boats by the time they were teenagers. In 1955, at the age of 16, Jamie built his first solo boat, a 15-foot cypress runabout for Lloyd Guthrie. Houston's first boat was a 17-foot juniper skiff, with a flared bow, that he built in 1961 at the age of 17. Since then the Lewis brothers have combined to build more than 200 commercial and sportfishing boats.

With more than four decades of experience each, Jamie and Houston Lewis need only hand-drawn sketches to create their vessels. The exception is an occasional shrimp trawler, and Houston has said that they have built so many trawlers that they don't even need the sketches. Jamie describes their boatbuilding approach as "rack-of-the-eye" design using traditional construction techniques. Their boats are in demand by both commercial fishermen and sportfishermen.

In 1985, Jamie and Houston formally named their business Lewis Brothers Boatworks. Jamie's son, James, has joined the crew and is ably carrying on the family tradition. They continue to build quality sportfishing boats that are crafted from start to finish using time-tested methods with great attention to detail. This has been the hallmark of Lewis Brothers Boatworks and their legacy will continue to grow.

Text continued on page 221

Top Left • 499: *Captain Buddy Harris, second from right, poses with a 310-pound marlin caught on the Offshore III. Morehead City, June 10, 1982.* Top Right • 500: *The sportfishing boat O Lucky Me was built by Myron and Buddy Harris at Harris Boat Works in Marshallberg. 1995.* Middle • 501: *Fishing party on the Offshore III with a nice catch. Morehead City, 1968.* Bottom • 502: *Captain Myron "Ace" Harris, left, on his charter boat Offshore. Morehead City, circa 1985.*

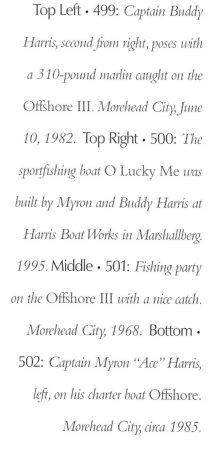

Left • 503: *Fishing party on the* Offshore, *with Captain Myron Harris, poses with a mixed catch. Morehead City, circa 1980.*

Bottom • 504: *The* Offshore III *was built by Myron and Buddy Harris in 1967. She is running out of Beaufort Inlet with Buddy Harris at the helm. 1985.*

Marshallberg is home to Myron "Ace" Harris and his son Buddy Harris, both well-known charter fishermen and boatbuilders. Myron was born in 1920 and during his teenage years he was a renowned baseball player, thus the nickname "Ace." He attended college on a baseball scholarship and became a math teacher after graduation. Myron began operating a charter boat, the *Sammy H.*, from Marshallberg during the summer of 1952. He continued to teach in the winter and charter fish in his time off. In 1956, Myron built his first charter boat called the *Offshore,* and, at age 13, Buddy started working as a mate on this boat.

Right • 505: *Captain Buddy Harris, kneeling center, and a fishing party on the* Offshore III. *Morehead City, 1968.*

In 1960, Myron retired from teaching to follow his dream. While operating his charter boat, the *Offshore*, he built the *Gale Ann*, a charter boat for Jimmy Harker on Harkers Island, and the Morehead City charter boat, *Ebb Tide*. In 1965, Myron and Buddy built the *Offshore II* and, a year later, they moved their boat from Marshallberg to the Morehead City waterfront. In 1967, Myron and Buddy formed Harris Boat Works in Marshallberg where they built a charter boat for Buddy called the *Offshore III*.

Since founding Harris Boat Works, Myron and Buddy Harris have built more than 30 sportfishing boats, mostly for charter fishing. Their sportfishing and boatbuilding legacy includes the *Virginian*, *O Lucky Me*, *Doghouse*, *Energizer* and *Catcher*, all built using plank-on-frame construction methods with contemporary epoxies, glues and finishes.

Myron Harris died in 2005 at the age of 83. Buddy Harris continues the charter fishing and boatbuilding heritage that started with his grandfather Sam Harris in the mid-1930s. Buddy remains a legendary character on the Morehead City waterfront. If only boats could talk!

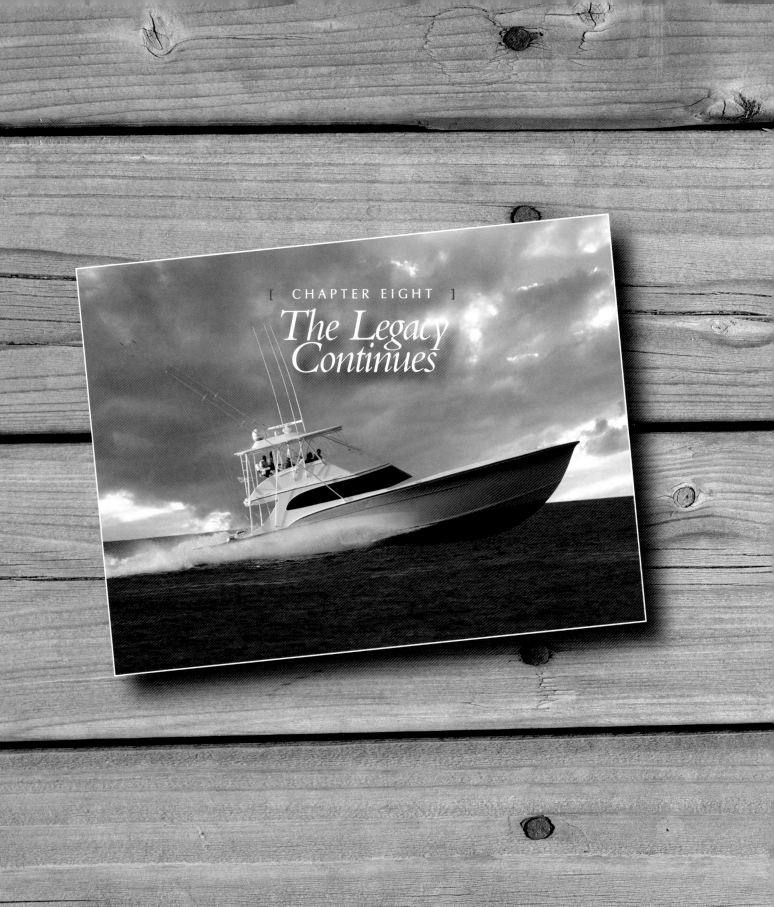

CHAPTER EIGHT

The Legacy Continues

The Legacy Continues

The small charter fleet at Grayson's Marina on Harkers Island sits silently on a beautiful, clear autumn afternoon in 1985. Captains Randy Ramsey and Jim Luxton relax on Jim's charter boat as they discuss what they will be doing in the coming winter months and, more important, what their future might be in the charter fishing business. Both are young men, in their early twenties, and they love the water, but charter fishing 170 days or more a year is a demanding lifestyle with a reward that is often more personal than financial. They have talked to all the old-time charter fishermen, and they know what lies ahead.

As they ponder their options, Randy suggests that maybe they should buy more modern boats so they can compete with the others in the fleet. Jim agrees and the tenor of the conversation becomes more animated. But how are they going to afford a new boat? They had no idea.

After a few more suggestions, the pair ended right back where they started. Randy surmised that he could go back to work with Myron and Buddy Harris in their Marshallberg boat yard; Jim figured he could probably commercial fish throughout the winter, just as he had done the previous year. They could guide a few duck hunting parties and resume charter fishing the following spring.

For some reason, this plan was not good enough for either of the two young men. If they couldn't afford to buy a boat, maybe they could build one. They could fish it for a couple of years and then sell it. Build an offshore fishing boat—it was a great idea, but with a limited knowledge of boatbuilding, just how would they do it?

Randy and Jim started researching the subject. They knew how boats handled from their charter fishing experiences and they agreed on the style of boat they wanted, so they turned to several local boatbuilders for advice. They visited Myron Harris, Julian Guthrie, Edward Davis and a few others to talk about boatbuilding and they were well received by each one. To get a better perspective, the pair decided to make a trip to Roanoke Island. They liked the style of boats being built on the northern Outer Banks, and besides, it was only a short trip.

As the two drove up the coast, neither was sure what kind of reception they would get since both were strangers to the region. Arriving on Roanoke Island, they stopped first at the boat shed of Warren O'Neal on the Manteo waterfront. Captain Irving Forbes, who was building a private sportfishing boat, now occupied the building. Randy and Jim introduced themselves and told Irving about their plans to build a boat. To their surprise, he welcomed them into his shop and spent several hours going over his designs and construction techniques. They crawled all over his boat and were free to ask any question. Irving suggested that they talk to Captain Buddy Cannady because he

If they couldn't afford to buy a boat, maybe they could build one. They could fish it for a couple of years and then sell it. Build an offshore fishing boat—it was a great idea, but with a limited knowledge of boatbuilding, just how would they do it?

Top • 506: Randy Ramsey, left, discusses the maintenance to be performed on his first boat, Sensation, at his Jarrett Bay facility. Beaufort, 2002. Bottom • *507: The private sportfishing boat Builders Choice is under construction at Jarrett Bay Boatworks. Williston, 1990.*

had constructed several charter boats and sold them after a year or two of fishing, just as they were planning. Captain Forbes provided directions and the pair headed off.

They found Cannady's shop just down the road and were greeted by the smell of juniper wafting from an old barn. They knew they were in the right place. Inside, they found Buddy Cannady in a contorted position lodged between the ribs of a giant sportfishing boat. If he could extricate himself, he said, he would be right out.

Randy and Jim looked around at the dirt floor and the dusty walls and figured if Cannady could build a boat, maybe they had a chance. Little did they know that Captain B.C. was one of the most knowledgeable and experienced boatbuilders in the region. He was also one of the most experienced charter captains, and his credentials belied his work environment.

Cannady spent a couple of hours with the duo and offered support and encouragement while he showed them his approach to boatbuilding. Randy and Jim could tell that Captain B.C. knew what he was talking about. This is how they wanted to build a boat.

Having taken enough time, the fledgling boatbuilders thanked Buddy and headed for the door. Cannady asked if they had talked to Omie Tillett. "Don't come this far without going to the summit," Cannady called out. It was just a few miles to the Oregon Inlet Fishing Center where Omie was out fishing, so they decided to take a chance.

Captain Tillett was offshore commercial fishing for King mackerel that day and wouldn't be in until dark, so Randy and Jim decided to wait at the landing just to meet him. It was twilight when Omie returned, and as he approached the dock he wondered who the two men were. He even left his engine running as a signal that he had many chores to perform. Randy and Jim introduced themselves and told Omie that they were charter fishermen and they wanted to build a boat.

They couldn't have said anything better. Captain Tillett shut down the engine on *Sportsman* and climbed onto the dock. Omie gave each one a bear hug as if he had just found a long, lost brother. They were stunned, but he does, in fact, consider all fishermen and boatbuilders to be brothers. After a brief conversation, Omie invited them to come by the next day to talk about boats.

Randy and Jim showed up at the appointed time to meet Captain Tillett. They talked about boatbuilding and Omie shared his ideas and building techniques. He even divulged some of his philosophical "nuggets" while providing insight into his strong faith and great inner strength.

After a couple of hours with Omie, the pair was overwhelmed by his knowledge and generosity and they thanked him for his time. As they moved towards the door, Omie motioned to Randy and said, "Go over to see my friends Tom Daughtry and Glenn 'Peanut' Haught. They have something for you." Omie provided directions and offered to help in any way as they started their business.

Just around the corner from Omie's house in Wanchese was Sportsman Boatworks. Omie started this company and he had built some of the most famous sportfishing vessels on the Outer Banks. He sold it to Tom Daughtry after developing allergies to the resins and dust.

Tom welcomed Randy and Jim and spent several hours openly showing them the details of boatbuilding. As Randy and Jim prepared to leave, Tom said that Omie wanted to make sure they went to see Peanut.

When they arrived at Glenn's house, Randy and Jim were warmly greeted. "A friend of Omie's is a friend of mine," he said.

The conversation quickly focused on boats. Peanut was the designer for several of Omie's boats and he talked easily about proportions, scale and functionality. Randy and Jim were impressed with what they had seen and heard, but they were still overwhelmed by the daunting task of building a boat. Where would they start?

They were ready to leave when Peanut informed them that he and Omie had decided to offer them the plans for Omie's famous charter boat, the *Temptation*, just to help them get started.

Randy said, "Great, that's a nice gesture but we can't afford it."

Peanut chuckled and replied, "How about $500, if you are interested?" "Interested? Where do we sign?" they said.

With the plans for the *Temptation* in hand, Randy and Jim rented the old Hi-Tide Boatworks building in Williston, once the boat shop of Julian Guthrie. As they made preparations to construct their first boat, Randy called West Marine Systems to order six barrels of epoxy. The salesman informed him that before he could send an invoice, he had to have a business name, one small detail they had overlooked. Randy held his hand over the receiver and turned to Jim. "What's our business name?" he asked. Through the large door at the end of the building they could see Jarrett Bay, and right then they decided to call their business Jarrett Bay Boatworks.

The conversation quickly focused on boats. Peanut was the designer for several of Omie's boats and he talked easily about proportions, scale and functionality. Randy and Jim were impressed with what they had seen and heard, but they were still overwhelmed by the daunting task of building a boat. Where would they start?

A little more than year later, in January 1987, Randy Ramsey and Jim Luxton launched their 53-foot charter boat the *Sensation*, a twin to the Oregon Inlet charter boat *Temptation*. Intended to be their only boat, the *Sensation* was the first of many finely crafted boats built by Jarrett Bay Boatworks. Randy freely credits Irving Forbes, Buddy Cannady, Tom Daughtry, Glenn "Peanut" Haught and several other generous boatbuilders with his success. He still holds a special admiration and respect for his friend and mentor, Captain Omie Tillett.

Overview

From the mid-1980s until today, custom boatbuilding on the Outer Banks has evolved into an industry with a world-class reputation. Boatbuilders have incorporated the classic Carolina styling with new materials and computer designs. They continue to explore new approaches to achieve strength, ride and efficiency in their custom boats.

From the mid-1980s until today, custom boatbuilding on the Outer Banks has evolved into an industry with a world-class reputation. Boatbuilders have incorporated the classic Carolina styling with new materials and computer designs. They continue to explore new approaches to achieve strength, ride and efficiency in their custom boats.

Boatbuilders who have emerged on the northern Outer Banks during this period include Buddy Smith, Craig Blackwell, Ritchie Howell, Paul Spencer, Bobby Croswait, Jim Sculley, Dean Johnson, John Bayliss and Glenn Bradley.

On the southern Outer Banks, Randy Ramsey, Gary Davis, Jamie Chadwick, Leonard Rigsbee, Billy Dupree, Robby Brittingham, Roy Barnes, Bill Schwabe, Mason Cox and Chip King have led the evolution of custom sportfishing boats.

These fine craftsmen have started their own sportfishing and boatbuilding legacy along the North Carolina Outer Banks.

Northern Outer Banks

Since 1984 and the start of Island Boatworks, Buddy Smith has been building sportfishing boats in the northern Outer Banks community of Frisco. Island Boatworks began when Smith and partner Mark Willis collaborated with a goal to build a fast, good-riding offshore sportfishing boat. Smith and Willis incorporated computer modeling and an analysis of weight distribution to locate the best position for the engines and fuel tanks. They also used the cold-molded techniques in the construction of their boats.

Buddy Smith fabricates the keel with 18 layers of laminated Douglas fir while the hull consists of three diagonal layers of premium plywood with fiberglass between each layer. Each boat is finished with epoxy, sanded and primed with six coats of primer. Two coats of color and one coat of clear sealant complete the exterior.

Unlike most of the sportfishing boats built on the Outer Banks, Buddy Smith designs a "reverse tumblehome" into his boats. The aft sections taper up and out rather than out and around like other builders. Smith believes this feature reduces drag against the water, producing a faster boat with the same horsepower.

Top Left • 508: *The 57-foot* Outlaw *was built at Island Boatworks. 1997.* Top Right • 509: *Buddy Smith working on a boat part at his drill press at his Island Boatworks shop. Frisco, 1998.* Bottom • 510: *Buddy Smith, Island Boatworks, built the sportfishing boat* Elixer. *2000.*

Buddy Smith has built 21 boats from 30 to 65 feet since 1984, including his first boat, the *Citation*. Among the others are *Delta Dawn, Excaliber* and *Elixer.* His son Joe has joined Buddy Smith at Island Boatworks, and they continue to build faster and more efficient sportfishing boats.

The community of Manns Harbor is home to Blackwell Boatworks. Craig Blackwell has been involved in boatbuilding since 1973 when he constructed sailboats in his native state of Michigan. He worked for West Marine Systems where he learned the cold-molding process and then moved to North Carolina in 1980 to work with Buddy Davis. Blackwell is an expert at setting up jigs and he willingly assisted other local boatbuilders with this process. Blackwell enjoys the camaraderie of the boatbuilding community on the Outer Banks, and his peers acknowledge him as an important part of this tradition.

Top •

511: *Craig Blackwell built the sportfishing boat C-Ya at his Manns Harbor shop. 2005.*

Middle • 512:

The sportfishing boat Lori D was built at Blackwell Boatworks. 1999. Bottom • 513:

The sleek sportfishing boat Triple A was built at Blackwell Boatworks. Manns Harbor, 2004.

In 1989, Craig Blackwell started Blackwell Boatworks and began building Carolina-style sportfishing boats. He creates his own hull designs that include more S-frame, tumblehome and hawk than other local boatbuilders. The combination of these features creates a distinctive style that sets his boats apart. In search of the right combination of strength and weight, Blackwell also experiments with exotic materials, composites and core materials.

Blackwell Boatworks has launched more than 50 boats from 28 to 78 feet during its 17-year history. Included in this prestigious list of boats are the *C-Ya*, *Triple A* and *Megabyte*. Craig Blackwell continues to build three or four boats each year while embodying the cooperative spirit prevalent among boatbuilders on the Outer Banks.

Ritchie Howell follows in the footsteps of other noted charter fishermen and talented boatbuilders. An avid fisherman, Howell became captain of the *Gannett* at the Oregon Inlet Fishing Center in 1982. He charter fished for 16 years and worked under the guidance of Bobby Sullivan and Paul Mann in their boatbuilding shops. During this time, he gained valuable experience and insight into the traditional Outer Banks boatbuilding process.

In 1998, Ritchie Howell started Carolina Yachts in Wanchese. He uses the cold-molded process and credits Paul Spencer with influencing his style and construction techniques. Howell's years of offshore fishing experience enable him to incorporate amenities designed for fishermen into each of his sleek custom boats.

Carolina Yachts has launched 10 large sportfishing boats from 47 to 65 feet, and three smaller boats of 28 to 32 feet. Each one has the trademark Carolina styling and sea-keeping abilities.

Paul Spencer has been involved in sportfishing and boatbuilding on the northern Outer Banks since 1968. Born in 1956 at Manns Harbor, Paul began working at the Oregon Inlet Fishing Center when he was 12 years old. He started with Captain James Mann on the inshore charter boat *Chris Ann* and then with Captain Chick Craddock on *Lollypop*. Spencer continued to mate on charter boats in the summer, including stints with captains Omie Tillett and Sheldon Midgett. He became captain of his first charter boat *Fish-N-Fool II* and later *Outlaw* in the early 1990s.

Along with his experience charter fishing, Paul Spencer worked with Billy Holton, Omie Tillett and Sheldon Midgett building boats in the winter. In 1996, at the urging of Sheldon Midgett, Spencer built his first boat, the *Sizzler*. Following the lead of Captain Buddy Cannady, Paul Spencer charter fished the *Sizzler* for a couple of years and then sold her. Buoyed by this success, Paul founded Spencer Yachts in 1999 and his next two boats, *Anticipation* and *Liquidator*, thrust him into full-time boatbuilding.

Text continued on page 233

Top Left
• 514: *The sportfishing boat* Rebel *running offshore. Ritchie Howell designed and constructed this vessel. 2003.*

Top Right • 515: *A Carolina-style sportfishing boat, the* Sea Warrior, *was built by Ritchie Howell at Carolina Custom Yachts in Wanchese. 2002.*

Bottom • 516: *The* Rebel *returns to port after a day of fishing. 2003.*

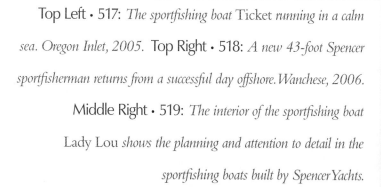

Top Left • 517: *The sportfishing boat* Ticket *running in a calm sea. Oregon Inlet, 2005.* Top Right • 518: *A new 43-foot Spencer sportfisherman returns from a successful day offshore. Wanchese, 2006.* Middle Right • 519: *The interior of the sportfishing boat* Lady Lou *shows the planning and attention to detail in the sportfishing boats built by Spencer Yachts.*

Bottom Left • 520: *Paul Spencer built the* Rumor Mill *at his shop in Wanchese. Circa, 2001.* Bottom Right • 521: *Paul Spencer stands beside the new pod drive system installed on a 43-foot sportfisherman just prior to launch. Wanchese, 2006.*

Spencer began building boats in his Manns Harbor workshop and has now added a major new facility in Wanchese. He has developed a production system that accommodates up to 14 custom sportfishing boats, in various stages of completion, at one time. His talented crew includes local boatbuilders Irving Forbes and Gerald Craddock, among many other fine craftsmen.

Above • 522: *Bob Croswait builds sportfishing boats from 26 to over 60 feet. This 29-foot boat has the same Carolina styling and characteristics as his larger boats. Wanchese, 2006.*

Paul Spencer credits Sheldon Midgett, Irving Forbes and Billy Baum for helping him get established as a boatbuilder, and he praises many others for their encouragement, support and sharing of information. With the completion of hull number 52, Paul Spencer is carrying on the Outer Banks boatbuilding tradition with great style.

Captain Bob Croswait has been working on and around boats for more than 30 years on the northern Outer Banks. Beginning in 1974 under the leadership of Buddy Cannady, Croswait learned the intricacies of plank-on-frame boatbuilding while constructing more than 30 sportfishing boats. Bob also worked under the direction of custom boatbuilder Billy Holton from whom he learned the cold-molded construction techniques. This combination of experience has provided Bob Croswait with a broad perspective on boatbuilding, allowing him to use either approach in constructing his custom sportfishing boats.

In addition to his boatbuilding experience, Croswait has considerable fishing expertise. He worked as a mate on the *Billfisher* with Captain Mike Merritt and then as captain of the *Challenger, Edge Runner, Limited Edition* and *Right Hook* over a period of 17 years at the Oregon Inlet Fishing Center. In 1999, Bob started Croswait Yachts and began building boats full-time. His workshop is located in Wanchese where he builds custom boats ranging from 27 to 67 feet in length. Croswait also offers custom repairs and renovations as a part of his enterprise. The influence of Buddy Cannady is apparent in the Carolina-style boats designed and built by Bob Croswait, evidence that the Outer Banks boatbuilding heritage continues to evolve.

Text continued on page 235

Top Left • 523: *Smaller sportfishing boats in the Carolina style have become very popular. Bob Croswait designed and constructed the Deja Blue. Wanchese, 2006.* Top Right • 524: *The sportfishing boat Striker was built by Bob Croswait. Wanchese, circa 2001.* Middle • 525: *A new 58-foot Sculley sportfishing boat gets a trial run. Wanchese, 2006.* Bottom • 526: *The sportfishing boat Water Witch was built by Sculley Boatbuilders in Wanchese. 2003.*

When Jim Sculley formed Sculley Boatbuilders in 1999, he was following his dream to build a great riding, custom sportfishing yacht complete with all of the amenities desired by offshore fishermen. Jim Polatty, a skilled boatbuilder who had been working for Davis Boatworks since 1984, joined Sculley, as did his son, Jimmy. Their first boat, a 58-footer named *Mick's Fin*, was the result of extensive design, testing and engineering along with the study and use of contemporary materials and finishes. Launched in 2002, this custom sportfisherman opened the door for subsequent boats including the *Wahoo, Rompeola* and *Water Witch*.

Jim and Jimmy Sculley were nurtured on the water, and both have a passion for sportfishing. Jim Sculley grew up fishing on his father's commercial fishing boat in Newport, California. After moving to the East Coast, he owned Fisherman's Wharf Marina at Rudee Inlet near Virginia Beach for 10 years. Jim and Jimmy often fished the waters out of Oregon Inlet where they developed an appreciation for the Carolina-style boats and the builders who made them. Jim Polatty added the engineering and boatbuilding experience to the Sculley team, and together they have built 14 custom sportfishing boats that are fished around the world. Using the cold-molded process, Sculley Boatbuilders stresses the importance of engineering and quality in its custom boats. Jim Polatty is proud that their boats are finished inside and out with the same attention to detail and craftsmanship.

Jim Sculley has broadened the legacy of Carolina-style sportfishing boats with a foray into the world of televised competition fishing on the ESPN Billfishing Extreme Release League. Team Sculley finished first in the 2004 competition on a 60-foot Sculley boat called *Waterproof*. With this success, Sculley Boatbuilders is poised to help move North Carolina boatbuilding to another level.

Top •
527: *A Sculley Boatbuilders sportfishing boat returns from a day of fishing. Oregon Inlet, 2005.*

Bottom • 528: *Jim Sculley is particularly proud of his custom interiors. A sailfish is depicted on etched glass as the salon of this Sculley sportfishing boat is readied for its owner. Wanchese, 2006.*

Top • 529: The master stateroom in a Johnson Boat Works sportfishing boat shows the attention to detail in Dean Johnson's work. Wanchese, 2005.

Another noted boatbuilder on the northern Outer Banks is Dean Johnson. Captain Johnson was born in Wanchese in 1953 and started working as a mate on the *Cherokee* with Captain Irving Williams in 1969. He then fished with Buddy Davis on the *Skipper* and with Buddy Cannady

Middle • 530: Dean Johnson takes one of his new custom sportfishing boats for a trial run. Wanchese, 2002. Bottom • *531: Mate Dean Johnson, left, and Captain Buddy Davis display a marlin Dean caught on the charter boat* Skipper. *Oregon Inlet Fishing Center, circa 1971.*

on the *Capt. B.C.* In 1977, Dean acquired his Captain's license and ran the *Streaker,* a Will Guthrie-built charter boat; the *Duke of Dare,* a Rose Brothers boat; the *Fight-N-Lady,* built by Sheldon Midgett; as well as the *C.J. IV* and the *Surfside,* both Ricky Scarborough boats.

Dean Johnson worked with Captain Omie Tillett to build the *Carolinian,* with Ricky Scarborough on the *Surfside* and with Paul Spencer on the *Reel Magic.* These fishing and boatbuilding experiences led to the start of Johnson Boat Works and Dean's first vessel, the *Top Shelf,* in 2002. Johnson was aided in the design by his father-in-law, Billy Baum, who has earned a reputation for his excellent boatbuilding knowledge and skills. Dean Johnson proceeded to build the *Easy Rider, Pipe Dream, Tough Catch* and *Reel Deal.* He is working on hull number seven. All of his boats are have been custom sportfishermen over 57 feet long. Dean describes his boats as "long and lean with a laid-back cabin and a great ride." His enthusiasm and approach to boatbuilding embodies the character of many others who preceded him. He uses his talents to carry on the Outer Banks traditions.

Captain John Bayliss has been a part of sportfishing and boatbuilding on the northern Outer Banks since 1975 when he was a mate on the Hatteras-based charter boat *Early Bird* with Captain Emory Dillon. Bayliss then worked with Captain Chip Shafer on the *Temptress* and with Captain Sam Stokes on the *Fight-N-Lady*.

In 1980, John Bayliss became captain of the *Tarheel*, a charter boat built by Ricky Scarborough. For 16 years, Bayliss fished charters and tournaments from Maryland to Mexico and developed a reputation as an outstanding fisherman and boat captain. In 1996, he became captain of the *Hatterascal*, the famous sportfishing boat for Hatteras Yachts, and his fishing reputation continued to grow.

Captain Bayliss decided to pursue his lifelong ambition to build custom fishing yachts. In 2002, he founded Bayliss Boatworks in Wanchese and immediately began construction on a 60-foot sportfisherman that he delivered in July 2003. Since that time, Bayliss Boatworks has completed six sportfishing yachts: *Uno Mas*, *Southpaw*, *Vintage*, *Old Reliable*, *Ultra* and *Canyon Express*. Each is constructed using computer-cut jigs and the cold-molded construction process.

Captain John Bayliss is passionate about fishing and boatbuilding. He utilizes the current computer technology to test his hull shapes, weight distribution and center of buoyancy. With years of experience on the water, John Bayliss understands the needs of offshore sportfishermen. He designs and builds quality, custom sportfishing boats to fit the needs of each client.

Glenn Bradley moved to the Outer Banks in 1975 and, four years later, began work in the Wanchese boat shop of Ricky Scarborough. Working under Scarborough, Bradley learned to build boats using plank-on-frame construction techniques. Bradley credits Ricky Scarborough with teaching him how to design and construct quality sportfishing boats.

In 1993, Bradley worked under the guidance of Captain Sunny Briggs where he learned how to construct boats using the jig techniques. He also credits Sunny with teaching him to ensure quality in the finishes and details of his boats.

Equipped with the knowledge and skills acquired from Ricky Scarborough and Sunny Briggs, Glenn Bradley began constructing small commercial skiffs. He built more than 40 of these popular juniper skiffs for fishermen and hunters. Bradley also helped out at several boat shops in the winter where he worked on 10 large sportfishing boats.

In 2004, Glenn Bradley started his own business, Bradley Custom Boats in Wanchese. His custom-built sportfishing boats, from 23 to 32 feet in length, are constructed using the plank-on-frame method.

Top • 532: *The* Reel Magic *a sleek sportfishing boat was designed and constructed by Dean Johnson at Johnson Boat Works. Wanchese, 2002.* Bottom • 533: *A Bayliss custom sportfishing boat, the* Ultra, *runs offshore. 2005.*

Text continued on page 240

Top Left • 534: *The sportfishing boat* Old Reliable *was constructed by John Bayliss at Bayliss Boatworks in Wanchese. 2005.*

Top Right • 535: *The private sportfishing boat* Southpaw *returns to Bayliss Boatworks after a trial run. 2004.* Middle • 536: *The interior of the* Southpaw *is elegantly appointed. John Bayliss is noted for his masterful design and quality fabrication. Wanchese, 2004.*

Bottom • 537: *Captain Omie Tillett christens the sportfishing boat* Ultra *as John Bayliss watches. Wanchese, 2005.*

Top • 538: *With its Carolina flare and S-frame, Glenn Bradley has a planked hull ready for the next step. Wanchese, 2005.* Middle • 539: *A 28-foot sportfishing boat is under construction at Bradley Custom Boats in Wanchese. 2005.* Bottom • 540: *A 26-foot sportfishing boat built by Glenn Bradley is ready to fish. 2005.*

Top Left • 541:

The beautiful master

stateroom in a Jarrett

Bay Boatworks

sportfishing boat is

custom designed and

fabricated with great

attention to detail and

function. 2005. Top

Right • 542: *A classic Carolina-*

style sportfishing boat built by

Jarrett Bay Boatworks runs hard

in the ocean. 2004. Bottom

• 543: *Randy Ramsey stands*

in front of a sportfishing boat

built at Jarrett Bay Boatworks.

Beaufort, 2005.

Southern Outer Banks

One boat-builder who has made a significant impact on the recent history of sportfishing and boatbuilding on the southern Outer Banks is Randy Ramsey.

Born in 1962, Randy knew that he wanted to be a charter fisherman even before he finished high school. He moved from Kinston to Morehead City in 1977 and immediately started pursuing his dream.

At the age of 18, Randy acquired his Coast Guard certification and enrolled in the diesel mechanics curriculum at Carteret County Community College. He was well on his way toward his goal of becoming a charter captain.

In 1983, Randy began his charter fishing career at Grayson's Marina on Harkers Island where he met Jim Luxton and the two decided to build their own charter boat. Randy had worked for Myron and Buddy Harris in the winter and he was familiar with boat construction. After talking with local builders on the Outer Banks, Ramsey and Luxton formed Jarrett Bay Boatworks.

In 1986, they rented the old Hi-Tide Boatworks building in Williston and in early 1987, launched their first boat, the 53-foot *Sensation*. The two then decided to build another boat when they were not fishing. Before long, they had two more orders for charter boats.

Their first private sportfishing boat was built in 1988, a 43-footer named *Bar None,* for Jack Huddle in New Bern. Randy also credits Huddle with providing support for Jarrett Bay Boatworks during their early years.

Several more charter and private boats were constructed at the Williston site until 1991 when Jarrett Bay Boatworks expanded and moved to Marshallberg. In 1993, Randy stopped charter fishing and began building boats full-time at this site. He also made a transition from plank-on-frame construction to cold-molded boats that same year. In 2001, Jarrett Bay Boatworks expanded again and established the Jarrett Bay Industrial Park near Beaufort.

During the past 20 years, Jarrett Bay Boatworks has constructed 54 classic Carolina-style sportfishing boats. Some of the great boatbuilding families of southern Outer Banks including Gary Davis, Keith Willis, Jamie Chadwick, Leonard Rigsbee, Robby Brittingham and Mason Cox have played important roles in creating the Jarrett Bay Boatworks legacy.

Jarrett Bay Boatworks now builds about four boats each year with the styling, attention to detail and craftsmanship that is a trademark of boatbuilders on the southern Outer Banks. Randy Ramsey is living his dream.

Top • 544: *The crew on the* Double Take, *a Jarrett Bay Boatworks sportfishing boat, fights a marlin. 2003.* Bottom • 545: *A Jarrett Bay Boatworks custom sportfishing yacht returns to Beaufort after a trial run. 2005.*

Top Left • 546:

The sportfishing

boat High Hopes

was built by Gary

Davis at Sleepy Creek

Boatworks. Marshallberg,

1990. Top Right • 547:

The Ms. Merle *is a 40-foot*

sportfishing boat built by Gary

Davis. 1994. Bottom • 548:

Gary Davis sands on one of

his early sportfishing boats

at Ray Davis Boat Works.

Marshallberg, 1982.

Gary Davis is a boatbuilder with a family heritage that dates through several generations on the southern Outer Banks. He began his boatbuilding career in Marshallberg in 1974 at the age of 16. Gary built a commercial skiff with the help of his grandfather, boatbuilding pioneer Ray Davis, and his uncle Edward Davis. He started work at Ray Davis Boat Works in Marshallberg in 1978 and mastered the building techniques for plank-on-frame construction.

In 1980, Gary Davis founded Sleepy Creek Boatworks and began building sportfishing boats, commercial vessels and sailboats using traditional techniques and designs. In 1989, Gary built his first boat on a jig, the *Laura J*, and then the *High Hopes*. Two years later, he started making all of his boats on a jig and constructing larger sportfishing boats. He built the *Fighting Lady*, *Bill Collector*, *Chaos* and *Blue Max*. Davis also built the party boat *Miss Hatteras* in 1992.

During the 18 years of Sleepy Creek Boatworks, Gary Davis built 52 beautifully designed and crafted boats at his Marshallberg boat shed. In 1998, he merged with Randy Ramsey at Jarrett Bay Boatworks where Gary Davis is now the production manager. Ray Davis would be amazed and proud if he could see the magnificent sportfishing boats that his grandson produces.

The Chadwick family—Eugene, Walter and Jamie—is another prominent boatbuilding family on the southern Outer Banks. Their boatbuilding lineage started with Eugene, born in 1918, who built commercial vessels along the waterfront on Harkers Island from 1935 until 1965 while working with the likes of Brady Lewis, M.W. Willis and the Rose brothers. Eugene started his own boat yard, Chadwick Boatworks, in 1955 across from Rose Brothers Boatworks, and he built his first sportfishing boat the same year.

Walter Chadwick, Eugene's son, was born in 1943 and started working at Chadwick Boatworks in 1956. Walter and Eugene constructed sportfishing boats and commercial boats until Eugene retired in 1965. During this 10-year period, they employed as many as 30 carpenters and built more than 100 boats, including many of the Morehead City charter boats. Eugene died in 1978, leaving the family's boatbuilding traditions to be carried on by Walter and Jamie.

Top • 549:

A stylish sportfishing boat built by Jamie Chadwick gets her finishing touches just before launch. 2005. Bottom • 550:

The boatbuilding crew at Chadwick Boatworks poses in front of a sportfishing boat. Left to right are Walter Chadwick, Eugene Chadwick, Gene Autry Willis, Frederick Willis, Buck Jones, Bobby Rose and Clifton Davis. Harkers Island, 1956.

Jamie Chadwick was born in 1966 and started working with Walter when he was 14 years old. In 1984, Jamie joined M. W. Willis and Sons Boatworks in their boat-repair business while building commercial boats from 22 to 37 feet in his backyard. In 2002, Jamie resurrected the name Chadwick Boatworks and opened his own boatbuilding workshop in Otway, on the road to Harkers Island.

A very talented boatbuilder with a hands-on approach, Jamie Chadwick is involved in every step of the construction process. He draws his own designs, scales his own measurements, builds his own jigs and cuts his own frames. He sands, planes, fiberglasses and paints, ensuring that only one boat is constructed at a time. His building techniques are derived from the skills he learned working with his father and from an innate understanding of boatbuilding. The result is a strong, sea-worthy and stylish Carolina sportfishing boat.

Text continued on page 245

Top Left • 551:

*Boatbuilder Jamie
Chadwick describes how
he designs and fabricates
his custom sportfishing
boats. Otway, 2005.*

Top Right • 552:

*Water curls up the side
of a Jamie Chadwick
sportfishing boat as she
heads offshore. Morehead
City, 2004.* Bottom •

553: *The Southern Exposure, built by Jamie Chadwick, gets a final wash down just prior to delivery. 2004.*

Captain Leonard Rigsbee is a charter fisherman and boatbuilder much like others before him. He started fishing in 1980 on the party boat *Carolina Princess* with Captain Woo Woo Harker. Rigsbee credits Harker with teaching him about offshore fishing and dealing with people on a charter boat.

Leonard Rigsbee progressed to become captain of his own charter boat, a 1971 Myron Harris-built craft called *Cap-N-Squid*. During the winter months, Leonard worked with Randy Ramsey at Jarrett Bay Boatworks.

Captain Rigsbee founded his boatbuilding company in 1998, calling it Cap-N-Squid as a tribute to his first charter boat. He began work on his new charter boat in 1998, appropriately named *Cap-N-Squid*, and launched her in 1999. Leonard charter fished this vessel for a year and then sold her, only to begin work on yet another *Cap-N-Squid*. He charter fished this boat until 2001 when he began building boats full-time.

Top • 554: *A large sportfishing boat awaits planking in the boat shop of Leonard Rigsbee. Otway, 2004.* Middle • 555: *The second Cap-N-Squid was built by Leornard Rigsbee with help from Will Guthrie. Leonard Rigsbee is at the helm of this charter vessel. 1999.* Bottom • 556: *The original Cap-N-Squid was a 42-foot charter boat built by Myron and Buddy Harris in Marshallberg. 1971.*

With the help of Randy Ramsey and Will Guthrie, Leonard Rigsbee also constructed *Westwind, Impulse, Sea Creature, Godspeed* and *Git-R-Done*. His boats are built using jigs and the cold-molded process. Captain Rigsbee quickly credits Woo Woo Harker, Randy Ramsey and Will Guthrie with providing the advice and support to get him started in fishing and boatbuilding. Not surprisingly, Leonard Rigsbee goes by the nickname "Cap-N-Squid."

Harkers Island is the home of Billy Dupree and Outerbanks Boat Works. Dupree owned a paint and body shop in Raleigh before moving to Harkers Island. In 1994, he began using his experience in automotive paints to help local boatbuilders with their custom paints and finishes.

Top Left • 557: Mitchell Lewis, left, and Billy Dupree check the measurements on a Carolina-style sportfishing boat. Harkers Island, 2005.

Middle Right • 558: Boatbuilder Mitchell Lewis, grandson of Brady Lewis, uses the time tested "rack of the eye" method for checking the lines. Harkers Island, 2005.

Bottom • 559: Billy Dupree is at the helm of a 26-foot sportfishing boat he built at his Outerbanks Boat Works shop. Harkers Island. 2005.

In 2000, Dupree founded Outerbanks Boat Works and began constructing sportfishing boats from 26 to 34 feet in length. His boats are designed and built with the same craftsmanship and styling that goes into the larger sportfishing boats. He uses the traditional plank-on-frame methods as well as the cold-molded process. His boats are finished to the same high standards of their big brothers.

Mitchell Lewis, grandson of Brady Lewis, began work at Outerbanks Boat Works in 2002, bringing additional boatbuilding skills to the construction process. Since opening, Dupree and Lewis have built more than 20 boats, inboards and outboards, and they currently have plans for a new express model.

Robby Brittingham started building boats with Randy Ramsey and Jim Luxton at Jarrett Bay Boatworks in 1991. When Jarrett Bay switched from plank-on-frame to the cold-molded process in 1993, Robby was involved with this transition. In 2001, after Jarrett Bay Boatworks vacated their building in Marshallberg, Robby founded Heritage Boatworks at this site and started building boats full-time.

Heritage Boatworks offers custom sportfishing boats ranging from 20 to 70 feet in length, all built using the cold-molded process. Brittingham has built eight boats since 2001, all of them stylish and well constructed. He is involved in every step of the process from design to fabrication and his boats are finished with great detail.

Robby Brittingham builds his boats with a little less flare and narrower S-frames than other local boatbuilders in an effort to improve the speed, efficiency and ride. He also adds more tumblehome aft.

Roy Barnes and Bill Schwabe, founders of Lightning Yachts, have long and varied careers contributing to a unique perspective on boatbuilding. Roy Barnes worked on the charter boat *Gale Ann* for Captain Jimmy Harker and later constructed his own charter boat, a 38-footer named *Sweet Thang*, that he fished out of Swansboro.

Bill Schwabe is an electrical engineer who got interested in boatbuilding at an early age when he helped his father rebuild a classic wooden boat. Bill then got hooked on offshore fishing when he moved to North Carolina in 1985. He fished in the summer and helped build sportfishing boats in the winter at East Bay Boatworks and Jarrett Bay Boatworks.

Top • 560: *A sportfishing boat is painted at Heritage Boatworks in Marshallberg. 2005.* Middle • 561: *A 38-foot sportfishing boat is readied for launch at Heritage Boatworks. Marshallberg, 2004.* Bottom • 562: *A Heritage Boatworks sportfisherman crosses Core Sound on its way to the ocean. Marshallberg, 2003.*

Top • 563:

A sportfishing boat gets its first coat of paint at Lightning Yachts. Beaufort, 2005.

Bottom • 564:

The sportfishing boat Nu-Twist heads to the Gulf Stream for a day of offshore fishing. Built by Lightning Yachts, this vessel is designed with a traditional look and fabricated using the latest materials and techniques. Beaufort, 2004.

Barnes and Schwabe collaborated with Ricky Gillikin to build their first sportfishing boat, *White Lightning*, launched in 1998. This charter boat was constructed using foam and honeycomb for the bulkheads and decking to create a stronger, lighter, more fuel-efficient and faster boat. With Bill Schwabe's engineering experience and the boatbuilding skills of Ricky Gillikin and Roy Barnes, their effort was successful.

Barnes and Schwabe then built a boat shop at Jarrett Bay Industrial Park and began fabricating sportfishing boats. They are currently working on hull number six and they continue to use the latest composites, resins and construction techniques to produce fast, strong and efficient sportfishing boats. They incorporate many of the materials developed in the aerospace industry into boatbuilding.

In 2001, Mason Cox founded Shearline Boats in Morehead City with a goal to build classic Carolina-style custom sportfishing boats while using the latest computer technology and contemporary materials. Shearline boats are built using computer-cut jigs and fabricated using the cold-molded process. They use the best materials available and their finish is yacht quality.

Mason Cox and his partner, Chip King, are particularly adept at using three-dimensional computer designs allowing the customer and the boatbuilder to view the boat before it's built. This saves time, materials and money, as well as providing an opportunity to make changes before the final plans are made.

Shearline Boats is currently working on hull number 25, a 60-foot offshore sportfishing boat. Previously, their boats ranged from 18 to 43 feet and were mostly center consoles.

Top • 565: *Roy Barnes works in the bow of a large sportfishing boat under construction at Lightning Yachts. Barnes and Roy Schwabe are the founders and co-owners of Lightning Yachts. Beaufort, 2005.* Bottom • 566: *The stylish sportfishing boat Nu-Twist refuels. 2005.*

Top Left • 567:
The Tight Lines
running offshore shows
the Carolina styling
designed into Shearline
boats. Morehead City,
2005. Top Right •
568: *Shearline Boatworks*
builds custom sportfishing
boats in Morehead City.
The Patriot is a 26-foot
vessel that is ready for
fishing. 2004. Bottom • 569:
A Shearline boat, Gambler,
returns after a day of offshore
fishing. 2005.

Trends & the Future

It was Friday, June 16, 2006 and the North Carolina Wildlife Resources Commission had just finished the dedication ceremony for the new Wildlife Education Center in Corolla. Commissioners Wes Seegars and Eugene Price were standing around with other dignitaries discussing the duck hunting heritage of Currituck Sound when Wes was interrupted with a question that challenged his judgment and even his sanity. How could he possibly attend a meeting with only one day left in the Big Rock Blue Marlin Tournament? Wes chuckled and confidently replied that he was, of course, going to win. After all, he did have one day left.

With a little more teasing and a few good-natured insults, Wes was more than ready for his four-hour drive to Morehead City. As he stood in the doorway, someone shouted one last taunt, "Don't let an out-of-state boat win this tournament." It was a veiled reference to the New Jersey-based *Can Do Too* that landed a nice 451.5-pound blue marlin on the first day of the tournament. Wes wheeled around and a big grin crossed his face. "I'll take that as a personal challenge," he said as he headed for the parking lot. The group wished him well, but most were thinking, "Yeah, right. Fat chance. No way." He was certain to have a great time and everyone secretly envied his enthusiasm and positive outlook, but win the tournament? *Get real.*

Even before he arrived in Morehead City, Wes was making preparations for the big day. The weather looked good and he asked his wife Jacque to ride along and watch him catch the winner. Much to his surprise, she enthusiastically agreed and the stage was set for a magical day.

The *Chainlink*, a 54-foot Jarrett Bay, slipped out of her berth at the Morehead City Yacht Basin precisely at 5:30 a.m. Captain Ralph Griffin was at the helm with mate Jonathan Oglesby in the cockpit, both seasoned anglers and experienced tournament fishermen. They understood the axiom "It's not over 'til it's over," and they were intense with their preparations for the final day. In addition to Wes and Jacque, sons Ben and John Seegars and their friends Jeff and Todd Nunn were also onboard.

With their plans well established the night before, Captain Griffin headed for a warm eddy of the Gulf Stream that was located just south of the Big Rock and about 55 miles offshore. They had been watching the northward movement of this body of water on satellite printouts since Sunday when it was east of Charleston, South Carolina. It was now within reach of the *Chainlink* and they were determined to see if it held a big blue marlin. As they skimmed across the placid ocean, no one talked about the two hook-ups gone awry on Monday—one had been on for three minutes and the other for eight minutes—or the paucity of fish in between. This was a new day.

Even before he arrived in Morehead City, Wes was making preparations for the big day. The weather looked good and he asked his wife Jacque to ride along and watch him catch the winner. Much to his surprise, she enthusiastically agreed and the stage was set for a magical day.

Above • 570: *The crew on the* Chainlink *works hard to keep Wes Seegars pointed in the right direction. Wes is hooked up to the marlin that won the Big Rock Blue Marlin Tournament. June 17, 2006.*

Captain Griffin found the warmer water right where it was supposed to be. Jonathan scurried around the cockpit with teasers and ballyhoo in hand and soon, at exactly 8 a.m., the radio crackled with an announcement that it was time for the lines to go overboard. The fishing was on and the excitement level could not be higher.

As the *Chainlink* settled into its trolling ritual, Wes commented about the noticeable absence of sargassum. No grass often equates to no fish and, for the first time, a little doubt crept into his mind.

At 8:40, Captain Griffin screamed that a big blue marlin was behind the port teaser on the short line. Jonathan Oglesby grabbed the Penn 80 that had been rigged with a jumbo horse ballyhoo and he readied for a pitch to the marlin. Captain Griffin jerked on the multi-colored teaser hard enough to cut his hand, and it worked. The big blue got excited, lit-up and moved to within 30 feet of the transom. Jonathan tossed the naked ballyhoo right in front of her. The giant marlin veered off, circled around and disappeared. Hearts stopped and jaws dropped. In an instant, the big fish reappeared directly behind the bait and everyone onboard watched as she inhaled what now looked like tiny bait.

After scrambling into his bucket harness, Wes waited an interminable time, almost 10 seconds, before pulling up on the rod. The marlin responded with a steep, 45-degree run toward the bottom. Four hundred yards of 100-pound test line were smoked off the reel and Wes was suddenly looking down at his backing. Captain Griffin had already decided not to pressure the marlin during her first run and he was not as worried as Wes seemed to be. In a few seconds, Wes felt the familiar marlin head shake and he yelled up to Ralph that the strike was solid.

At 8:50, Captain Griffin radioed headquarters with the exhilarating announcement that tournament fishermen love to hear: "The *Chainlink* is hooked up." In a display of sportsmanship typical of offshore anglers, other boats immediately responded with congratulations and words of encouragement for a successful battle.

For the next two hours, Wes and Ralph seesawed with the big blue marlin. Being very careful not to back over the line, use too much drag or otherwise do something foolish, Wes worked the marlin to the boat. As soon as Jonathan touched the leader, the blue took one look and decided that it was time to leave. In a flash, 400 yards of line were peeled off the reel but this time the dive was not quite as steep. Captain Griffin knew it was time to apply some pressure so he started backing down. Wes gained yardage but the giant was moving so they had to be very careful.

An hour and a half passed and the fish was coming up again. Jonathan grabbed the leader and sure enough, the marlin took off again. Seven times this scenario repeated itself but each run was noticeably shallower. Wes was winning but not by much.

At 2 p.m., the call for lines out of the water was issued. The tournament was over unless a boat was already hooked up. The rules said that they could continue fighting their fish until it was lost, released or boated, no matter how long it took. Wes had been tied to this marlin for five and a half hours and figured that it just might take forever.

A few boats circled wide and offered support before heading to shore. By 3 o'clock, the *Chainlink* was all-alone on the ocean, more than 10 miles from where they hooked-up, and the big fish was still deep. Thirty minutes later, on her eighth trip to the boat, the marlin was exhausted. So was Wes, but the fight was over. At 3:30 p.m., seven long hours after the marlin struck, Captain Griffin radioed that the *Chainlink* had a fish onboard.

After a brief celebration, the marlin was covered with ice and wrapped in towels for a dash to the weigh-in. Wes figured that the fish would place but he was not sure if they had a winner. Captain Griffin, however, offered an experienced and prophetic estimate: 502 pounds he surmised.

Above • 571: *Captain Ralph Griffin, left, and angler Wes Seegars, right, with the 501.5-pound blue marlin that won the Big Rock Tournament. June 17, 2006.*

The run home seemed quick. Along the way, tournament headquarters radioed to see if Captain Griffin would disclose the length of the fish thus providing a good estimate of the weight for those on shore. He respectfully declined adding to the suspense that was already building. The crew on the *Chainlink* had no way of knowing that live updates were being broadcast on local radio and television stations as well as over the Internet. Wes figured that only a few people would be left to see the weigh-in since it was going to be after 6 o'clock before they got to the scales.

As the *Chainlink* approached Beaufort Inlet, Wes could see hundreds of boats sitting by the channel and he wondered what was happening. When he got closer, horns sounded, people waved and a flotilla formed behind his boat. At the scales, Wes was awestruck to see more than 3,000 people, including many friends who had heard about the catch and had driven several hours to see the weigh-in. As the marlin was hoisted on the scale, Captain Griffin took a quick look and turned to shake Wes's hand. The marlin weighed 501.5 pounds and they had won the 2006 Big Rock Blue Marlin Tournament.

When congratulations were offered to Wes, he talked about how important it was to have Jacque, Ben and John out fishing with him that day and about how humbling it was to receive such an outpouring of support from friends, competitors and even strangers. Not a word about winning the tournament or the prize money. That's just the way he is. And yes, June 17, 2006, was truly a magical day for the Seegars family, one they will never forget.

Top • 572: *Many beautiful and functional custom sportfishing boats are built using the time-tested plank-on-frame method. 2006.* Bottom • 573: *The cold-molded construction process also results in a beautiful and functional custom sportfishing boat. 2006.*

Overview

A major trend in the construction of custom boatbuilding is toward bigger, faster and stronger offshore fishing boats. This push will soon result in sportfishing yachts that will exceed 90 feet in length with speeds of 50 miles per hour and more. Custom boatbuilders on the Outer Banks are currently nearing these milestones, and even larger and faster sportfishing boats are on the horizon.

Some of the significant trends in boatbuilding are the result of new materials, construction techniques, interior designs and propulsion. Space-age composites, laminates, urethanes, coatings and finishes are in development that will allow custom builders to fabricate larger vessels that can withstand greater speeds. New construction techniques include vacuum intrusion, vacuum bagging and injection molding. Interiors are lavish and custom-made with state-of-the-art integrated electronic systems. Propulsion systems include, among others, pod drives, jet drives, turbines, and hybrid electric–diesel engines. In the future, propulsion systems will strive for fuel efficiency, environmental sensitivity and low maintenance. Boats may even be fueled by alternative energy sources.

Offshore sportfishing has also evolved with an appreciation for the protection and sustainability of fishery resources. Catch-and-release practices, circle hooks, tagging programs and fishing tournaments have led to a better awareness among anglers and the public about offshore fishery stocks. Fishery research has been expanded and management groups now view highly migratory pelagic species from a worldwide perspective.

Trends in Custom Boatbuilding

When Warren O'Neal launched the *Sportsman* in 1961, he could not have imagined how sportfishing boats would evolve into the sleek, fast, luxurious fishing machines of today. Contemporary boatbuilders along the Outer Banks utilize the latest designs, materials and components to fabricate offshore fishing boats tailored to all fishing and cruising needs. Each sportfishing yacht is designed and built based on the needs of the customer, and the allure of owning a unique boat portends well for the future of custom boatbuilding.

During the past 50 years, the trend in custom offshore sportfishing boats has been driven by what seems to be a boatbuilders trilogy: bigger, stronger and faster. The hull shape, proportions and characteristics are paramount in the push for speed, ride and interior room. As with all boats, these features are always a compromise. Sunny Briggs summed up the challenge for boatbuilders when designing a hull: "If the deep-Vee forward is sharp, the ride is good. However, if it is too sharp, the boat handles poorly in a following sea, and, if it is too shallow, she pounds in a head sea. The answer is: she has to be just right."

Top • 574: *A scale model of a 53-foot Sculley custom sportfishing boat is "tank-tested." Computers analyze data from different hull configurations operated at different speeds. This information will be used to design a hull with the desired performance goals. 2006.*

Bottom • 575: *The bottom of the hull is also analyzed using computer modeling and tank-testing. 2006.*

In order to get this "just right" combination, many boatbuilders utilize computer technology and mathematical modeling to predict hull dynamics and behaviors. Builders can get a good idea of the hull performance before a boat is even built by tank-testing various shapes and weight distributions at different speeds. Other boatbuilders rely on time-tested hull shapes proven effective through their years of boatbuilding experience. Again, a boating compromise.

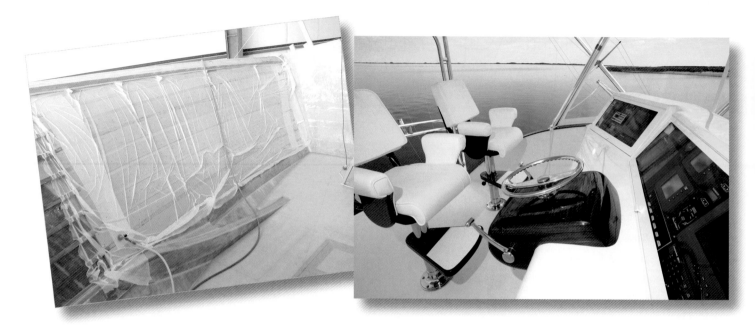

Left • 576: *Many custom boatbuilders have begun using a vacuum process to control the penetration and amount of resin used during fabrication. 2006.*

Right • 577: *Custom finishes and rich detailing are an important aspect of contemporary sportfishing yachts. 2006.*

Materials used in the fabrication of offshore sportfishing boats have been improved significantly during the last 50 years, and particularly since 1990. New composites have been added to the assemblage of resources boatbuilders use in their quest for bigger, stronger and faster boats. Much technology now used in the fabrication of custom sportfishing boats has been adapted from the aerospace industry. Aramid fibers, polymers, foams, laminates, carbon fabrics and core materials produce lighter and stronger hulls, decks, bulkheads and superstructures. Also, noise, vibration, structural fatigue and moisture intrusion can be greatly reduced by these new products.

Thermoplastics, hybrid sandwich materials, water-resistant adhesives, embedded monitoring systems and even self-repairing, "smart materials" are in development or already in use. With advances in materials engineering, custom boatbuilders will need to understand and utilize composites, laminates and polymers to keep pace in the rapidly changing world of boatbuilding.

Construction techniques have also evolved along with the new materials. Vacuum infusion, where vacuum pressure forces resin into a dry laminate; vacuum bagging, where excess resin is pulled out of a wet laminate; and fabrication of injection-molded components are all techniques currently being used in custom boatbuilding.

As construction techniques become more complex, the demand for a skilled labor force increases. Workers will need to be more educated and better trained in order to effectively utilize sophisticated technologies.

Finishes for sportfishing boats have also progressed rapidly. Contemporary fluoropolymer coatings resist the corrosive effects of salt water and fading from ultraviolet light, while maintaining their color and gloss. Polyurethane coatings are utilized to protect metal and wooden components used in boat construction, and antifouling paints are more effective and environmentally friendly. Varnishes continue to improve and gelcoats are stronger and more vibrant than ever.

Electronics and communication systems on offshore sportfishing boats now rival airplanes in both effectiveness and complexity. Satellite telephones and telemetry, computer monitoring of engine performance, video capabilities, audio components and all sorts of navigational aids are just a few of the systems available to offshore fishermen and boaters. Integrated systems that monitor and control all of the functions on the vessel are now in use.

Some of the most extreme transformations in custom boatbuilding have occurred in the interior of the boat. The trend in custom offshore sportfishing boats is toward luxury with all of the personal comforts imaginable. Richly appointed exotic woods, masterfully crafted cabinets and furniture, designer fabrics, artist-created inlays, premium appliances and amenities too numerous to mention have become standard features. Calling many of today's custom sportfishing boats "opulent" is an understatement; a more appropriate description might be "over the top."

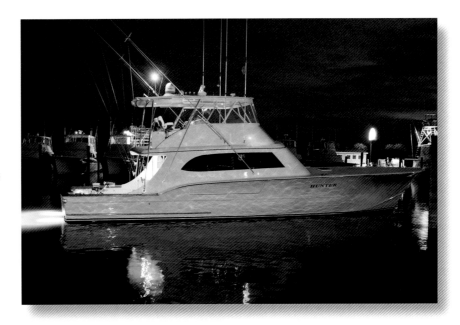

Above • 578: *Custom lighting accentuates the styling of Carolina sportfishing yachts. 2006.*

Among all of the changes in boatbuilding over the past 50 years, propulsion ranks at the top as the most important. When Buddy Davis describes the future of boatbuilding, he succinctly says, "It's all about the power. Always has been, always will be."

Even though some new technology in this area has emerged over the past 50 years, improvements in propulsion have generally been limited to modifications on the standard diesel, gasoline and outboard motors. The advent of turbo-charged diesels, stern drives and four-stroke outboards are examples of innovations with significant impacts for boaters. Improvements have also been made in engine efficiency, horsepower, reliability and emission control.

Among the propulsion technologies currently being developed and refined are pod drives, vented tunnel drives, pump jets, four-stroke outboard engines mounted inside the boat, gas and diesel turbines, fuel cell-driven electric engines, hybrid diesel-electric engines and jet drives.

Boat owners are looking for a rare combination of power, reduced weight, lower capital cost and improved efficiency. These seemingly contradictory goals provide a challenge for the makers of propulsion systems. The tried and true diesel engine, with ongoing research, modifications and improvements, will likely remain the mainstay for offshore sportfishing boats in the foreseeable future.

Text continued on page 265

Top Left • 579: *Underwater lighting and well-placed accent lights add allure and charm to the dockside presence of custom sportfishing yachts. 2005.* Top Right • 580: *Satellite communications offer uninterrupted linkage for telephones, fax machines, computers and other electronics. 2005.*

Bottom Left • 581: *The bridge is loaded with navigation aids and electronics for fishing. 2006.* Bottom Right • 582: *Custom towers along with elaborate communication and navigation systems are an important part of contemporary sportfishing boats. 2005.*

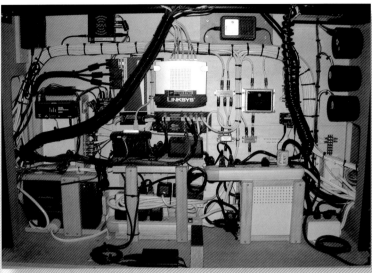

Top Left •
583: *Control panels provide a central location for information about the various systems on the vessel. 2006.* Top Right • 584: *An integrated audio-visual system links the audio and video components throughout the entire boat. 2006.* Middle • 585: *The interior is designed in a collaborative effort among the owner, boatbuilder, cabinet-maker, and interior designer. The result is amazing. 2006.*

Above • 586: *Contemporary materials, such as solid surface countertops, are both practical and beautiful. 2006.* Bottom Left • 587: *Custom features, like storage compartments, are designed into each interior. 2005.*

Top Left • 588: *Style and luxury are carried throughout contemporary custom sportfishing yachts. Bathrooms are among the most richly appointed areas. 2006.* Top Right • 589: *The master stateroom contains custom features seldom found in even the most luxurious homes. 2006.* Middle Left • 590: *Many custom sportfishing yachts include a guest bedroom in the forward compartment. 2006.* Middle Right • 591: *An impressive view is standard. 2006.* Bottom • 592: *With the ever-increasing demand for speed, and thus larger engines, the engine compartment must be well designed and constructed. 2006.*

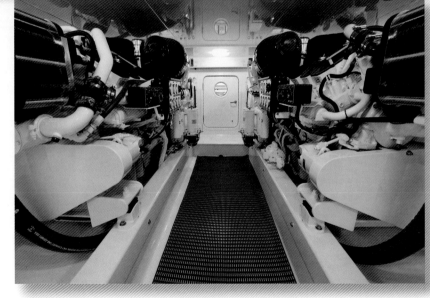

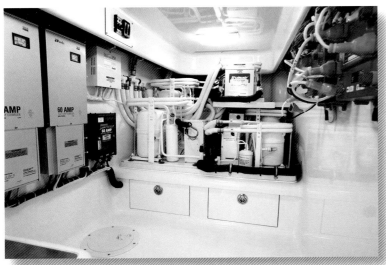

Top • 593: *Mechanical and electrical systems on contemporary sportfishing yachts are complex so easy access is a necessity for maintenance and repairs. 2006.*

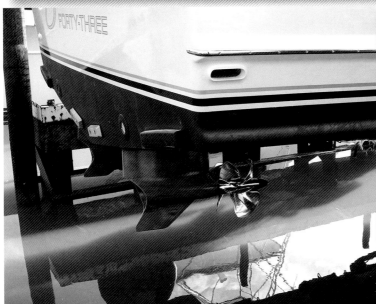

Middle Left • 594: *The pod drive is one of the new technologies in propulsion systems. 2006.* Middle Right • 595: *With a joystick, mounted right, the speed and direction of the vessel can be controlled with one lever. 2006.* Bottom • 596: *Tests indicate that pod drives provide increased fuel efficiency and maneuverability. This 43-foot Spencer sportfisherman is equipped with a pod system. 2006.*

Top Left • 597: *A lighted reel locker allows fishermen to easily select a rod and reel combination for the type of fishing being planned. 2006.* Bottom Left • 598: *A custom rod-holder is mounted beneath a bunk bed to maximize space. 2006.* Top Right • 599: *Sportfishing amenities are the most important aspect of custom sportfishing yachts. 2006.*

Bottom Right • 600: *The cockpit provides plenty of fishing space for both anglers and crew. 2006.*

Trends in Offshore Sportfishing

Offshore sportfishing has also seen its share of changes in the last 50 years. Among the most important advances has been the widely accepted concept of "catch-and-release." Along the Outer Banks, this practice dates to 1958 when Dr. Jack Cleveland caught and released a blue marlin onboard the *Albatross II* with Captain Bill Foster. The fish weighed approximately 400 pounds and the report of this feat made a national newspaper, the *New York Mirror*. Soon after, in 1962 at Oregon Inlet, Mrs. Marie Olds caught and released another blue marlin onboard the *Sportsman* with Captain Omie Tillett.

Anglers now realize that the large pelagic gamefish, particularly blue marlin, white marlin and sailfish, are a limited resource and efforts are made to land fish quickly and with as little damage as possible. Also, techniques have been developed to help resuscitate tired fish and survival rates are improving. Almost all offshore tournaments reward catch-and-release practices along with stiff penalties for anglers who bring undersized fish to the scales.

Another improvement in offshore fishing is the utilization of circle hooks. These hooks bend sharply inward toward the shank, almost forming a closed circle. When a fish strikes, the angler pulls, rather than jerks, on the rod and the circle hook rolls into the corner of the fish's jaw. This prevents deep hook sets and greatly improves the survival of

Top Left • 601: *A tuna tower provides a great vantage point.* 2006. Top Right • 602: *Captain Omie Tillett, right, and mate Sunny Briggs, center, award a catch-and-release flag to Mrs. Marie Olds. Oregon Inlet Fishing Center, 1964.* Bottom • 603: *Circle hooks have become popular with offshore anglers who practice catch-and-release techniques. 2006.*

Top • 604: *A giant bluefin tuna is fitted with an archival tag during the Tag-A-Giant research project near Cape Lookout. 2005.* Middle • 605: *A tag is inserted near the dorsal fin of a bluefin tuna and she is released from the charter boat* Calcutta. *2005.* Bottom • 606: *A pop-up tag is capable of relaying information via satellite to the research team at the Tag-A-Giant. 2005.*

released fish. Commercial fishermen and long-liners developed circle hook technology, but many offshore anglers use them when fishing with live or natural baits.

Research and tagging of pelagic gamefish has recently attained a higher priority with fishery resource managers. International commercial fishing pressure on large pelagics, combined with increased recreational fishing pressure, has made the task of managing fish roaming the open ocean very difficult. In addition to national and international fishery management groups, several private, nonprofit organizations now assist in this research effort.

Supplementing the many studies on population dynamics of marlin and sailfish, the Hopkins Marine Station, Stanford University and Monterey Bay Aquarium have undertaken an Atlantic bluefin tuna tagging program along the Outer Banks of North Carolina. Known as "Tag-A-Giant," this project is designed to improve research, policies, conservation and sustainability of these highly migratory gamefish.

Each year in January, when giant bluefin tuna congregate off Cape Hatteras and Cape Lookout, a research team embarks on an intense tagging program that partners scientists with fishermen in a remarkable quest. Since its origin in 1994, the Tag-A-Giant project has tagged and released over 1,000 bluefin tuna, and the numbers continue to grow.

Since the recapture rate of migratory, open ocean species is low, the Tag-A-Giant project uses archival and satellite tags to track the movements of bluefin tuna. Archival tags are

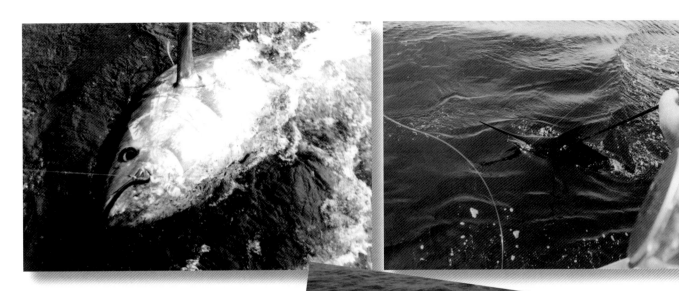

mini-computers inserted into the stomach of a captured bluefin. The internal part of the tag measures and stores data on the depth and internal body temperature of the fish while a slender stalk that protrudes from the body measures water temperature and light levels. The information is recorded on a micro-computer and yields data about the migratory patterns and physiology of the fish. However, in order to recover this computer, a fisherman must catch the fish and return the tag to the research team.

Pop-up satellite tags measuring location, depth, light levels and water temperature are also used by the research team. These tags are inserted to the back of a bluefin tuna and include a micro-computer with powerful radio transmitters capable of broadcasting data to an Argos satellite. At a preset time, an electrical impulse severs the small wire holding the tag in place and it pops to the surface. Information can then be relayed via satellite to the research team.

The Tag-A-Giant project is one example of researchers, policy-makers and fishermen combining efforts to conserve and perpetuate a sustainable fishery resource. These research trends, coupled with wise policy decisions, will enhance offshore fishery resources and offshore sportfishing opportunities for future generations.

Studies conducted by the Virginia Institute of Marine Sciences, Texas A&M University, the Southeast Fishery Science Center and the Billfish Foundation indicate that billfish landings peaked in the early 1960s and have fallen steadily since. Recent studies indicate that billfish stocks are in jeopardy primarily due to loss from commercial long-line fishing. Target species for long-liners are tuna and swordfish, but marlin and sailfish are a significant bycatch.

Top Left • 607: *With a circle hook and a tag, this bluefin tuna is ready to be released. Data collected from these studies will provide fishery resource managers with better information about the migration patterns of pelagic species. 2005.* Top Right • 608: *A tag is placed in a marlin just before release. 2005.* Bottom • 609: *A small dolphin is fitted with a tag and ready to go back into the water. 2005.*

Top • 610: *The Fabulous Fishermen participated in Morehead City parades to promote local charter fishing.* 1956. Middle • 611: *The Mary-Z was the boat on which Captain Bill Olsen and angler Jimmy Croy landed the first documented blue marlin in Morehead City. September 14, 1957.* Bottom • 612: *The Fabulous Fishermen produced promotional decals and patches that date from 1956. The initial logo was a red flag that displayed two fishhooks with two small fish.*

In 2004, the Atlantic Billfish Research Plan was released by the Southeast Fisheries Science Center. It documents the declining populations of Atlantic billfishes and calls for additional research and an emphasis on international management of fishery resources.

Offshore fishing tournaments have also played an important role in the conservation and development of our fishery resources. Dating to the mid-1950s, the Big Rock Blue Marlin Tournament has been a leader in this effort.

In 1956, a small group of friends informally banded together to promote charter fishing in Morehead City. This association consisted of anglers, outdoorsmen, charter fishermen and business people who wanted to increase the visibility of fishing opportunities along the southern Outer Banks. They called themselves the "Fabulous Fishermen."

Members of this group included Bob and Mary Simpson, Jerry Schumacher, Tony Seamon, Dick Parker, Ottis Purifoy, Hubert Fulcher, Tom Potter, George Bedsworth and Arthur Lewis. Also included were the wives of several charter captains.

Bob Simpson and Jerry Schumacher, both outstanding photographers, provided photographs, and the others wrote articles and distributed information about what was biting and where people could fish. In order to effectively publicize the charter fleet, the Fabulous Fishermen knew that they had to come up with a gimmick to get the news media involved. After only a few meetings, they decided to offer a prize for the first blue marlin landed at Morehead City. The Fabulous Fishermen promoted their idea throughout the region and the race was on.

In the summer of 1956, offshore fishermen began to see blue marlin cruising the waters in an area discovered by Captain George Bedsworth and Ed Purifoy called the Big Rock. Even though several were hooked, none were landed. In August 1956, a white marlin was brought to shore, but not what the Fabulous Fishermen wanted.

Finally, on September 14, 1957, word was relayed from offshore by Hubert Fulcher that angler Jimmy Croy had landed a blue marlin on the *Mary-Z*. Bump Styron, manager of the Morehead City Yacht Basin, contacted radio broadcaster Bob Campbell and word of the marlin was spread over the airwaves. As the *Mary-Z* made her way back to the Morehead City Yacht Basin, a crowd of about a hundred people assembled for the festivities.

Tony Seamon quickly made a trip to Roses Department Store and the manager donated a red wagon for the promotion. Seamon then stopped by First Citizens Bank to pick up two bags of silver dollars that had been waiting for this occasion for over a year. Accounts vary about the exact amount but Tony Seamon, Jr. recalls counting 500 silver dollars into that little red wagon. Others remember 250, 300 or 325 as the number, but whatever the amount, it all went into the wagon until it overflowed.

As the *Mary-Z* neared port, the Fabulous Fishermen mobilized the news media and several reporters were on hand. As the crowd waited, Tony Seamon, Jr. pulled the red wagon loaded with silver dollars from the Sanitary Restaurant, up Evans Street, to the Morehead City Yacht Basin. Police cars, with sirens blaring, led the way. In a ceremony hosted by Bump Styron, Jimmy Croy was presented with the silver dollars, and the media flooded area newspapers with word of the 143-pound blue marlin landed at Morehead City.

In 1958, the Fabulous Fishermen incorporated and became the Fabulous Fishing Club. They hosted the Fabulous Fishing Club Blue Marlin Tournament the same year and their goals were accomplished.

In 1959, the tournament was re-named the Big Rock Blue Marlin Tournament and it has been growing ever since. In 2008, the tournament will celebrate its 50th anniversary. All indications are that there will be many more great years to come.

Top • 613: *Fish are attached to an old truck as the Fabulous Fishermen ride in a parade down Arendell Street in Morehead City. 1956.* Bottom • 614: *In 1958, a round Fabulous Fishing Club Blue Marlin Tournament patch was produced and, in 1959, the Big Rock Blue Marlin Tournament patch was developed.*

Top Left • 615: *Sportfishing boats return through the channel from Oregon Inlet after a day of fishing in the Pirates Cove Billfish Tournament. 2004.*

Top Right • 616: *Charter boats wait for another day at the Oregon Inlet Fishing Center, 2005.* Bottom • 617: *Dawn and it's time to go fishing. 2006.*

In addition to the Big Rock Blue Marlin Tournament, more than 30 other offshore fishing tournaments are held in North Carolina each year. King mackerel, wahoo, sailfish and even inshore fish are targeted, with the ultimate winners being the charities that these tournaments support.

The Governor's Cup Billfishing Conservation Series is a team sportfishing competition that decides the winners by compiling points awarded from seven billfish tournaments. An award is presented for catch and release, circle hook landings and for following minimum-size requirements. Since its beginnings in 1990, the Governor's Cup Series has involved 679 anglers who have caught and released 1,591 billfish.

The economic contributions made by boatbuilders and offshore fishermen to the economy of the Outer Banks and adjacent counties are significant. According to a 2005 report prepared by the North Carolina Employment Security Commission, the benefits of boatbuilding industries, recreational fishing and related marine services total more than 1,200 businesses, 20,000 jobs and $275,000,000 in annual wages. These impressive figures demonstrate the importance of boatbuilding and sportfishing to the economy of the Outer Banks.

A great future builds on a great past. With a solid foundation derived from a host of legendary boatbuilding and sportfishing pioneers, this extraordinary heritage will continue to flourish along the North Carolina Outer Banks.

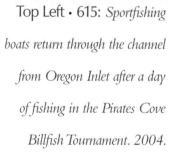

Appendices, Glossary, Photography Credits & References

Appendix 1:
Map of the Outer Banks

Northern Outer Banks, Virginia to Oregon Inlet

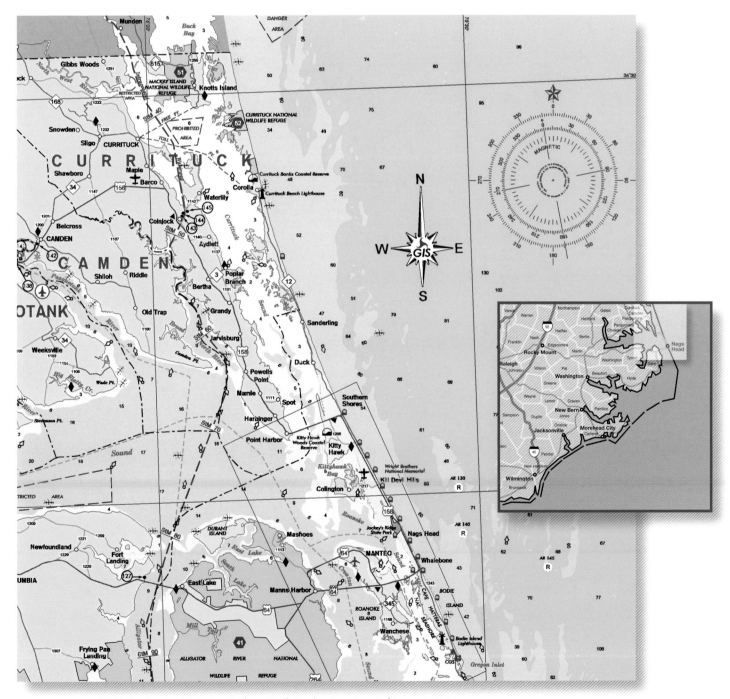

(North Carolina Coastal Boating Guide • North Carolina Department of Transportation)

Appendix 1:
Map of the Outer Banks

Northern Outer Banks, Oregon Inlet to Ocracoke Inlet

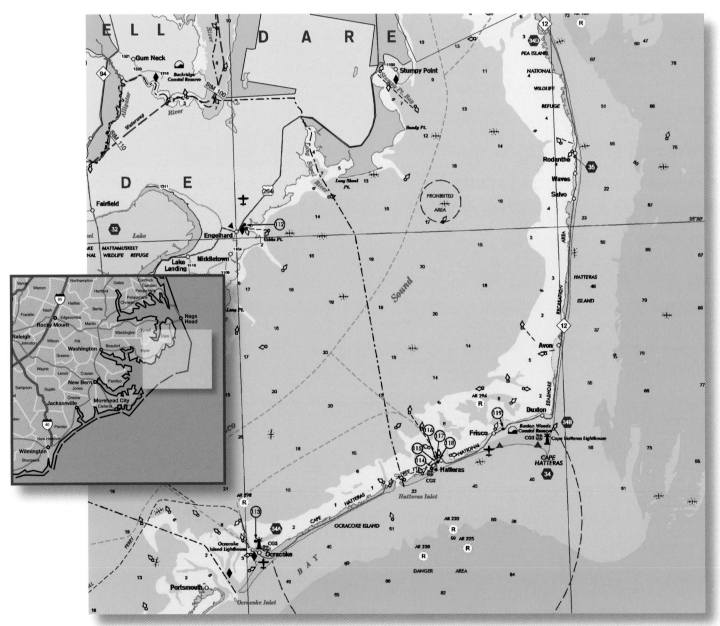

(North Carolina Coastal Boating Guide • North Carolina Department of Transportation)

Appendix 1:
Map of the Outer Banks

Southern Outer Banks, Ocracoke Inlet to Beaufort Inlet

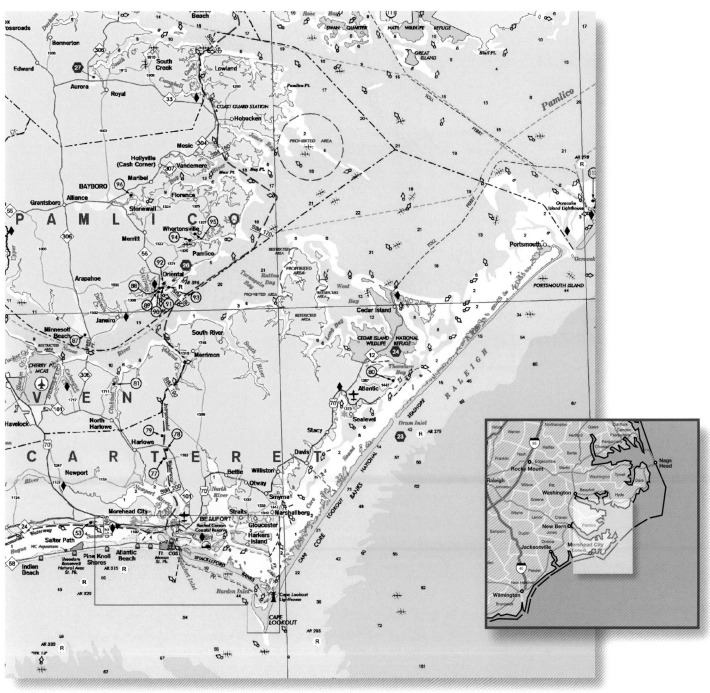

(North Carolina Coastal Boating Guide • North Carolina Department of Transportation)

Appendix 2:
Evolution of the Carolina-Style Sportfishing Boat

Photo 1: *Along the southern Outer Banks, the sharpie* Bessie B *represents the beginnings of the Carolina style. Her classic lines feature a straight stem, round stern and long sweeping sheer line. These characteristics are important in the development of Core Sound sink-net boats. Beaufort, 1900.* Photo 2: *On the northern Outer Banks, the shad boat was the most popular inshore vessel for commercial and sportfishing. With its straight stem, low bulging sides and sweeping sheer line, many characteristics of the shad boat were also incorporated into the Core Sound sink-net boats. Manteo, 1905.* Photo 3: *The Albatross is an example of a Core Sound sink-net boat built for sportfishing. These vessels were ideal for inshore and near-shore commercial and sportfishing.*

They had a trunk cabin, straight stem, sweeping sheer line and round stern. Hatteras, 1938. Photo 4: *The next generation of sportfishing boats included charter vessels that had a sweeping sheer line, straight stem and square stern. Emerging in the 1940s and 1950s, the* Gulf Breeze *embodies these features. Morehead City, 1948.* Photo 5: *The* Sportsman *incorporates many of the designs in contemporary sportfishing boats. The flare, broken sheer line, square stern, deep-Vee forward and wide tumblehome first appeared together in this vessel. Oregon Inlet, 1961.* Photo 6: *Contemporary boatbuilders utilize the latest designs, construction techniques and technologies to create magnificent offshore fishing vessels like the* Pisces IV. *Oregon Inlet, 2005.*

Appendix 3:
Characteristics of the Carolina-Style Sportfishing Boat

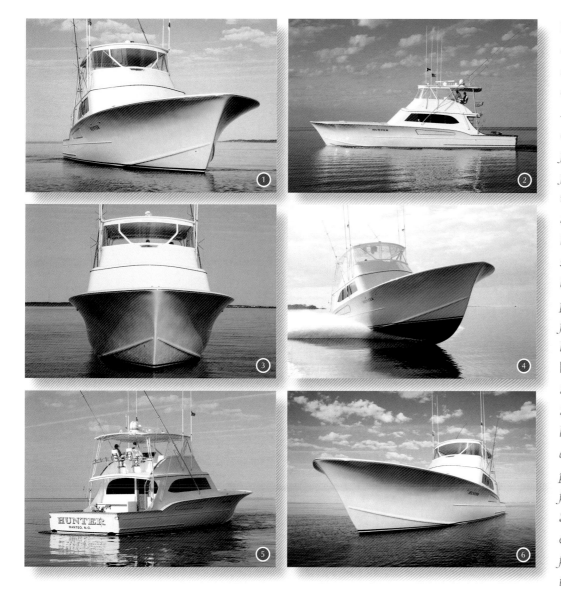

Photo 1: *Flare: The upward and outward curvature of the hull at the bow is a feature that exemplifies the Carolina style. An exaggerated flare helps deflect waves and spray away from the hull. The "Carolina flare" is recognized around the world.* **Photo 2:** ***Broken Sheer Line:*** *The broken sheer line is a curved step-down of the sheer line as it sweeps from the bow to the stern. This feature provides a pleasing transition from the inset cabin to the low, straight cockpit gunwales.* **Photo 3:** ***S-Frame:*** *The S-frame, sometimes known as S-curve, refers to the shape of the hull from the sheer line, past the chine to the keel. The S-frame provides more interior space for living quarters.* **Photo 4:** ***Sharp Entry:*** *The sharp entry, or deep-Vee forward, is a design feature on Carolina-style boats that allows the boat to knife through waves. The sharp entry combined with a hull that flattens toward the stern results in a vessel that performs well in both head seas and following seas.* **Photo 5:** ***Exaggerated Tumblehome:*** *The tumblehome is when the width of the beam, most often measured at the transom, is wider than the width of the uppermost deck. The tumblehome is a feature that adds a pleasing look to the boat.* **Photo 6:** ***Hawk and Exaggerated Spray Rails:*** *Carolina-style boats have a noticeable "hawk" or hook where the bow stem, flare and foredeck converge. The hawk curves upward to provide stability and pleasing lines to the bow of the boat. Exaggerated spray rails not only help deflect ocean spray down and away from the boat but they also provide extra lift for the hull.* (Photographs of the Hunter built by Paul Mann)

Appendix 4:
The Plank-on-Frame
Construction Process

Photo 1: *Captain Bobby Sullivan checks the level and width of the stem for his charter boat Marlin Fever. Captain Sullivan demonstrates the plank-on-frame techniques he learned from his grandfather, Allen Hayman.*
Photo 2: *The stem and keel are laid out and the stations have been measured and erected. In plank-on-frame construction, the boat is built from the keel up.* **Photo 3:** *The frames are in place and the flare has been shaped. The curved battens attached to the sides of the hull provide support for the frames.* **Photo 4:** *Captain Sullivan is reinforcing the S-frames and checking his measurements. At this stage the boat is almost ready for planking.* **Photo 5:** *The hull has been planked with juniper boards from the sheer line to the chine.* **Photo 6:** *Fiberglass has been added for extra strength and waterproofing and the hull has been faired.* **Photo 7:** *The boat is ready to be launched. Her flared bow, deep-Vee hull, S-frame, and exaggerated spray rails are evident.*
Photo 8: *Sleek and stylish, the Marlin Fever heads offshore.*

(Photographs of the Marlin Fever built by Bobby Sullivan)

Appendix 5:
The Cold-Molded
Construction Process

Photo 1: *The cold-molded boatbuilding technique is demonstrated at the shop of Captain Sunny Briggs. Cold-molded boats are constructed from the keel down, or "upside-down." The jigs and stations have been set up and battens have been added.* Photo 2: *The keel has been laid and the jigs are connected and reinforced.* Photo 3: *The flared bow, S-frames and deep-Vee are evident as the first layer of premium plywood is added. The hull will receive at least three layers and the sides will get at least two layers, each glued diagonally to provide extra strength.* Photo 4: *The hull has received two layers of fiberglass for added strength and waterproofing.* Photo 5: *The hull and sides have received two layers of compound to seal the plywood and workers are sanding the boat.* Photo 6: *Workers remove the hull from the building and flip her over so interior, deck and superstructure work can begin.* Photo 7: *The engines, deck and cabin have been installed and work continues on the interior.* Photo 8: *The Ann Warrick has been completed and she heads offshore for a day of fishing.*

(Photographs of the Ann Warrick built by Sunny Briggs)

Appendix 6:
Diagram of a Sportfishing Boat

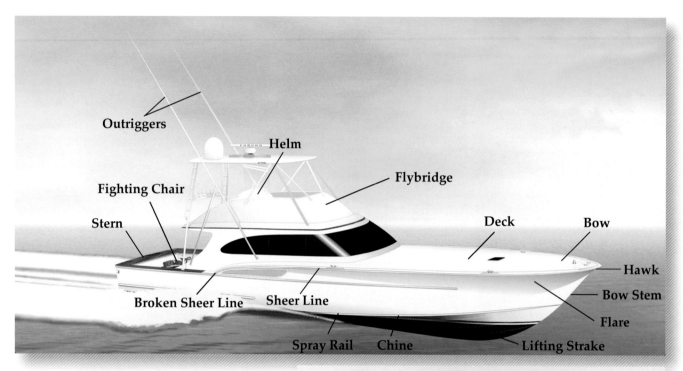

Outriggers

Helm

Flybridge

Fighting Chair

Stern

Deck

Bow

Hawk

Broken Sheer Line

Sheer Line

Bow Stem

Flare

Spray Rail

Chine

Lifting Strake

Top & Bottom: *These diagrams illustrate a few of the commonly used terms that describe parts of a sportfishing boat. Definitions are included in the Glossary.*

(Illustrations of a Sunny Briggs 55-foot sportfishing boat provided by Applied Concepts Unleashed, Inc.)

Mezzanine

Cockpit

Transom

Cabin

Gunwale

Waterline

Tumblehome

Tuna Door

Glosssary of Boatbuilding
& Sportfishing Terms

- *Aft:* Near, at, or towards the stern of a boat.
- *Amidship:* Down the middle of a boat along the line of the keel.
- *Backing:* A thin, strong line used to fill up the spool on a reel before attaching the primary fishing line.
- *Backing down:* Driving the boat in reverse while pursuing a fish.
- *Ballast:* Any material used to improve stability and control of a boat.
- *Ballyhoo:* A small shiny fish that is a popular offshore trolling bait.
- *Batten:* A long strip of wood used by boatbuilders to create a fair, or smooth, curve.
- *Beam:* The width of a boat.
- *Bilge:* The compartment on the internal part of the hull and the lowest part of the boat.
- *Billfish:* Any of several species of pelagic fish including sailfish, spearfish, swordfish and blue, black or white marlin.
- *Bow:* The forward part of the hull of a boat. Designed to cut through the water and to keep waves from washing over into the hull.
- *Break or break line:* An abrupt change in temperature, depth, bottom topography, water clarity, current or other feature.
- *Broken sheer line:* A broken sheer line is a curved step-down of the sheer line as it sweeps from the bow to the stern.
- *Bulkhead:* The internal walls of a boat. An upright partition that separates one compartment from another.
- *Cabin:* The enclosed portion of a boat that provides shelter and other amenities.
- *Centerboard:* A metal or wooden board that is housed in a casing along the centerline of a sailboat. The centerboard provides stability and can be raised or lowered depending on the water depth.
- *Chine:* The distinct change in the angle of the hull where the bottom and the side intersect.
- *Circle hook:* A hook where the point bends drastically toward the shank to form almost a complete circle. Useful for reducing fish mortality.
- *Cockpit:* An opening in the deck from which the boat is handled or where an angler fights a fish.
- *Cold-molding:* A construction process involving the application of two or more wooden panels, strips or composites at opposing 45-degree angles that are held together by glue (commonly epoxy glue).
- *Composite:* A material or structure that has been created by melding two or more different materials together to form a stronger product.
- *Covering board:* The top plank or covering on the deck or gunwales.
- *Cross bracing:* Wooden strips placed diagonally across the frames to provide extra strength.

Continued

- *Deadrise:* The angle measured between the keel and horizontal when viewed in a cross-section.
- *Deck:* The top surface of the hull that prevents water from entering the boat. It also provides structure and strength to the hull.
- *Draft:* The depth of the keel, the lowest point of the boat below the waterline or the depth of water it takes to float a boat without touching bottom.
- *Drag:* The mechanical device on a reel that limits how fast a fish can strip line from the reel.
- *Fair:* Smooth, or pleasing to the eye.
- *Fighting chair:* A chair, usually equipped with a restraining belt or harness, used by fishermen to fight a large fish.
- *Flare:* The up and out curvature of the hull above the waterline.
- *Flybridge:* An elevated structure on a boat that extends across the vessel and contains controls for navigation and visual advantages for sportfishing.
- *Following sea:* A sea in which the waves are moving in the same direction as the boat (with the waves).
- *Fore:* Near, or at, the bow of a boat.
- *Frame:* A board, or other support, in the hull that extends from the keel to the sheer line or deck.
- *Freeboard:* The height of the boat above the waterline.
- *Gaff:* A steel hook of varying sizes, mounted on a pole or stick. A gaff is used for snagging fish brought along side the boat.
- *Gale:* A storm warning where winds are clocked between 32-63 miles per hour.
- *Galley:* The kitchen area of a boat.
- *Gimbal:* A device mounted to a fighting chair that allows for the rotation of a rod in multiple dimensions while transferring the weight of the rod from the arms and wrists of the angler to the chair.
- *Gunwale:* The upper longitudinal structural member of the hull.
- *Hawk:* Carolina-style boats have a noticeable "hawk," or hook, where the bow stem, flare and foredeck converge. The hawk curves upward to provide stability and pleasing lines to the bow of the boat.
- *Head sea:* A sea in which the waves are moving in the opposite direction as the boat (into the waves).
- *Helm:* The wheel or portion of the boat that controls the steering.
- *Horse ballyhoo:* A large ballyhoo rigged for marlin fishing.
- *Hull:* The body or shell of a boat.
- *Keel:* The center part of a boat's spine that runs along the length of the bottom from stem to stern.
- *Leader:* A strong line or wire inserted between the lure and the fishing line. The leader provides extra strength and abrasion resistance.
- *Lifting strake:* Longitudinal wooden or composite strips added to the hull to provide lift.
- *Lighter:* To load and unload vessels or to transfer cargo directly from one vessel to another.
- *Lit-up:* Pelagic fish like marlin, sailfish, wahoo and dolphin have a tendency to brighten into brilliant neon colors when excited or hooked.

- *Long–liner:* Commercial fishing boats loaded with a huge spool of heavy monofilament line that target tuna and swordfish.
- *Marlin tower:* A low platform over the flybridge, shorter than a tuna tower, where a spotter looks for fish, grass or other objects in the water.
- *Mate:* The person on a sportfishing boat that assists the captain. Usually the mate provides primary assistance for the fishing activities.
- *Mezzanine:* The mezzanine is an "interior balcony" that is a mid-level deck generally between the cockpit and the cabin.
- *Outrigger:* Long poles used on sportfishing boats to hold trolling lures out to the side.
- *Partyboat:* A fishing boat for hire that carries more than 6 people and often as many as 100. Most partyboats fish with heavy tackle for bottom fish.
- *Pelagic fish:* An offshore fish that migrates in the open ocean waters.
- *Port:* The side of a boat to the left of a person facing forward.
- *Rigging:* The ropes and chains used to support and operate masts, booms, dredges, and other commercial gear.
- *Run:* Either of two meanings: a group of fish of the same species that migrate together; or, pulling line off a reel by a hooked fish.
- *Scuppers:* Openings in the transom, above the waterline, that allows water to drain off the deck.
- *Sheer line:* The curved shape of the top of the hull. The sheer line can be straight, broken, sweeping or any combination of the three.
- *Shoal:* A sandbar or shallow area surrounded by deeper water.
- *Shutter plank:* The board that finishes the planking of a boat.
- *Sink–net:* A type of net that is weighted and set beneath the surface. Sink-nets are used on commercial fishing vessels.
- *Spray rail:* Longitudinal strips that deflect spray downward when the hull travels over the water. Usually positioned along the chine.
- *Starboard:* The side of the boat to the right of a person facing forward.
- *Stem:* A continuation of the keel upwards at the front of the hull.
- *Stem post:* The principal vertical timber in a boat's bow.
- *Stern:* The farthest aft part of the boat.
- *Swivel:* A strong connector between the mainline and the leader, or the bait, designed to eliminate line twist.
- *Teaser:* A bait, or string of baits often without hooks, used to attract gamefish to the surface or into the baits with hooks.
- *Transom:* The flat, vertical aft end of a boat.
- *Tumblehome:* Typically measured at or near the transom, tumblehome is when the width of the beam is more than the width of the uppermost deck.
- *Tuna door:* A door located in the transom through which large, heavy fish can be pulled onboard. This door opens from the cockpit and prevents anglers from having to pull big fish over the gunwales.
- *Tuna tower:* A high platform over the flybridge, taller than a marlin tower, where spotters look for fish, grass or other objects in the water.
- *Waterline:* The horizontal line between the bow and stern where the water touches the hull.

Photography Credits

Photography Credits:

Graphic Images Provided By:
- Applied Concepts Unleashed *(www.acunleashed.com)*
- Black Bart *(www.blackbartlures.com)*
- Melton International Tackle *(www.meltontackle.com)*
- Sea Striker *(www.seastriker.com)*

References

- Alexander, John and James Lazell. *Ribbon of Sand: The Amazing Convergence of the Ocean and the Outer Banks.* Chapel Hill, North Carolina: Algonquin Books of Chapel Hill, 1992.

- Alford, Michael B. *Traditional Work Boats of North Carolina.* North Carolina Maritime Museum. Beaufort, North Carolina, 2004.

- Barfield, Rodney. *Seasoned by Salt: A Historical Album of the Outer Banks.* Chapel Hill, North Carolina: University of North Carolina Press, 1995.

- Beal, Candy and Carmine Prioli, Editors. *Life at the Edge of the Sea: Essays on North Carolina's Coast and Coastal Heritage.* Wilmington, North Carolina: Coastal Carolina Press, 2002.

- Grundvig, Nelse and Dave Inscoe, Editors. *Report on Marine Industry Economic Activity.* Labor Market Division. North Carolina Employment Security Commission. Raleigh, North Carolina, 2005.

- Moffatt and Nichol. *A Study of the Benefits of Oregon Inlet to the Economy of Dare County and the Surrounding Region.* Dare County. July, 2006.

- Parker, Reuel B. *The New Cold-Molded Boatbuilding: From Lofting to Launching.* Camden, Maine: International Marine, 1992.

- Schoenbaum, Thomas J. *Islands, Capes and Sounds: The North Carolina Coast.* Winston-Salem, North Carolina: John F. Blair Publishing, 1982.

- Southeast Fisheries Science Center. *Atlantic Billfish Research Plan.* Version 1.4. National Marine Fisheries Service. National Oceanic and Atmospheric Administration. Department of Commerce. January 30, 2004.

- Steward, Robert M. *Boatbuilding Manual, Fourth Edition.* Camden, Maine: International Marine, 1994.

- Stick, David. *Graveyard of the Atlantic.* Chapel Hill, North Carolina: University of North Carolina Press, 1952.

- Stick, David. *The Outer Banks of North Carolina, 1584-1958.* Chapel Hill, North Carolina: University of North Carolina Press, 1958.